Miriam F. Stimpson teaches courses in
modern architecture and furnishings
at Brigham Young University, Utah.

A Field Guide
of Modern

A SPECTRUM BOOK

Prentice-Hall, Inc., Englewood Cliffs, New Jersey 07632

MIRIAM F. STIMPSON

to Landmarks Architecture in Europe

Library of Congress Cataloging in Publication Data

Stimpson, Miriam.
  A field guide to landmarks of modern architecture
in Europe.

  "A Spectrum Book" —T.p. verso.
  Bibliography: p.
  Includes index.
  1. Architecture, Modern—19th century—Europe—
Directories. 2. Architecture, Modern—20th century—
Europe—Directories. 3. Architecture—Europe—
Directories. I. Title.
NA957.S75 1985   724.9'1   84-22306
ISBN 0-13-316555-8
ISBN 0-13-316548-5 (pbk.)

A Field Guide to Landmarks of Modern Architecture in Europe

A SPECTRUM BOOK

10   9   8   7   6   5   4   3   2   1

Printed in the United States of America

ISBN 0-13-316555-8

ISBN 0-13-316548-5 (PBK.)

Interior design: Maria Carella
Production coordination: Fred Dahl
Manufacturing: Frank Grieco
Cover design: Hal Siegel
Cover art: Le Corbusier's pilgrimage chapel at Ronchamp, France (1950)
by Tina Jackson

Prentice-Hall International, Inc., *London*
Prentice-Hall of Australia Pty. Limited, *Sydney*
Prentice-Hall Canada Inc., *Toronto*
Prentice-Hall of India Private Limited, *New Delhi*
Prentice-Hall of Japan, Inc., *Tokyo*
Prentice-Hall of Southeast Asia Pte. Ltd., *Singapore*
Whitehall Books Limited, *Wellington, New Zealand*
Editora Prentice-Hall do Brasil Ltda., *Rio de Janeiro*
Prentice-Hall Hispanoamericana, S.A., *Mexico*

Contents

Foreword

...We cannot escape buildings and the subtle
but penetrating effects of their character, nobel or mean,
restrained or ostentatious, genuine or meretricious.

SIR NIKOLAUS PEVSNER

Architecture as a form of artistic expression may be arguable to some, given the utilitarian role of so much in our built environment. The notion must be supported by the appreciation that architecture is not a blanket term for all that is built—there are many facets to this form, and much is publicly accepted as architecture that has no claim. "A bicycle shed is a building," wrote Sir Nikolaus Pevsner, "but Lincoln Cathedral is a piece of architecture." (Whether a bicycle shed might become a piece of architecture is another question.) That a work of architecture has the capacity to elevate our spirits is no surprise; however, this capacity is not limited to, for example, a Gothic cathedral. The "pieces of architecture" included in Miriam Stimpson's *A Field Guide to Landmarks of Modern Architecture in Europe* are testaments to what was seen, particularly in the early days of modernism, as the architecture of a new age, requiring new forms to reflect a new spirit.

Out of the nineteenth-century writings and teachings of John Ruskin and William Morris came the strengthened notion of the importance of the craftsman, and the corresponding call for better design in all the arts. Morris decried the "short-sighted, reckless brutality" of towns and buildings, and argued for architecture that is not "a weight upon the spirit." Emphasizing the power of good design to improve the lives of both maker and user, Morris called for art and well designed objects available to all the people. His theories, plus the gradual acceptance among artists and architects of the machine as a powerful instrument, and of new technologies as realities of the times, became the framework upon which the architecture of the twentieth century developed.

Out of the hundreds of buildings presented in Miriam Stimpson's *Field Guide* are several that are seminal in their contribution to the architecture of this century—and are particularly worth a visit.

In England, the work of C.F.A. Voysey (Annesley Lodge, 1895, and The Orchard, Chorley Wood, 1899) with horizontal bands of windows, broad expanse of white wall, and lack of stylistic reference, exerted great influence on the Continent as well as in Britain. The Scottish architect Charles Rennie Mackintosh, with his Glasgow School of Art (1897), linked the Art Nouveau trend on the Continent with an original and clear spatial sense. The school's library manifests this, with structure, furniture, and furnishings designed by Mackintosh contributing to the overall sculptural volume.

At this time, Art Nouveau artists and architects—particularly in Belgium and France—found aesthetic inspiration in the flowing lines found in nature. Often reinforced concrete was used as an expressive building material; Victor Horta's Hôtel Tassel (Brussels, 1893) is an outstanding example. On the interior, iron is used ornamentally in stair supports, railings, and columns. The structural and expressive use of reinforced concrete is seen in Auguste Perret's house at No. 25 rue Franklin, Paris (1902–1903). In Barcelona, The Church of the Sacred Family (begun 1903) by Antonio Gaudi displays an intensely personal form of Art Nouveau.

Vienna was an important center for architects interested in the principles of the new age. Otto Wagner's glass-vaulted Post Office Savings Bank (1904–1906) illustrates his conviction to these ideas. His pupil Josef Hoffmann's Palais Stoclet in Brussels (1905–1911) and Adolf Loos' Steiner House (Vienna, 1910) show the influence of Wagner as designs in the "modern" style: stripped of ornamentalism, with strict geometric forms, devoid of any reference to historical styles.

The outstanding industrial building of this period is Peter Behrens' AEG turbine factory, built in Berlin (1909), which gave conscious monumental stature to this building type for possibly the first time. The steel frame is clearly expressed, and the form of the building is dramatic and beautifully proportioned.

Another direction in modern architecture in northern Europe was Expressionism, influenced by Art Nouveau. Dynamic building shapes, flowing lines, and a sense of personal inventiveness typify this style. They are found in Chile-Haus (Hamburg, 1923) by Fritz Hogar and the Schocken Department Store by Eric Mendelsohn.

Coincidentally with the Expressionist movement in architecture, the design principles that later were the basis of the Modern movement became evident. The Fagus shoe factory built by Walter Gropius (after leaving the office of Peter Behrens) and Adolf Meyer with its strong geometric form, "walls" of glass within a steel frame, and flat roof—is a new level of development in this style.

In the early days of the International Style, the masters of twentieth-century architecture emerge. Mies van der Rohe's Tugenhat House (1930) is a domestic adaptation of the architectural themes he explored for the first time in the German Pavilion (now reconstructed) for the 1929 Barcelona Exhibition. These themes include the open plan, a strong spatial composition, elegant furniture (particularly the now well-known "Barcelona" chair), and the sculptural use of structural details.

The Finnish architect Alvar Aalto's Tuberculosis Sanatorium (Paimo, 1929–1933) is designed in the Modern idiom, yet with features that reveal the architect's Scandinavian heritage. His work exhibits a strong feeling for materials, especially wood; bold colors, used to enhance the architectural design; allowance for natural light and fresh air in the building; and an interest in shaped forms in both detail, plan, and overall building volume.

Perhaps the greatest voice of the International Style was that of the Swiss architect Le Corbusier. The Villa Savoye, built in a field in Poissy, near Paris (1930), is a country house for the new age. The design includes his "five points for a new architecture": The house is raised on pilotis (slender columns); the roof garden replaces the ground plane from which the house is lifted; the interior plan is free-flowing, since the interior walls are no longer load-bearing; horizontal bands of windows allow light throughout the room; and the building's facade is clearly expressed as a "skin" over the steel "skeleton."

Le Corbusier's Salvation Army Building (1929) and Swiss Pavilion (1930), both in Paris, utilize these points on a grander scale, and for entirely different building types. The Unite' d'Habitation at Marseille (1947) marks a new development in his design, with the use of rugged concrete, bold forms, and dramatic roofscape. Le Corbusier's most startling work is the pilgrimage chapel at Ronchamp (1950) seen on the cover of this book. Thick white concrete walls, curving brown concrete roof, small windows of varying sizes (with stained glass designed by Corbusier) placed compositionally in the deep wall, and sculptural light towers—the chapel reveals the powerful expressive voice of this modern master.

Many—indeed most—of the buildings described on these pages are accessible through published drawings or photographs and have popular familiarity in this sense. But a building, as a three-dimensional volume with a particular spatial quality, naturally offers much more through an actual visit. Not only does one move through the building, but one also sees the building in its context, observes the overall form and mass, realizes how the architect has established the major paths through the building, watches how light (both natural and manmade) enhances the aesthetic and architectural experience, notices the craftsmanship of details, sees how the hierarchy of spaces within the building is accomplished, discovers how the structure affects the overall design, and in general forms an impression that cannot be gleaned solely from the study of illustrations or diagrams.

Miriam Stimpson's *A Field Guide to Landmarks of Modern Architecture in Europe* offers the "guidebook" information one needs to find, identify, and appreciate these buildings. What we can bring to a visit is "eyes that see"—to explore what is best in architecture, and envision what is possible.

S.M. DAVIS

Preface

This handbook guides the reader to the finest monuments of modern architecture in Europe. Numerous excellent guides direct the traveler interested in architecture to traditional landmarks of Europe, but not a single comprehensive reference lists the important structures built in Europe during the past hundred years.

This illustrated guide makes it easy to find the most famous modern buildings in Europe. Structures are presented in alphabetical order, by country and city. Maps are included at the beginning of each chapter. Illustrations and descriptions are given for each building, and the descriptive notes are kept brief to maximize accessibility. Additional hallmarks of modern architecture are listed at the end of each chapter.

More than 2500 buildings were examined for this compilation. The structures were selected on the basis of correspondence with professional architectural and historical organizations, embassies, Chambers of Commerce, and national tourist bureaus, to whom I give special thanks. Additionally, extensive research through architectural periodicals and books aided in the selection of the buildings.

Only a few private houses have been included, those that have played a significant role in the development of modern residential design. The majority of structures illustrated are public and commercial buildings, many open to the public.

Acknowledgments

Verkehrsverein Luzern, Schweiz. Pilatusstrasse 14
VVV Peeland, Parkweg 15, 5700 AD Helmond, Holland
Verkehrsamt, Berlin, Europa Center, 1000 Berlin 30
Consulate General of Denmark, Danish information Off., 280 Park Ave. New York, NY
Fremdenverkehrsamt der Landeshauptstadt Munchen, Rindermarkt 5, Munchen 2
Frigoscandia AB Head Office, Rushallsgatan 21 S-251 09 Helsingborg, Sweden
Swiss National Tourist Office, Union Square, 250 Stockton Street, SFO, Calif
Tourist Information Brussels, Rue du Marche-aux-Herbes 61, 1000 Bruxelles
Stadtverkehrsburo Salzburg, Auerspergstrasse 7, Saltzburg A-5024
Verkehrsverein Basel, Blumenrain 2, Basel, Switzerland
Office du Tourisme de Strasbourg et de sa region, Palais de Congres, F. 67082, Strasbourg
Bund Deutscher Architekten, Bundessekretariat, Ippendorfer Allee 14b, 5300 Bonn 1
Technische Hogeschool Eindhoven, Den Dolech 2, Postbus 513, 5600 MB Eindhoven, Holland
Verkeershuis, Postbus 552, 6800 an Arnhem, Holland
VVV Rotterdam Tourist Office, Stadhuisplein 19, 3012 AR, Rotterdam, Holland
Rijksdienst voor de Monumentenzorg, Nederlands Documentatie Centrum voor Bouwkunst
    Droogbak Ia—1013 GE Amsterdam
Wiener Fremdenverkehrsverband, Comite de Tourisme de la Ville de Vienne,
    A-1095 Wien, Kinderspitalgasse 5, Austria
Stockholm Information Service Gustav Adolfs Torg 18, 2 tr, 111 52 Stockholm, Sweden
    Kansallis-Osake-Pankki, Aleksanterinkatu 10, 15110 Lahti 11, Finland
Aalborg Turist Forening, Osteraagade 8, 9000 Aalborg, Denmark
City of Nottingham, Public Relations Office, 54 Milton St. Nottingham, England
Fremdenverkehrsverband, Innsbruck, lgls u. Umgebung, Innsbruck, Austria
Frankfurter Verkehrsverein e.V., Frankfurt am Main, Germany
Lahti Tours Ltd, Lahtimatkat, Lahti, Finland
Glasgow Chamber of Commerce, Glasgow, Scotland
Office de Tourisme, 14 Place Stanislas, Nancy, France
Stadtverwaltung Kaiserslautern, Postfach 1320, Kaiserslautern, Germany
Verkehrsamt der Stadt Koln, am Dom Unter Fettenhennen 19, Koln, Germany
City Information Service, Box 1 MC, Newcastle upon Tyne, United Kingdom
Liverpool Tourist Information Centre, Liverpool, England
Helsinki Chamber of Commerce, Kalevankatu 12, SF-00100 Helsinki, Finland
Maison du Tourisme, Dauphine-Grenoble, Grenoble, France
Verkehrsverein Mannheim, Verkehrspavillon, Mannheim, Germany
Lahden Ev.Lut. Seurakunnat, Tiedotustoimisto, Lahti, Finland
Hedmarksmuseet, OG Domkirkeodden, Hamar, Norway
Tromso Information Center, Tromso, Norway
EPT Como, Italy
Institut Francais d'architecture, 6 rue de Tournon, Paris, France
London Chamber of Commerce & Industry, 69 Cannon Street, London, England
Fundacio Joan Miro, Centre d'Estudia d'Art Contemporani, Barcelona, Spain
Ministere de la culture, Musee National Message Biblique, Nice, France
Dusseldorf Verkehrsverein, Dusseldorf, Deutschland
Landeshauptstadt Dusseldorf, Dusseldorf, Deutschland
Prefecture de la Region Rhone-Alpes, Secretariate General, Lyon, France
Patronat Municipal De Turisme de Barcelona, Barcelona Espana

City Information Centre Bristol, England
Verkehrsamt der Stadt Koln, am Dom Unter Fettenhennen 19, Koln 1, Deutschland
Geneva Chamber of Commerce, Rue Petiot 8, Geneva, Switzerland
Embassy of the United States of America, Oslo, Norway
Tampere Tourist Information, Finland
Werbe-Und Verkehrsamt Stadt Bonn, Bonn, 2 Drucksache
Turku City Tourist Office, Kasityolaiskatu 3, Turku 10, Finland
Pro Monza, Palazzo Comunale, Monza, Italy
American Consulate General, Sodra Hamngatan 2, Goteborg, 20, Sweden
The Swedish Institute, Box 7434, Stockholm, Sweden
Espoo Tourist Office, Tapiontori 02100 Espoo 10 Finland
Chambre De Commerce et D'Industrie De Nice et Des Alpes-Maritimes, Nice, Cedex, France
Netherlands Consulate General, 601 California Street, San Francisco Calif.
Embassy of Finland, 3216 New Mexico Ave., N.W., Washington, D.C.
Ministry for Cultural Affairs, Recreation and Social Welfare, BBKB, Amsterdam, The Neth.
Norse Arkitekters, Josefinesgt. 34, Oslo, Norway
Embassy of Ireland, 2234 Massachusetts Avenue. N.W., Washington, D.C.
Norwegian Information Service, 835 Third Avenue, New York, N.Y.
Consulate General of Switzerland, 235 Montgomery St., San Francisco, Calif.
Consulate General of the Federal Republic of Germany, 601 California St. SFO, Calif.
Royal Netherlands Embassy, Washington, D.C.
Swiss Society of Engineers and Architects, Zurich, Switzerland
The Embassy of Italy, 1601 Fuller St., N.W., Washington, D.C.
German Information Center, 410 Park Ave., New York, N.Y.
Royal Netherlands Embassy, 4200 Linnean Ave., N.W., Washington, D.C.
Danish Tourist Board, 75 Rockefeller Plaza, New York, N.Y.
Syndicat D'Initiative, Amiens, France
Stadt Nurnberg, Hochbauamt, 8500 Nurnberg
Austrian Institute, 11 East 52nd St., New York, N.Y. 10022
Department of State, U.S.A., Washington, D.C.
Tourist Information Office, Stationsplein 210, Leiden, Holland
Stadsarkitekten-Radhuset-8100 Arhus, Denmark
Ecole special d'architecture, Paris, France
Stadt Kassell Der Magistrat, Kassel, Germany
Ente Provinciale Per il Turismo, Florence, Italy
Bund der Architekten der DDR, Berlin, Deutschland
Paderborn Verkehrsverein, Paderborn, Germany
Landeshauptstadt Saarbrücken, Stadtamt 13, Saarbrücken, Germany
Bologna Tourist Center, Via Leopardi 1, Bologna, Italy
British Tourist Authority, Los Angeles, California

ILLUSTRATORS: Tina Jackson, principal illustrator. Kinateder & Smart, Associates, Architects, Sally Sharp, Bret Bleggi and Brenda Braun.

Austria

AUSTRIA

Vienna •
Perchtoldsdorf •

• Salzburg

• Innsbruck

THE MODERN MOVEMENT IN AUSTRIA

OTTO WAGNER

The history of modern design in Austria begins with the contributions of Otto Wagner, Professor of Architecture at the Academy of Art in Vienna, who taught or influenced most of the architects of his generation. At first he was an exponent of Art Nouveau style, utilizing organic lines, forms, and colors—the Majolica House is an outstanding example.

THE SECESSION

A group of young Viennese architects and designers, including Josef Marie Olbrich (who built the Secession Gallery), Otto Wagner, and Josef Hoffmann, determined to break ties with traditional decoration. They developed modern ideas that helped to bring art and design into the twentieth century by utilizing freer and simpler forms. Their frequent exhibitions, often featuring the work of such well-known European architects as Mackintosh from Scotland, helped to introduce modernism to the public. Adolf Loos, who exerted influence on other individual architects and movements throughout Europe and America, was also involved with this group.

THE WIENER WERKSTÄTTE

Many of the original members of the Secession organized this workshop with the express purpose of executing furnishings and accessories for their many projects. The design direction of this workshop was toward more geometric expression.

PERIOD FROM WORLD WAR I TO WORLD WAR II

Although the organization of the Wiener Werkstätte dissolved after World War I, the leading members continued to develop modern theories of design.

PERIOD AFTER WORLD WAR II

Today modern architecture stands side by side with traditional buildings. A number of important modern architects of a new generation have exerted their influence. Hans Hollein is one of the best known and has gained an international reputation for his innovative designs. When Vienna was selected by the UN as the headquarters for UNIDO, the Vienna International Centre was launched, giving new direction to architecture in Austria.

Note: Excellent guides are available at the Vienna Tourist Centre, including *Art Nouveau in Vienna* and *VIC The Vienna International Centre*.

SALZBURG

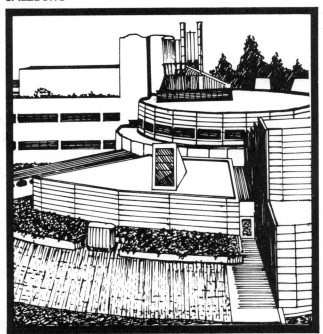

Austrian Radio and Television (ORF) Studio Osterreichischer Rundfunk (ORF) (1970-72)

ARCHITECT: Gustav Peichl
LOCATION: Nonntaler Hauptstrasse 49d, 5020 Salzburg

This unique pie-shaped studio features a striking circular rotunda. Gleaming metal ducts, frankly exposed, become a contributing part of the design. Brilliant red-painted pipes and trimmings punctuate the raw concrete background and metal. An unusual arrangement of "sculptured discs" and other modern forms nestles in a beautiful natural setting. Other ORF studios using the same plan by Peichl have been built in Innsbruck, Dornbirn, Linz, and Eisenstadt.

SALZBURG

Church at Parsch (1956)

ARCHITECTS: Arbeitsgruppe 4
LOCATION: Gaissmairstrasse 6, Salzburg-Parsch

Arbeitsgruppe 4, students of Holzmeister, have been concerned with a new approach to architecture that is both constructive and flexible. The Church at Parsch breaks with traditional church building in Austria in its use of modular design; the focal point is a dramatic window rising from the central chapel area.

SALZBURG

The Grosses Festspielhaus (1926-36/60)

ARCHITECT: Clemens Holzmeister
LOCATION: In Hofstallgasse

Holzmeister designed many well-known structures in Austria, especially churches, in traditional local styles. The Grosses Festspielhaus is his most famous design, much visited by tourists who come there to enjoy the music of Mozart and other composers. The concert hall is doubly interesting for Holzmeister's remodelings, improving acoustics and efficiency of space.

VIENNA

Austrian Travel Bureau (1978)

ARCHITECT: Hans Hollein
LOCATION: Vienna 1, Opernring 5

Hollein has a reputation as one of the most imaginative modern architects in Europe. The interiors of the Austrian Travel Bureau abound with exotic stylized palm trees. An Indian dome, a ruined Greek column, and other symbols of travel are incorporated under a domed grid reminiscent of Otto Wagner's earlier Post Office Savings Building. The structure is an interesting example of post-modern architecture.

VIENNA

Central Savings Bank (Zentralsparkasse) (1980)

ARCHITECT: Gunther Domenig
LOCATION: 1100 Wien, Favoritenstrasse 118

A sophisticated organic structure, the bank evokes a surrealist feeling by utilizing a glass skin supported by modern versions of the classical orders of architecture. The focal point is the awesome staircase. Organic trusses support the weight and carry out the design theme.

VIENNA

Church On The Steinhof (1905-7)

ARCHITECT: Otto Wagner
LOCATION: 1014, Baumgartner Hohe 1

This famous early modern architect said, "We must create, not imitate," and "We must design what the public ought to like, not what it does like!" The Church on the Steinhof, a strong departure from traditionalism, ranks with Frank Lloyd Wright's Unity Temple in Oak Park, Illinois, as a landmark in ecclesiastical architecture at the turn of the century. Outraged Viennese citizens threw fruits and vegetables at the new structural exterior in protest, decrying it as "blasphemous."

VIENNA

Consilium Memorial Church At Lainz, Vienna (1968)

ARCHITECT: Josef Lackner
LOCATION: 1130 Wien, Lainzerstrasse 138

Lackner was a student of Holzmeister, architect of the Grosses Festspielhaus in Salzburg. Lackner's treatment of steel and concrete in the Consilium Memorial Church takes on a sculptural quality that provides admirable interior and exterior modern design. The altar is enhanced by the surrounding seating areas and choir-loft.

VIENNA

Karntner Bar (American Bar) (1907)

ARCHITECT: Adolf Loos
LOCATION: Vienna 1, Karntner Durchgang

Loos, who has been called the forerunner of Le Corbusier, had a stormy and unhappy career. He alienated many architects in Vienna, but held true to his radical modern ideas. The American Bar demonstrates his modern theories, employing simple geometric forms to unify both interior and exterior design.

VIENNA

"Loos House" (Goldman Building) (1911)

ARCHITECT: Adolf Loos
LOCATION: Vienna 1, Michaelerplatz 3

The residential portion of the Loos House is sheathed with inexpensive marble, the lower commercial section treated even more plainly. The austerity of the structure provoked abuse from the Viennese. But the beautifully designed interior staircase on the main floor has been photographed for numerous books and periodicals.

VIENNA

Majolica House (Majolika Haus) (1898)

ARCHITECT: Otto Wagner
LOCATION: Vienna 4, Wienzeile 38a-40

At the turn of the century Wagner designed in the Art Nouveau style (Jugendstil), a decorative approach based on nature motifs. The Majolica House is considered one of the most beautiful architectural works employing this style. The structure is faced with distinctive pink and green majolica tile, so expensive that Wagner actually ended up paying for
part of it. (Note the interesting adjoining apartment house with Egyptian motifs.)

VIENNA

Postsparkasse
(Postal Savings Bank) (1904-6)

ARCHITECT: Otto Wagner
LOCATION: On Biberstrasse by the
Wiesingerstrasse (Georg-Coch-Platz 2)

Wagner is considered the founder of the
modern movement in Austria. He was
appointed professor of architecture at the
Vienna Academy in 1894 and taught most of
Austria's important pioneer architects. He was
also a founding member of the Secession, a
group of artists who broke away from
traditionalism. The Postal Savings Bank
demonstrates a remarkable use of structural
design, frankly exposing aluminum, marble,
and granite.

VIENNA

"Primavesi" House
(SKYWA) (1915)

ARCHITECT: Josef Hoffmann
LOCATION: Vienna 13, Gloriettegasse 14-16

With Kolo Moser, Josef Hoffmann in 1903
founded that offshoot of the Secession,
the Wiener Werkstätte. Within the formal
workshop environment, Hoffmann developed
simple geometric expressions in furniture
and other mediums that helped introduce
modernism into the twentieth century.
Influenced by Charles Rennie Mackintosh in
Scotland and Wagner in Vienna, Hoffmann felt
the need for unity between architecture,
furniture, and decoration. The garden fence
of the Primavesi House is a delightful
decoration that is mirrored in the detail of
other architectural features on the house.
Hoffmann's most famous work is the Palais
Stoclet in Brussels.

VIENNA

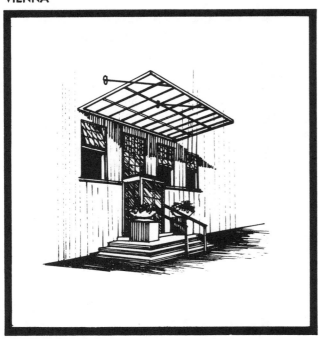

Purkersdorf Sanatorium (1903-5)

ARCHITECT: Josef Hoffmann
LOCATION: Purkersdorf, Wiener Strasse 72-80

The original Purkersdorf Sanatorium designed by Hoffmann has been almost completely altered. Hoffmann believed that a structure, from foundation to the ridge of the roof, should be one work of art; he designed not only all details of the building, but its furnishings as well. For the modern sanatorium he designed his popular Purkersdorf Chair, now in production from I.C.F. (International Contract Furnishings).

VIENNA

Retti's Candle-Shop (1965)

ARCHITECT: Hans Hollein
LOCATION: Vienna 1, Kohlmarkt 10

Hollein is one of the most important architects in Austria today. He has given this old candle shop a stunning modern "face lift" through the use of gleaming aluminum panels. Enclosed glass cases, though small, effectively display candles. The eye-catching entrance is set in a deep key-shaped space.

VIENNA

Schullin's Jewellers (1974)

ARCHITECT: Hans Hollein
LOCATION: Vienna 1, Kohlmarkt 7

The spectacular jewelry shop with its sculptural split over the doorway glistens with gold color. Hollein has created an expressive design that looks like a jewel itself. The structure shows why Hollein has gained international recognition for creative and effective architecture.

VIENNA

Secession Gallery (1897)

ARCHITECT: Josef Maria Olbrich
LOCATION: Vienna 1, Griedrichstrasse 12

Olbrich, who trained under Wagner, was a founding member of the Secession in 1897 and designed the Secession Gallery for this artistic organization. The motto of the group is inscribed over the doorway: "To each time its art, to each art its freedom." The huge golden ornamental dome has lovingly been called the "giant golden cabbage." Details of the building are stylized; the doorway in particular is noteworthy for its Art Nouveau motifs.

VIENNA

Steiner House (1910)

ARCHITECT: Adolf Loos
LOCATION: Vienna 13, St. Veitgasse 10

Loos had significant influence on the course of early modern architecture. Loos wrote articles stating his modern theories, designed simple furniture, and taught courses in modern design. The stark, white stucco Steiner House with its boldly rounded forms, ridiculed in Austria when it was built, is today considered a landmark—Loos' most important residential work.

VIENNA

The Karl Marx Hof (Heiligenstadt Houses) (1927)

ARCHITECT: Karl Ehn
LOCATION: Vienna 19, Heiligenstadterstrasse

This famous housing project has been compared to a mighty fortress symbolizing socialist solidarity. Karl Marx Hof has 1,325 apartments and is over a kilometer long. The complex outraged many people at the time it was built. Today the complex looks dated and reminds Vienna of the cruel Civil War of 1933.

VIENNA

Vienna International Center
(1971-present)

ARCHITECT: Johann Staber and others
LOCATION: The Parkland on the Danube

A vast architectural complex, Austria's most ambitious building project incorporates facilities for housing, education, recreation, eating, shopping, health, and entertainment. A major emphasis of the Center is headquarters for international organizations; a number of institutions headquarter here, including OPEC, IAEA, and UNIDO. Bold, curving concrete buildings synthesize form, materials, and function.

VIENNA

The Vienna Stadthalle (1958)

ARCHITECT: Roland Rainer
LOCATION: Marzpark

Advancements in modern design came to a halt during the grim period of World War II. Rainer made a substantial contribution to architecture and town planning during the post-war years, building upon ideas set forth by Loos and Frank. The impressive Vienna Stadthalle is consistent in a simplicity of materials and form suitable to its function.

ADDITIONAL MODERN STRUCTURES OF INTEREST

INNSBRUCK

Church At Neu-Arzi (1958)
ARCHITECT: Josef Lackner
LOCATION: Spingeserstrasse 14 A-6020

This church, especially its interior space, is considered one of the most interesting religious structures designed in Austria after the war.

Kirche Vols (Vols Church) (1967)
ARCHITECT: Josef Lackner
LOCATION: Inquire at Stadtisches Verkehrsburo, Burggraben 3

Sharply angled forms with a white stucco finish significantly contrast with the magnificent surrounding mountains.

LEOBEN (STEIERMARK)

Forschungsinstitute Und Rechenzentrum Leoben (1973)
ARCHITECTS: Gunther Domenig/ Eilfried Huth
LOCATION: 27 miles NNW of Graz

This extraordinary contemporary structure has an arrangement of three building components stacked at varying angles to each other.

NEU-RUM (TIROL)

Auferstehungskirche Neu-Rum (Church At Neu-Rum) (1976)
ARCHITECT: Horst Herbert Parson
LOCATION: Close to Innsbruck, Inquire Stadtisches, Verkehrsburo, Burggraben 3

Precisely cut stepped forms of white and dark forms highlight this unique religious structure.

PERCHTOLDSDORF

Perchtoldsdorf Town Hall (Interiors) (1976)
ARCHITECT: Hans Hollein
LOCATION: 7 miles SW of Vienna

A brilliant renovation of an old town hall by Austria's internationally known modern designer.

PUCHENAU OBEROSTERREICH

Romisch-Katholisches Seelsorgezentrum Puchenau (1976)
ARCHITECT: Roland Rainer
LOCATION: Hills of Upper Austria (Linz is closest large city)

This small, well-planned center for the Roman Catholic Church features a design based on octagonal forms with supportive facilities branching outward from the central chapel.

SALZBURG

Bildungshaus St. Virgil (1976)
ARCHITECT: Wilhelm Holzbauer
LOCATION: Inquire at Stadtverkehrsburo, Auerspergstrasse 7

Constructed of concrete and glass, this religious building is interestingly arranged, featuring circle, diagonal, and block forms.

St. Joseph's College (1964)
ARCHITECTS: Arbeitsgruppe 4
LOCATION: Aigen, Salzburg, Gyllenstermstrasse 8

A unification of horizontal lines and rectangular forms underlies the design of this unpretentious educational facility.

VIENNA

Block of Flats (1888)
ARCHITECT: Otto Wagner
LOCATION: No. 12 Universitatsstrasse

One of the earliest modern structures in Austria.

Clima Villenhotel (1960's)
ARCHITECT: Ernst Hiesmayr
LOCATION: Nussberggasse 2c, Haus 1,
A-1190

A unique cluster of small, medium, and large apartments, situated in the Viennese woods. Based on International Style prototypes.

Karlsplatz Station (1898)
ARCHITECT: Otto Wagner
LOCATION: on the Karlsplatz

With the design of this station, Wagner won recognition in Europe as an important exponent of the modern style.

Museum Des 20, Jahrhunderts (Museum of 20th Century) (1962)
ARCHITECT: Karl Schwanzer
LOCATION: III Schweizergarten

This light, airy glass and steel museum features large exhibit spaces centered around a central atrium.

Pfarrzentrum Leopoldau (1971)
ARCHITECT: Karl Schwanzer
LOCATION: Inquire Stadinformation, Rathaus, Schmidthalle (Branch in Karlsplatz-Passage)

This modern religious center is distinguished by repeating circular forms providing a unique design composition.

Philips Eurocenter (1971)
ARCHITECT: Kurt Hiawenicska
LOCATION: N.Oe. Suedstrasse 14, Objekt 24, Laxenburg

A huge but orderly complex based on principles of the clean white International Style.

Rehabilitation Centre (1967-73)
ARCHITECT: Gustav Peichl
LOCATION: der Allgemeinen Unfallversicherungsanstalt Koeglergasse 2-2

An efficiently planned modern center with facilities geared for patients suffering from brain damage.

Stadt Des Kindes (Children's Village) (1974)
ARCHITECT: Anton Schwighofer
LOCATION: Meuhlbergstrasse 7, A-1140

Huge "stacked cubes" are reminiscent of the architecture popular during the 1920s utilizing white surfaces, flat roofs, and corner windows. The complex was designed to accommodate children from various undesirable environments.

Vienna Subway System (1980s)
ARCHITECT: Wilhelm Holzbauer with others
LOCATION: in the Karlsplatz

An "extension" of Otto Wagner's Stadtbahn of 1893/1906. This new sleek subway features a redline design combined with white materials.

Wagner's House (1886-8)
ARCHITECT: Otto Wagner
LOCATION: No. 26 Huttelbergstrasse

Recently restored, the Wagner House in the woods is a beautiful example of Wagner's early modern style and representative of the Secessionist Movement in Vienna.

VIENNA-MAUER:

Zur Heiligsten Dreifaltigkeit Church (1976)
ARCHITECTS: Fritz Wotruba/Fritz G. Mayr
LOCATION: Inquire Stadinformation, Rathaus, Schmidthalle in Vienna (Branch in Karlsplatz-Passage) 6 miles SW of Vienna

Constructed of raw concrete, this unusual church appears as a mountain of building blocks arranged at varying levels.

Belgium

BELGIUM

- Roeselare
- Leuven (Louvain)
- Brussels
- Nivelles

MODERN ARCHITECTURE IN BELGIUM

ART NOUVEAU

Belgium became involved with new design approaches when Henri van de Velde became "spokesman for the Art Nouveau." This style, inspired by nature, employed motifs drawn from organic forms and lines. The design for van de Velde's Bloemenwulf House is one of the first departures from traditional architecture in Belgium. He also had his own furniture factory outside of Brussels and taught at the Arts and Crafts Academy at Weimar, Germany—a forerunner of the famous Bauhaus design school. Victor Horta's townhouses in the Art Nouveau style aroused international interest when they were built. These townhouses are still admired today.

PERIOD AFTER WORLD WAR I

After Art Nouveau lost favor, Belgium contributed little to the modern movement.

BRUSSELS' WORLD FAIR OF 1958

Belgium again gained international attention when it hosted the World's Fair in 1958. This significant exhibition featured buildings designed by some of the world's leading architects. Many of these structures are still standing and may be visited today. The large sculptural Atomium, designed as the symbol of the fair, still looms over the Brussels' skyline.

ARCHITECTURE IN BELGIUM DURING RECENT DECADES

Architecture in Belgium today is primarily modern structural design, although the influence and quality of the buildings throughout Europe are minimal. The work of Lucien Kroll and Atelier, presently the most prominent architectural firm in Belgium, is exceptional.

BRUSSELS

Bloemenwulf House (1895)

ARCHITECT: Henri van de Velde
LOCATION: Avenue Vanderaey, B - 1180, Brussels (Uccle)

Henri van de Velde became spokesman for the Art Nouveau style in Europe. With the design of Bloemenwulf House, the home he built for his family, he attempted to integrate the entire interior and exterior design according to precepts of the new style. The flowing roof line recalls a vernacular style from the past. The interiors and furnishings especially reflect the new design approach based on themes from nature.

BRUSSELS

Banque Lambert (1964)

ARCHITECTS: Skidmore, Owings and Merrill (USA)
LOCATION: Avenue Marnix 24 B-1050 Brussels (Ixelles)

This prominent American architectural firm has offices around the world. The architects were early followers of the great Mies van der Rohe in Chicago during the 1940s and 1950s. SOM's office and administrative structures are among the world's best designed buildings. The uniform design of the Banque Lambert is a fine example of the firm's work.

BRUSSELS

Horta's House and Studio (1890s)

ARCHITECT: Victor Horta
LOCATION: 23-25 Rue Americaine,
Saint-Gilles

Many tourists and students of architecture visit Horta's well-preserved home and studio. Horta was one of the first architects in Europe to employ Art Nouveau motifs in architecture. Original furnishings and accessories were also designed by the architect and are on display for the public. The Art Nouveau detailing, including stained glass, hardware, and staircase, is exquisite.

BRUSSELS

Hotel Tassel (1893)

ARCHITECT: Victor Horta
LOCATION: 6 Rue Paul-Emile-Janson

Horta's reputation spread throughout Europe after he completed his Art Nouveau townhouses in Brussels. The much-photographed interior and exterior of the Hotel Tassel features superb Art Nouveau detailing, particularly the wrought iron interior staircase. All furnishings and fittings were designed to be consistent with the flowing organic forms of the new nature-based style.

BRUSSELS

Hotel Van Eetveld (1898)

ARCHITECT: Victor Horta
LOCATION: 4 Avenue Palmerston

One of Horta's finest Art Nouveau creations, the Hotel Van Eetveld has an admirable glass facade with flowing iron forms and mosaic panels. The interior dome, staircase, and decorative detailing are excellent examples of the new "modern style" at the turn of the century ("modern" in the sense that it borrowed nothing from the past; today we consider modern to be structural rather than decorative). With the work of Horta and van de Velde, Brussels became the architectural capital of Art Nouveau.

BRUSSELS

Palais Stoclet (1905-11)

ARCHITECT: Josef Hoffmann (Austria)
LOCATION: 279 Avenue de Tervueren, Woluwe-Saint-Pierre

The wealthy Stoclet family commissioned this famous Austrian architect to design their luxury home after a vacation trip to Vienna. Hoffmann, a member of the Secession and Wiener Werstätte in Vienna, became internationally recognized as a result of this brilliant work. A strong early influence on Art Deco designers, the exterior features plain white surfaces outlined in black. The interior design, with its beautiful mosaic compositions, furnishings, and fittings, was created by Hoffmann and the Wiener Werkstatte.

BRUSSELS

Philips Pavilion (1958)

ARCHITECT: Le Corbusier (France)
LOCATION: Avenue des Nations, Fair
Grounds: Heysel

This bold and dynamic structure, commissioned for the Brussels' World Fair in 1958, was designed by Le Corbusier, the internationally famous Swiss-born French architect whose work and philosophies influenced architects around the world to establish the International Style. The design of this sculptural structure expresses strong movement and rhythm unfolding into sharp peaks.

BRUSSELS

The Atomium (1958)

LOCATION: North Brussels at Fair Grounds in Heysel, Laeken

Looming above the skyline of north Brussels, the spectacular Atomium is an unusual sight. The dramatic structure symbolizes the atom in the form of a crystalline metal molecule that has been magnified 200 milliards times. It was built for the Universal Exhibition in 1958. Fascinating exhibits on the use of atomic energy are housed on the first three levels of the structure. This is a work of architecture enjoyed by both children and adults.

BRUSSELS

USA Pavilion (1958)

ARCHITECT: Edward Durell Stone (USA)
LOCATION: Avenue des Nations and
Avenue Frondaisons

Stone, one of America's leading modern
architects, was commissioned to represent the
United States at the Brussels' World Fair. The
architect was known for his "classic" and
"pretty" approach to modern architecture,
often featuring slender vertical lines and
pierced concrete screens. The design of the
USA Pavilion is typical of his light and airy
colors and forms. Stone designed the JFK
Center for the Performing Arts in Washington,
D.C.

LEUVEN (LOUVAIN)

Medical Faculty Building (1969-74)

ARCHITECTS: Lucien Kroll and Atelier
LOCATION: University of Louvain campus

Sited on the campus of one of the finest
universities in Europe, the Medical Faculty
Building was designed as a hilltop "town" to
accommodate numerous functions employing
different building systems and materials. A
variety of interesting detail can be observed
throughout the impressive complex. This
structure is one of the architect's best-known
projects.

NIVELLES

Manufacturing Plant for Torin, S.A. (1963-4)

ARCHITECTS: Marcel Breuer and
Hamilton Smith (USA)
LOCATION: 17 miles S of Brussels

This strongly-expressed structure reflects the architect's individualistic style. The entire structure of this plant, including roof slabs and pre-stressed beams and supports, is of prefabricated concrete made in Holland. Sculptural window panels were designed to protect the inhabitants from sun glare. Breuer received a number of commissions in Europe decades after he fled from Nazi Germany.

SLEIHAGE

Église Des Peres Du S. Sacrament (1960s)

ARCHITECT: Andre Desmedt
LOCATION: Near Roeselare, West Flanders

One of the most interesting modern structures built in Belgium since World War II, the innovative church has twelve sides with twelve triangular windows. The steel roof is topped with a dynamic spirelet. The interior of the entire church, except for the windows, is black. The black marble facings are particularly stunning.

ADDITIONAL MODERN STRUCTURES OF INTEREST

BRUSSELS

Alma Metro Station (1980s)
ARCHITECTS: Atelier Kroll
LOCATION: Woluve-St-Lambert Station

A whimsical and almost shocking architectural treatment, this transportation building was designed by one of Belgium's leading design firms.

Apartment Hotel (1950s)
ARCHITECT: Rene Stapels
LOCATION: Avenue Louis

A lovely luxury residence hotel of light and airy proportions, the interior design and furniture for this impressive complex are from the American firm of Knoll International.

Berlaimont Building (1963-70)
ARCHITECTS: De Vestel and Gilson
LOCATION: At Rond-point Schuman (rue de la Loi 200)

This large building complex in the shape of a four-pointed star is the headquarters for the EEC—the European Communities. The structure is one of Belgium's finest new buildings. The influence of Le Corbusier is evident in the design concept.

Brussels International Trade Mart (1975)
ARCHITECT: John Portman (USA)
LOCATION: Inquire: Natl. Tourist Office, Grasmarkt 61

This new commercial structure was designed by America's prominent architect, well-known for his Hyatt Regency hotels in the United States (Bonaventure in Los Angeles, Renaissance Center, Detroit, Hyatt Regency, San Francisco, etc.)

Foncolin Building (1958)
ARCHITECT: Andre Jacqmain
LOCATION: Rue Montoyer 3

The Foncolin Building is an early example of structural commercial design in Belgium. The uniform composition of concrete slabs, windows, and slender steel supports produces a pleasing streamlined effect.

Gare Central (1937-52)
ARCHITECT: Victor Horta
LOCATION: Downtown central Brussels

This admirable structure was one of the last important works by the great Art Nouveau designer. The building was completed after Horta's death.

Modern Art Museum (1984)
ARCHITECT: Bastin de Namur
LOCATION: Place Royale

The new Modern Art Museum is beautifully planned as an effective background for an impressive collection of modern art.

Palais Des Beaux Arts (1919-28)
ARCHITECT: Victor Horta
LOCATION: Rue Ravenstein 23

After the death of Art Nouveau, Horta renounced the use of decorative floral forms and moved in the more structured architectural direction demonstrated in this building. It functions as the heart of cultural and artistic life in Brussels.

Solvay House (1894)
ARCHITECT: Victor Horta
LOCATION: 244 Avenue Louise

Horta designed many townhouses in the Art Nouveau style; the four presented in this chapter are considered his best. The Solvay house is noted for its perfectly detailed organic forms, especially in the iron work. The symmetrical facade employs a concave-convex form reminiscent of ocean waves. The curvilinear "whiplash lines" of the railing complement the design.

GHENT

Intellect Building (1980s)
ARCHITECT: Denis Van Impe
LOCATION: Mageleinsstrat, on the corner

The Intellect Building is a fascinating and almost whimsical structure capturing traditional vernacular.

(NOTE: In an effort to promote interest in Belgium's Art Nouveau treasures and preserve these structures, The Junior Chamber Brussels, members of Jaycees International, has printed a brochure on Art Nouveau Architecture in Brussels. Included is information on the *CAUCHIE HOUSE,* located at Frankenstraat 5, *HOTEL DE ST. CYR,* located at Boulevard Clovislaan, *DE ULTIEME HALLUCINATIE,* located at Koningstraat 316, rue Royale, *SHOP-FRONT* at Koningstraat, 13, rue Royale and many other important works from this period. The brochure is available at T.I.B. (Office de Tourisme), located at Rue du Marche-Aux-Herbes 61, Brussels).

Denmark

DENMARK

Skagen

Ålborg

Viborg   Randers

Århus

Elsinore
(Helsingor)

Hillerød
Farum
Humlebaek
Ballerup
Vejle   Morso   Copenhagen
                              Roskilde   Rødovre
Odense   Koge   Glostrup
        Nyborg   Herlev
                         Korsor   Hoje-Tastrup
                         Vordingborg   Klampenborg
                                                   Søllerød
Nordborg   Hvidovre

Sønderborg

MODERN ARCHITECTURE IN DENMARK

THE DANISH NATIONAL ROMANTIC MOVEMENT

Twentieth-century architecture in Denmark began when the Danish National Romantic Movement introduced a simpler style, nationally oriented. The movement, led by Martin Nyrop, consisted of Andreas Clemmensen, Hack Kampmann, Martin Borch, and Peter V. J. Klint. Their approach became the major influence in Danish modern architecture until the 1920s. One of the most outstanding works during this period was Peter V. J. Klint's vast modern Gothic Grundtvig Church in Copenhagen.

DANISH ARCHITECTURE PRIOR TO WORLD WAR II

During the 1920s the influence of the Bauhaus and the modern movement elsewhere in Europe was moderately felt. Kay Fisker, who trained at the Royal Danish Academy, helped to introduce modern ideas for housing. C. F. Moller, who also trained at the Academy, is known for the building of Aahus University in partnership with Fisker and Povl Steegman.

ARNE JACOBSEN

Denmark's foremost modern architect is Arne Jacobsen, student of Kay Fisker at the Royal Danish Academy. He designed a "House of the Future" at the Copenhagen Exhibition of 1929 with Flemming Lassen, and won many competitions for structures during the 1930s. Two important buildings during this period were the Aarhus and Sollerod Town Halls. Jacobsen's works were greatly influenced by Le Corbusier in France and Gunnar Asplund in Sweden. Jacobsen is also a furniture designer; his "egg," "swan," and "ant" chairs are classics of modern design.

DANISH ARCHITECTURE AFTER WORLD WAR II

Jacobsen, after spending the war period as a refugee in Sweden, continued to exert influence as the leader of modern architecture in Denmark until his death in 1971. His main interest was in the design of private houses, but his S.A.S. Hotel and other commercial projects employing classical proportions and mathematical precision combined with warmth and humanity have won him international acclaim.

Denmark's major contribution to the modern movement after the war has been in the field of home furnishings, with the works of such leading designers as Hans Wegner, Finn Juhl, Kaare Klint, and Poul Kjaerholm. Jørn Utzon, both an architect and furniture designer, has designed one of the world's most spectacular modern structures—the Opera House in Sydney, Australia. Other popular current modern Danish architects include Gunnar Jensen, Finn Monies, Berge Glahn, Ole Helweg, Palle Jacobsen, Jorgan Bo, Friis & Moltke.

AARHUS

Aarhus University (1931-42)

ARCHITECTS: Kay Fisker, C. F. Moller, and Povl Stegmann

LOCATION: NDR. Ringgade 1-3, Aarhus University Campus, Katrinebjerv, Aarhus

Aarhus University is pleasantly situated on a gently sloping hill close to Aarhus. A lake, trees, and flowers add to the lovely environment. The University is growing, and the early buildings of Fisker and his partners, built of warm yellow brick, are noticeably different in their plain and uniform design. Many of the original buildings, bombed by the R.A.F. because they were occupied by the Nazis, have been rebuilt.

AARHUS

Residential College— Skjoldhog (1973)

ARCHITECTS: Friis & Moltke
LOCATION: Skjoldhojkollegiet Spobjergvej 5, 8220 Brabrand

Denmark has built three universities and a number of colleges since World War II. Most of these facilities employ the latest architectural techniques and materials. The Residential College—Skjoldhog, a project planned by Denmark's leading modern architectural firm, features an effective environment for student activities arranged around outdoor terraces.

AARHUS

Town Hall At Aarhus (1938)

ARCHITECT: Arne Jacobsen and Erik Moller
LOCATION: Raadhuspladsen

The Town Hall at Aarhus is Arne Jacobsen's most famous pre-war building, an early example of this internationally admired architect's excellent sense of proportion. The boxy, five-story glass structure is balanced by a soaring clock tower and, on the other end of the building, a ramp leading up to a projecting entranceway. A large carpet depicting a map of Aarhus is featured in the lobby.

AARHUS

The Music Center (1982)

ARCHITECTS: Kjaer & Richter
LOCATION: In a landscaped square W of the Town Hall

A masterfully designed complex, the new Music Center at Aarhus achieves a strong visual relationship between the old town and Arne Jacobsen's landmark Town Hall of 1938. Located in a sloping garden-park setting, a network of walkways helps integrate the building to its surroundings. A dazzling four-story glass-roofed arcade introduces the spacious lobby area containing a balcony-level restaurant and a gallery area hung with contemporary art. The entire interior and exterior materials are the finest and expertly finished. The main concert hall, employing a purple palette, is acoustically superb.

AARHUS

Training and Conference Centre—Scanticon (1970s)

ARCHITECTS: Friis & Moltke
LOCATION: Ny Moesgaardsvej, 8270 Hojbjerg

During the past decade another building concern for Danish architects has been efficient and well-planned conference centers—today Denmark boasts some of Europe's best. The Training and Conference Centre—Scanticon at Aarhus is designed for maximum privacy in sprawling tiers. The architects have used a waterproof concrete consisting of oven dried quartz sand, cement, and chemicals in the construction of this facility.

ÅLBORG

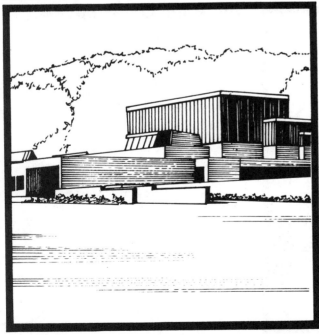

Ålborg Art Museum (North Jutland Museum of Modern Art) (1953-72)

ARCHITECTS: Alvar and Elissa Aalto, Jean-Jacques Baruel
LOCATION: 60 miles NW of Aarhus, 50 Kong Christians Alle'

Many interested in design make a pilgrimage to the northern tip of Denmark to see the work of Finland's world-famous architect, Alvar Aalto. A new stage in Aalto's life commenced with the design of the expressive Alborg Art Museum, a structure that departs from previous approaches. Aalto loved to contrast the natural and the technological, and the old and the new.

ÅLBORG

University Center
At Ålborg (1981)

ARCHITECTS: Dall & Lindhartsen
LOCATION: Alborg University Campus,
Fibigerstraede, Alborg st.

The University of Alborg is one of three
universities built in Denmark since World War
II. Architects have been quick to respond to
new educational requirements and facilities;
the old corridor school has long been
forgotten. The University Center at Alborg, the
newest addition on campus, has large atrium
spaces constructed of glass, steel, concrete,
and natural materials.

COPENHAGEN

Church At Bagsvåerd (1951)

ARCHITECT: Jørn Utzon
LOCATION: Taxvej 16, 2880 Bagsvaerd,
Copenhagen

After World War II, many younger-generation
architects in Denmark were inspired by
America's Frank Lloyd Wright. Jørn Utzon
concentrated on new materials and
construction techniques. He is internationally
famous for his Opera House at Sydney,
Australia, with its bold dynamics. The Church
at Bagsvaerd features severely stark forms, a
new direction in church design and one of
Utzon's first important works.

COPENHAGEN

Bella Centre (New Trade Center) (1970s)

ARCHITECT: Ole Meyer
LOCATION: On Amager
(New Exhibition Hall)

Tourists, students, and designers from all over the world visit the Bella Centre to see the latest design developments in Scandinavia. This cavernous complex of glass and metal beams serves as an exhibition and congress center for Copenhagen. The high-tech facility provides an excellent background for displaying modern Scandinavian wares.

COPENHAGEN

Church Of The Advent (1943)

ARCHITECT: Erik Moller
LOCATION: Sallingvej and Bellahojvej

A charming church constructed of traditional Danish brick on a triangular site. The soaring beamed ceiling centers over the meeting hall. Spacious windows, mostly on one side of the chapel, look out onto a pleasant garden. Seating consists of orderly rows of simple Danish wood chairs with rush seats.

COPENHAGEN

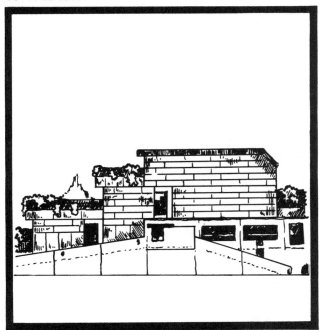

Farum Midtpunkt Housing Terraces (1970s)

ARCHITECTS: Sorensen, Moller-Jensen, and Arnfred
LOCATION: Farum Midtpunkt, Copenhagen

Numerous innovative housing developments have been designed in Denmark during the last decade. Typical of this creative planning is the Farum Midtpunkt Housing complex, where architects have tried to combine economic advantages of multi-stories with private outdoor living spaces. The design solution is one of the best of its kind in Denmark.

COPENHAGEN

Grundtvigskirken (1913-26)

ARCHITECT: Pedar Vilhelm Jensen Klint
LOCATION: Pa Bjerget

The Grundtvigskirken, with its staggering emphasis on the vertical line, remains one of the most dramatically designed churches in Europe. It seems a huge modern enlargement of a traditional Gothic church. Built with warm yellow brick, the expressive design of the facade has been compared to a massive church organ. Pedar is the father of Kaare Klint, one of Denmark's pioneer modern furniture craftsmen.

COPENHAGEN

Langelinie Pavilion (1958)

ARCHITECTS: Eva and Nils Koppel
LOCATION: At the foot of Amaliegade

The beautiful Langelinie Walk, meandering between the harbor and the old fortifications, is very popular in Copenhagen. The striking restaurant pavilion, with facilities for the Royal Danish Yacht Club, is constructed of steel, painted black, with wall panels of grey-blue. The open-air restaurant terrace commands a lovely view of the Langelinie Walk and harbor. Poul Henningsen, Denmark's most famous lighting designer, created the lighting fixtures throughout the three-story building.

COPENHAGEN

S.A.S. Air Terminal And Hotel Building (1959)

ARCHITECT: Arne Jacobsen
LOCATION: Banegaardspladsen

This twenty-one story steel-and-glass structure was built for Scandinavian Airlines Systems and is combined with the Royal Hotel. A long, low wing and the tower are raised on a reinforced concrete framework in the heart of Copenhagen. The hotel tower is sheathed in thin aluminum, with slender horizontal bands of gray-green glass windows emphasizing the horizontal line. Jacobsen, also a furniture designer, created for the hotel lobby two chairs, the "egg" and the "swan," that have become modern classics.

COPENHAGEN

Sports Center—
Kildeskovshallen (1970s)

ARCHITECTS: Karen and Ebbe Clemensen
LOCATION: Adolphsvej 25, 2820 Gentofte

This warm and inviting sports center of glass, steel, and wood is one of the finest examples of humanism in Danish architecture. Interior, exterior, and grounds are planned for total participation. Windows and outdoor terraces are designed to take full advantage of the sun.

COPENHAGEN

St. Knud Lavard Church (1957)

ARCHITECT: Carl R. Frederiksen
LOCATION: Lyngbygardsvej,
Kongens Lyngby

Situated in a northern suburb of Copenhagen, this simply expressed church is typical of the Danish artistic philosophy of clean functional approach. Slender lines and forms are repeated by the support columns and wooden benches. Effective lighting is provided principally by a continuous clerestory window band that wraps around the tops of the high walls.

Concert Hall—Tivoli (1956)

ARCHITECTS: Hans Hansen and
Fritz Schegel
LOCATION: Tivoli Park

The festive and delightful Tivoli Park is a
favorite spot for both tourists and Danes. The
present Concert Hall at Tivoli was built on
the site of a previous building destroyed
during World War II. At night the building
is viewed at its best, with floodlights
accentuating the slender columns, arches,
and stylized decorative facade. Numerous
fountains enclosed in tiered circular ponds, a
focal point in the square, are also beautifully
lit at night.

COPENHAGEN

U.S. Embassy (1951)

ARCHITECT: Ralph Rapson (USA)
LOCATION: Dag Hammarskiolds Alle' 24

Rapson, a prominent American architect who
taught at the University of Minnesota's School
of Architecture, was highly influenced by Le
Corbusier. His design for the U.S. Embassy is
simple, direct, and functional. Rapson felt that
an embassy should be a "well-designed office
building."

COPENHAGEN

Zero Energy House (1973)

ARCHITECT: Peter Narboe with the Institute of Housing Construction
LOCATION: Polytekniske Laereranstalt Ank. Engelundsvej 1,2800 Lyngby

This low-energy house was built at the Technical University at the time of the first oil crisis to study energy-saving ideas in building. In the center of the house a glass-covered room is heated only by the sun. The house also has solar collectors, heat-exchangers, and two maximum-insulation zones. The research project inspired new maximum-insulation housing designs.

COPENHAGEN

Stengard Church At Gladsaxe (1963-4)

ARCHITECTS: Rolf Graae and Vilhelm Wohlert
LOCATION: Stengaards Kirke i Gladsaxe, 2860 Soborg

The unifying element employed throughout this Lutheran Church is red untreated brick. Brick is used everywhere—exterior and interior walls, altar, pulpit, even the font. The play of light on the inside brick walls emphasizes the warmth and texture of this building material. Belfry towers loom high above layered tile roofs.

GLOSTRUP

Shopping Center
At Glostrup (1970s)

ARCHITECTS: Ejnar Graae and
Henning Helger
LOCATION: Glostrup, near Copenhagen

Increased suburban development in Denmark
during the past decades has created a need
for convenient shopping facilities. The well-
planned shopping center at Glostrup is typical
of the many excellent commercial facilities
recently built. The raw concrete exterior of
this complex was executed in dramatic
curvilinear form.

HERLEV

Copenhagen County
Hospital (1970s)

ARCHITECTS: The Council of Practicing
Architects
LOCATION: Herlev, near Copenhagen

The Copenhagen County Hospital is one of
the finest hospital designs in the world. Only
three materials were used for the exterior—
white concrete, brown anodized aluminum,
and glass. Interior colors were selected
according to function in a particular space,
adding to the smooth running of various
areas. The impressive structure has influenced
hospital building around the world.

HOJE-TASTRUP

The Hoje-Tastrup School (Late 1970s)

ARCHITECT: Ole Kortzau, with design by Henning Larsen's office.
LOCATION: Hoje-Tastrup suburb, about 10 miles from Copenhagen

This school complex is situated in a park area that was formerly a village garden. The rapidly growing suburb is an attractive residential area. The Hoje-Tastrup School in particular has received international recognition as representative of the finest Danish architecture today. A strong feature of this simple complex is a large folded roof above the central common area between the four principal buildings. It is colorfully covered with synthetic rubber in bold white and blue stripes.

HUMLEBAEK

Louisiana Museum (1958)

ARCHITECTS: Jorgen Bo and Vilhelm Wohlert
LOCATION: Ny Strandvej at Gammel Strandvef, 22 miles north of Copenhagen

The Louisiana Museum has an exceptionally beautiful location in a park lush with trees and flowers, positioned by an elegant nineteenth-century house overlooking the Ore Sound. A cluster of exhibition halls joins the house through a staggered corridor. Whitewashed walls, large warm wood beams, tile floors, and large plate glass windows provide the perfect background for the museum's contemporary Danish art and other exhibitions.

HVIDOVRE

St. Nikolaj Church At Hvidovre (1960)

ARCHITECT: Johan Otto von Spreckelsen
LOCATION: Skt. Nikolai Kirke, Strobyvej,
2650 Hvidovre

One of Denmark's favorite building materials, brick, has been expressively employed in this Roman Catholic church. The exterior of simple square and diagonal forms becomes an effective background for a small dark cross placed to one side of the entrance. The interior is dramatically lit by two narrow side windows that throw beams of light on the warm yellow brick, highlighting its texture.

KOGE

Koge Town Hall (1978)

ARCHITECTS: Arkitektgruppen i Aarhus
LOCATION: Center of town, 22 miles SSW of Copenhagen

The new Koge Town Hall was designed as an extension of the old town hall that is now used primarily as a reception area. The contrasting modern design of the new hall complements the older hall in an excellent marriage of old and new. The two buildings connect through a pedestrian mall from the old town square into a glass enclosure in the new Town Hall.

MORSO

Morso Town Hall (1980)

ARCHITECTS: Friis & Moltke
LOCATION: About 50 mi. W of
Copenhagen, just W of Holbaek

Friis & Moltke, Denmark's leading modern
architectural firm, has designed a number of
commercial structures outside Denmark.
Government changes created a need for new
town halls throughout Denmark during the
past decade. A symmetrical building designed
around a courtyard, end wings turning
upward, the new Morso Town Hall is a
dramatic break with earlier pre-war town
halls such as Arne Jacobsen's buildings of the
1930s.

ODENSE

St. Hans Tveje (1919)

ARCHITECT: Peder Vilhelm Jensen Klint
LOCATION: 85 miles WSW of Copenhagen

St. Hans Tveje Church, although not as
famous as Klint's Gruntvigskirken in
Copenhagen, is an interesting early example of applying Gothic metaphors to a
contemporary secular building. Like the
Gruntvigskirken, this structure features
building forms similar to a pipe organ.
St. Hans Tveje is a heavier and simpler
expression of this theme.

RANDERS

St. Clemens Church At Randers, Jutland (1963-4)

ARCHITECTS: Inger Exner, Johannes Exner and Knud Erik Larsen
LOCATION: 22 miles NW of Aarhus

Beautifully located on a sloping landscaped hillside, this impressive Lutheran Church has a prism-shaped nave that has been compared to a ship's stern. The soaring vertical windows provide effective sunlight and a panoramic view directly behind the altar. The natural materials of brick, wood, tile, and glass employed throughout the structure are typical of Danish construction.

RØDOVRE

Rødovre Town Hall (1955)

ARCHITECT: Arne Jacobsen
LOCATION: Rodovre Parkvej and Taarnevej, near Copenhagen

Completely clean and pristine, Rodovre Town Hall is almost cold in its uniform design. The main entrance features a canopy supported by steel columns. Long exterior walls are curtained with light green glass panels framed with steel. Black marble faces the end walls. Executed by Denmark's most illustrious early modern architect, Rodovre Town Hall is an important example of the urban planning developments promoted since World War II.

ROSKILDE (ZEALAND)

Museum For Viking
Boats (1970s)

ARCHITECT: Professor Erik C. Sorensen
LOCATION: On Roskilde Fjord

When a small fleet of Viking boats was uncovered in Roskilde Fjord, it was decided to build a museum to house the important historical find. The building was constructed with reinforced concrete using sturdy bearing columns and extended girders. Five boats are displayed in a structure that projects part way into the Roskilde Fjord and permits three viewing levels. Large windows on the north side of the building protect the boats from exposure to direct sunlight.

SKAGEN

Skagen Town Hall (1970s)

ARCHITECT: Ejnar Borg
LOCATION: Port City, 30 miles NE of Hjorring

The Danes feel that a town hall should be more than just an office building. It should also serve as the "town's house," extending a feeling of warmth and welcome to the citizens. The Skagen Town Hall is a model example of this philosophy of design meeting the needs of people. A spacious outdoor plaza hospitably introduces the inviting structure.

ADDITIONAL MODERN STRUCTURES OF INTEREST

AARHUS

Radio/TV Building (1973-81)
ARCHITECTS: C. F. Mollers with others
LOCATION: Halmstadgade 10-12

One of the finest facilities of its type in Scandinavia.

ÅLBORG

Carl Christensen Factory (1956)
ARCHITECT: Arne Jacobsen
LOCATION: Riihimakivej

One of Jacobsen's finest commercial designs.

BALLERUP

Toms Fabrikker A/S Factory At Ballerup (1961)
ARCHITECT: Arne Jacobsen
LOCATION: 8 miles NW of Copenhagen

Jacobsen's most admired commercial endeavor. Constructed of reinforced concrete and concrete cast with white ceramic tile.

COPENHAGEN

Bellahoj Housing Estate (1950-56)
ARCHITECTS: Mogens Irming and Tage Nielsen.
LOCATION: Belahojvej 44, 2700 Bronshoj

This prize-winning housing project is situated on Copenhagen's highest ground.

Bottling Plant—Carlsberg Breweries (Bryggerierne) (1970s)
ARCHITECT: Svenn Eske Kristensen
LOCATION: Vesterfaelledvej 100

An interesting cubistic design of brick.

Buddinge School And Community Center (1970s)
ARCHITECTS: Eva and Nils Koppel
LOCATION: Buddinge Hovedgade at Gladsakse Ringvej, NW of town

A thoughtful and intelligent solution to a difficult problem, this complex provides facilities for a cinema, a community center, a public library, and two schools located between two busy highways in a highly industrial section.

Commercial College Handelshojskolen (1970s)
ARCHITECT: H. Hannibal
LOCATION: Julius Thomsensplads 10

One of the many outstanding educational facilities in Denmark, Handelshojskolen has a remarkable auditorium demonstrating warmth and functionalism.

Copenhagen Town Hall (Kobenhavns Radhus) (1893-1902)
ARCHITECT: Martin Nyrop
LOCATION: Radhuspladsen

With its simple geometric design and unadorned red brick walls, this town hall is one of the first early examples of modern architecture in Scandinavia. Nyrop, a leader of the Danish National Romantic Movement, sought to establish architecture employing simple expressions.

Den Permanente (Modern Showroom)
LOCATION: Near Central Station

A fine permanent collection of modern design from leading Danish artists is displayed. (Also, some work is for sale.)

Headquarters Of Messrs. Jespersen & Sons A/S (1955)
ARCHITECT: Arne Jacobsen
LOCATION: Nyropsgade 18

An effective light curtain wall of wood with aluminum bars and windows of green glass.

Hotel Scandinavia (1970s)
ARCHITECTS: Bent Severin, Graae, and Helger
LOCATION: Amager Boulevard 70

An excellent example of a deluxe modern hotel in Denmark. The box-like structure rises above Denmark's skyline.

Jacob Asbaek House (Galleri Asbaek)
OWNER: Jacob Asbaek
LOCATION: Ny Adelgade 4

This restored traditional home features one of the best private modern art collections in the city.

Munkegard School (1956)
ARCHITECT: Arne Jacobsen
LOCATION: Vangedevej, Gentofte

This school, one of Jacobsen's most innovative projects, is based on a unique checkerboard plan.

Denmarks Nationalbank (1965–71)
ARCHITECT: Arne Jacobsen
LOCATION: Havnegade 5

Completed a few years before the death of Denmark's leading pioneer modern architect, the National Bank reflects Jacobsen's philosophy of simplicity and functionalism.

Panum Institute (1970s)
ARCHITECTS: Architects KKET
LOCATION: Blegdamsveg 3

A modern medical facility for Copenhagen University featuring a lively color scheme throughout.

Residential Area—"Vejlegardsparken" (Brondby Strand) (1970s)
ARCHITECT: Svend Hogsbro
LOCATION: 2660 Brondby Strand

A convenient and comfortable residential area in one of Copenhagen's newest developments.

Sports Center—Rundforbi (Late 1970s)
ARCHITECTS: Claus Bremer & Ole Helweg
LOCATION: Rundforbivej 140

An acute triangular plan. A well-designed sports center featuring an excellent color and light treatment.

Sports Center—Virumhallen (1970s)
ARCHITECTS: Gunnar Jensen and Finn Monies
LOCATION: Cedervaenget 19

This large sports center is functional and aesthetically appealing. The dynamic diagonal form of the roof is expressive of the stimulating sports activities housed within.

Voldparken (1951-57)
ARCHITECT: Kay Fisker
LOCATION: 2700 Bronshoj

Fisker helped establish standards for the new modern movement in Denmark. This housing development was influenced by International Functionalism.

ELSINORE

Kingowusene (1958-60)
ARCHITECT: Jørn Utzon
LOCATION: 24 miles N of Copenhagen

Close to the town made famous by Shakespeare's *Hamlet*, Utzon has planned sixty-three small houses in clusters around courtyards, with windows placed to take full advantage of the sunlight and countryside.

FARUM

The Baths At Farum (1970s)
ARCHITECTS: Knud Holscher and Svend Axelsson
LOCATION: 9 miles SSE of Hillerod

A beautifully-designed swimming facility.

HOLSTEBRO

Holstebro Art Museum (1981–84)
ARCHITECT: Hanne Kjaerholm
LOCATION: West Jutland, 23 miles NE of Ringkobing

High vaulted skylights 9 feet wide run throughout the interesting spaces of this classic modern white museum. The new airy museum is annexed to a stately white traditional villa.

KLAMPENBORG

Soholm Row Houses (1949)
ARCHITECT: Arne Jacobsen
LOCATION: 7 miles N of Copenhagen in Stradevejen, Klampenborg

This seaside development boasts a number of projects by Jacobsen, including a theater, the Bellavista Flats, and a restaurant.

NORDBORG

Factory Danfoss (1970s)
ARCHITECTS: N.P. Waino, P. Maroti, and P. O. Pedersen
LOCATION: On Als Island, 10 miles N of Sonderborg

A fine example of modern factory design in Denmark.

SØLLERØD (HOLTE)

Town Hall At Sollerod (1940)
ARCHITECT: Arne Jacobsen
LOCATION: 8 miles N of Copenhagen

A demonstration of Jacobsen's sensitivity for combining warmth and humanism with mathematical precision. Considered one of the architect's first important works.

VEJLE

High School At Vejle (Late 1970s)
ARCHITECTS: Gravers & Richter
LOCATION: 40 miles SSW of Aarhus

A streamlined design featuring large terraces for student enjoyment. The plan is admired for its efficient use of space and its attractiveness.

VIBORG

County College (1970s)
ARCHITECTS: Friis & Moltke
LOCATION: 37 miles NW of Aarhus

The firm of Friis and Moltke, one of the most prestigious in Europe, represents the finest current design and technology. The County College is one of the firm's best designs. Other well-designed universities in Denmark, built since World War II, are the *UNIVERSITY AT ODENSE*, the *UNIVERSITY AT ALBORG*, and the *UNIVERSITY AT ROSKILDE*, designed by various architects.

VORDINGBORG

Vordingborg Theater (1970s)
ARCHITECTS: Friis & Moltke
LOCATION: 50 miles SSW of Copenhagen

An excellent example of theater design in Scandinavia.

England

ENGLAND

Newcastle •
Sunderland •
Durham •

• York
Leeds •
                                    Kingston-upon-Hull
Manchester •
• Liverpool
• Runcorn   • Sheffield
Birkenhead •

                    • Nottingham
            Beeston •
                    • Loughborough   Norwich •
                    • Liecester
Birmingham •
            • Coventry
Warwick •
                              • Cambridge
                              Ipswich •
            • Oxford

                    Perivale •   London
            • Swindon Watford •
                    Thamesmead •
                    Leatherhead • Mitcham •
                    Guildford •   Gravesend
• Bristol
• Bath   • Gatwick
            Haslemere •
Southampton •   • Horsham
Beaulieu •   Brighton
            Chichester   Bexhill
        Portsmouth   Sayers Common

MODERN ARCHITECTURE IN ENGLAND

INDUSTRIAL REVOLUTION

New discoveries, inventions, and the development of iron as a building material contributed greatly to the design of new structures in England. Early modern buildings in England often featured amazing iron roofs enclosing large spaces. Generally, the remainder of the building was traditionally decorated. The Crystal Palace of 1851 was a spectacular structural example of modern design. Its remarkable construction of iron, glass, and wood was far advanced for the time and influenced architects around the world.

ARTS AND CRAFTS MOVEMENT

This artistic protest against the ugliness of machine-made products and the stress of the Industrial Revolution was led by William Morris. Morris advocated a return to hand-crafted furnishings of simple honest design. The Arts and Crafts members were inspired by the Medieval and Gothic periods, but interpreted the styles in a fresh and contemporary manner. Many designers throughout Europe and America were inspired by the teachings of this significant philosophy.

ART NOUVEAU

Early beginnings of the Art Nouveau Style, popular throughout Europe and America, evolved in England. The style, based on flowing organic forms from nature, flourished between 1890 and 1910. Flowers, vines, stalks, reptiles, a woman's form, and other motifs were employed in all mediums of art and architecture. Important exponents of the style included Sir Arthur Liberty, Charles Annesley Voysey, and some members of the Arts and Crafts Movement.

ART DECO

This style was inspired by many influences, including the Bauhaus in Germany, Mackintosh in Scotland, Hoffmann in Austria, and even such events as the opening of King Tut's tomb. The World Fair of 1925 in Paris officially launched the sleek, shiny, streamlined style, a pioneering response to modernism. Popular between World War I and World War II, the Art Deco style was employed for hundreds of striking buildings in England.

MODERN DEVELOPMENTS AFTER WORLD WAR II

Modern architecture after the war became highly individualistic, with prominent modern designers developing their own unique approaches. Perhaps more important, Britain's special architectural contribution has been working in close collaboration to produce fine public buildings—especially education and housing facilities. The British Government has supported extensive building programs that have produced admirable works. Architects in England have accepted new challenges dealing with unique building problems with respect for human requirements.

BEESTON

Pharmaceutical Factory

(1930-32)

ARCHITECT: Sir Owen Williams
LOCATION: Boots Co. LTD, 4 miles S of
Nottinghamshire

The most important work of Sir Owen
Williams, famous in England for pioneering
reinforced concrete, is considered to be the
Pharmaceutical Factory in Beeston. The
creative design for this complex features
expressive mushroom-shaped support
columns. Cantilevered glass exterior walls
allowing maximum lighting inside are
arranged in large horizontal bands that wrap
around the entire structure.

BEXHILL

De La Warr Pavilion (1936)

ARCHITECT: Eric Mendelsohn (USA) with
Serge Chermayeff
LOCATION: Bexhill-on-Sea, Sussex.
The Ocean front.

Mendelsohn was a refugee from the Nazis
when he designed this pavilion. He remained
in England for a few years before opening his
practice in San Francisco. This extraordinary
structure, his only important work in England,
has boldly designed balconies running the
perimeter of the flat and round forms of the
building. With large expanses of windows, the
airy building commands a sweeping view of
the ocean from its waterfront site. The design
was executed in collaboration with Serge
Chermayeff, who also later left England for a
career in America.

BRISTOL

Cathedral Church Of St. Peter And St. Paul (1973)

ARCHITECT: Percy Thomas Partnership
LOCATION: Pembroke Road

Seemingly simple in design, the architectural approach was based on strict adherence to a basic triangular module. A brilliant structural system of ascending rings of concrete walls made possible an enormous nave and sanctuary free of column supports. The white concrete is frankly exposed, revealing the texture of sawed-board formwork. The ceiling lighting is superior, and the total effect is one of exceptional beauty.

BRISTOL

Gane's Exhibition Pavilion (1936)

ARCHITECT: Marcel Breuer (USA)
LOCATION: On grounds at Ashton Court Estate, just SW of Bristol

Breuer, the internationally prominent Bauhaus member, left Nazi Germany in 1935 for London, where he practiced architecture with England's Francis R.S. Yorke until 1937, when he left England for America. The Gane's Pavilion is his most important work in England. Breuer expressed a new direction in architecture with the design of the pavilion by emphasizing mass through the use of Coltswold stone and large areas of glass. The pavilion was erected for the Royal Agricultural Show and promoted by Gane's Furniture. It is now owned by the City Council.

BRISTOL

Wills Tobacco Office And Factory (1976)

ARCHITECTS: Skidmore, Owings, and Merrill (USA)
LOCATION: Hartcliffe Estate, S of city center

The prestigious American firm is known throughout the world for its fine commercial buildings, a number of which have been erected in Europe. The Wills Tobacco Office and Factory is beautifully situated on a podium that spans an artificial lake. The efficient complex features a seven-story office wing intersected by a long horizontal wing connecting additional facilities.

CAMBRIDGE

Cripps Building (1967)

ARCHITECTS: Sir Philip Powell and Hidalgo Moya
LOCATION: St. John's College, Cambridge University

A flexible structure employing a reinforced concrete frame with clear spans for possible future expansion. Powell and Moya designed Cripps Building to complement the traditional surroundings. By its large-scale linear design, the complex creates courtyards by setbacks that are directly related to the considerations of the location.

CAMBRIDGE

History Faculty Building (1964)

ARCHITECT: James Stirling
LOCATION: Cambridge University

Scotland and England's world-renowned architect designed this striking glass and brick building to principally function as an adequate reading room for three hundred people. A glass roof is supported by lattice steel girders, providing effective lighting that floods the interior space with aesthetic appeal.

CAMBRIDGE

New Hall For Girls At Cambridge (1966)

ARCHITECTS: Chamberlain, Powell, and Bon
LOCATION: Cambridge University

The New Hall for Girls at Cambridge is a remarkable departure from the established criteria for modern architecture during this period. Most structures were designed by the rules set forth by Le Corbusier, the Bauhaus, and the International Style. The New Hall is an even sharper break with the traditional buildings found at Cambridge. The imaginative New Hall has brought a number of images to the minds of students, including "an orange peel dome."

CHICHESTER

Chichester Festival Theater
(1961)

ARCHITECTS: Powell and Moya
LOCATION: Oaklands Park, 62 miles SW of London

Theater-going crowds flock to this ancient Roman city to see live performances by some of England's and the world's most famous actors. It is England's first professional theater to be built with an open stage. The audience is seated around the stage on three sides. An intricate system of hexagonal ring girders in steel tubing supports the roof. The large auditorium is supported on six concrete ribs forming the cantilevered overhang extending over the entrance.

CHORLEY WOOD

The Orchard House (1900)

ARCHITECT: Charles Francis Annesley Voysey
LOCATION: Residential urban district, 5 miles W of Watford

This early modern architect and furniture designer was known as "the great simplifier" for his approach geared toward eliminating unnecessary decoration. Many historians feel Voysey was decades ahead of his time in finding contemporary expressions of design. He built a number of "English cottage houses" in England, often traditional in feeling but substantially structural in concept. This philosophy is reflected in the Orchard House, Voysey's most important "modern" work.

COVENTRY

St. Michael's Cathedral (1960)

ARCHITECTS: Sir Basil Spence and Partners
LOCATION: Cathedral Square

The Coventry Cathedral is one of England's most dramatic and compelling modern structures. Spence received a knighthood upon its completion. The Cathedral was built upon ruins of a previous Gothic Cathedral bombed during World War II. Much effort was put into preserving any salvageable ruins and capturing the spirit of the old architecture in soaring structural concrete designs.

DURHAM

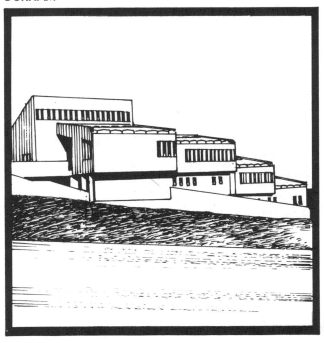

Dunelm House (1964)

ARCHITECTS: Architects' Co-Partnership
LOCATION: Durham University Campus

Dunelm House is situated dramatically on a sweeping bank of the River Wear, surrounded by traditional structures and artistically linked to an adjacent modern Footbridge by Ove Arup. The structure is sensitively tiered into the slope, taking full advantage of a limited space. The building, almost entirely of raw concrete, houses the student club and the university staff house.

HASLEMERE

Olivetti Training School
(1969-73)

ARCHITECT: James Stirling
LOCATION: Residential urban district,
12 miles SSW of Guildford

The Italian Olivetti Firm has commissioned many of Europe's most impressive modern buildings and James Stirling has designed some of England's most creative structures. This innovative school has been labeled "slick tech." The building is covered with a cream-colored shiny plastic. The edges of the building have been rounded to soften the materials and the architecture.

HULL

Gulbenkian Center (1967)

ARCHITECT: Peter Moro and Partners
LOCATION: Hull University Campus

Built a few years after the firm's successful Nottingham Playhouse, the Gulbenkian Center functions as a flexible drama studio for theater study. The pleasing arrangement of shapes and textures is an eye-catcher. The hexagonal structure is of raw concrete, glass, and red brick panels, with a copper roof. The facility includes a photo studio, auditorium and stage, TV and film studio, communications center, film preview theater, costume storage, and numerous other theater services.

IPSWICH

Willis Faber And Dumas Offices (1972-76)

ARCHITECTS: Norman Foster Associates
LOCATION: 70 miles NE of London

Norman Foster has blazed the trail in England with a series of high-tech, high-image glass skins that have dazzled Europe to an amazing advancement in the use of glass compared to traditional buildings or even to the Crystal Palace of 1851. The use of glass on the Willis Faber and Dumas Offices combines high technical bravura with efficiency and competence. The dark-tinted glass structure follows the curving contours of its corner site, with a sidewalk repeating the form. The much-photographed building has an interior with vast flowing spaces made possible by walls free of loadbearing.

LEEDS

Corn Exchange (1860-63)

ARCHITECT: Cuthbert Brodrick
LOCATION: Duncan Street

During the latter half of the nineteenth century early modern architects in England and elsewhere in Europe were concerned with new building functions—in particular, enclosing large interior spaces. New developments in iron construction made this feat possible. The Corn Exchange is a superior example of iron construction, noted for its modern elliptical dome.

LEICESTER

Engineering Building (1959-63)

ARCHITECTS: James Stirling and James Gowan
LOCATION: Leicester University Campus

The Engineering laboratories are remarkable for their architectural virility. Bold use of bright red brick, red tiles, concrete, and glass creates suitable space for teaching workshops, lecture theaters, research laboratories, staff rooms, and other facilities. Often schools of art, architecture, and engineering become vehicles for expressing new techniques and materials. The Engineering Building at Leicester appropriately expresses the latest engineering techniques.

LEICESTER

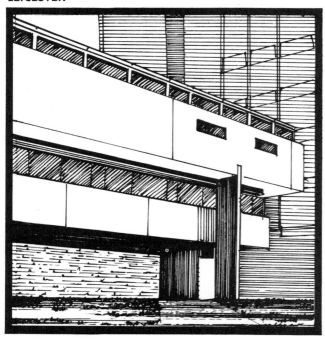

Attenborough Building (1970)

ARCHITECTS: ARUP Associates
LOCATION: University of Leicester

Many buildings designed in England during the past decade employ extreme repetition of the constructional elements, causing the eye to move in a uniform manner. The Attenborough Building features strong repeating horizontal forms relieved by occasional level changes.

LIVERPOOL

The Metropolitan Cathedral Of Christ The King (1962-67)

ARCHITECT: Sir Frederick Gibberd
LOCATION: Liverpool, Mersey, Mount Pleasant

Regarded as one of the most creative structures in England, Liverpool Cathedral is based on a circular plan. The focal point is a remarkable metal-and-glass lantern that sweeps high above the concrete podium. Inside, the lighting comes entirely from the colorful stained glass of the lantern, evoking a serene quality found in ancient medieval cathedrals. The new cathedral was built on the foundations of an intended classical church abandoned by Sir Edwin Lutyens.

LONDON

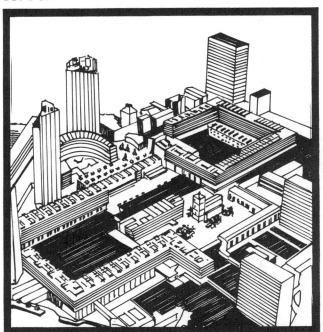

Barbican Center (1970s and 80s)

ARCHITECTS: Chamberlin, Powell, and Bon
LOCATION: London Wall

This well-planned commercial complex situated in the heart of London has become a popular meeting place for tourists and residents. The huge complex includes apartments, schools, a concert hall, a theater, a restaurant, and an art gallery. The massing of various functions has created a network of plazas, courtyards, landscaping, and even parking pleasantly planned to complement the structures.

Aviary At The London Zoological Gardens (1962)

ARCHITECTS: Lord Snowdon, with Cedric Price and Frank Newby
LOCATION: Regent's Park in north London

The chief attraction in Regent's Park is the Zoo. The highlight of the Zoo is the creative aviary by Princess Margaret's ex-husband. A good example of "non-architecture," this rhythmic birdcage is mostly air. Reminiscent of the Constructivist Movement in Germany during the 1920s, the architects have tried to design a structure that does away with enclosure. The unique design was created by supporting wire mesh over tension cables and a network of tubular aluminum.

LONDON

Bousefeld School (1956)

ARCHITECTS: Chamberlin, Powell, and Bon
LOCATION: Old Brompton Road at The Boltons

The delightful Bousefeld school has been highly praised for its brilliant use of space and functional facilities. Gardens, including a water garden, terraced levels, and play spaces, surround well-designed educational spaces. The architects employed a forty-square-inch module throughout the complex, with many of the components prefabricated. Bousefeld school is representative of the many excellent modern school plans throughout England.

LONDON

Bush Lane House (1976)

ARCHITECTS: ARUP Associates
LOCATION: 80 Cannon Street, E.C.4

Although British architects have considered rolled steel as a building material for decades, understanding its characteristics and potential developed slowly in England. There are still no structures comparable to the World Trade Center in New York or the Sears Building in Chicago. But there are noteworthy uses of rolled steel in London. The Bush Lane House, with its projecting skeletal frame and glass sheathing, is the only example in London of a tubular stainless steel, diagonal-external structure. The steel is filled with water for fire protection.

LONDON

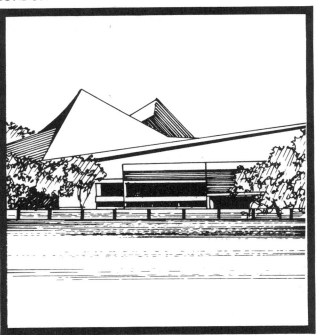

Commonwealth Institute (1960s)

ARCHITECTS: Matthew, Johnson Marshall
LOCATION: 230 Kensington High Street

A huge curved concrete roof dominates the architectural design of the Commonwealth Institute. The vast interior space functions as a museum exhibition hall. An interesting display representing all of the commonwealth countries flows effectively in the space. The clean structural background enhances the detailed exhibits.

LONDON

Coutts Bank (1973-77)

ARCHITECTS: Sir Frederick Gibberd and Partners
LOCATION: 440 Strand WC2, east of Trafalgar Square

The building's development started over 150 years ago when John Nash improved the West Strand structures. Further speculations followed. In 1903 the buildings were demolished and the Coutts Bank was erected. The new award-winning Coutts Bank has been restored and converted from the original structures. A four-story tinted glass entrance facade is dramatically slanted at the top. Interior spaces are vast and filled with plants. Materials, including travertine and bronze, provide a stately feeling.

LONDON

Crystal Palace (1851)

(Destroyed by fire in 1937)
ARCHITECT: Joseph Paxton with Prince Albert
LOCATION: Hyde Park, later moved to Crystal Palace Park on Thames

This masterpiece demonstrates the potential of iron as a building material, playing so significant a role in the development of modern architecture it must be mentioned even though it was destroyed. The daring project was created for the Great Exhibition of 1851. Constructed of wood, glass, and iron, the innovative Crystal Palace was an important example of structural, modular, and prefabricated design. The immense structure was four times the size of St. Peter's in Rome. With his method of construction, Paxton could have continued the building to any length—he stopped at 1,851 feet, the year of the exhibition. At opening-day ceremonies, Queen Victoria said: "This is my proudest moment."

LONDON

Daily Express Building (1931)

ARCHITECT: Ellis Clarke and Atkinson with
Sir Owen Williams
LOCATION: Fleet Street EC4

A superb example of Art Deco architecture in
the heart of London's newspaper land. The
typical shiny exterior of black and transparent
glass features rounded corners arranged in a
tiered design popular during the 1920s and
1930s. The dazzling entrance hall by Atkinson
is an expressive fantasy in metal design.
Gleaming sunburst designs and other motifs
found throughout the building are typical of
the Art Deco style. The building is one of the
world's best examples from this period.

LONDON

Dome Of Discovery (1951)

ARCHITECT: Ralph Tubbs
LOCATION: South Bank

This enormous building, with its vast, partly
column-free interior, was designed for the
Festival of Britain in 1951. The spectacular
dome of the structure is three hundred and
sixty-five feet in diameter, the largest dome of
this type in the world at the time. The Dome
of Discovery was an enormous success,
amazing crowds with its unusual design and
providing a fitting background for the
contemporary exhibits.

LONDON

Economist Building (1964)

ARCHITECTS: Alison and Peter Smithson
LOCATION: 25 St. James Street

The impressive Economist Building was designed by England's respected husband-and-wife architectural team. The Smithsons are known for planning their designs to fulfill human needs, taking full advantage of the latest technical advancements. The sleek Economist Building, their best-known work, is one of London's most photographed multi-story structures. The structure functions as offices for *The Economist* newspaper, a bank, and apartments. Each is accommodated in separate but adjoining buildings.

LONDON

Elephant House At The London Zoo

ARCHITECT: Sir Hugh Casson
LOCATION: London Zoo, Regent's Park

A unique design emphasizing shape and form, the cluster of buildings of ribbed concrete seems to capture the feeling of the massive elephant's body. Other interesting structures at the Zoo are the Penguin Pool and Gorilla House by Ove Arup and Tecton and Lubetkin. Casson, one of England's leading contemporary architects, was knighted for his work as director of architecture for the Festival of Britain in 1951.

LONDON

Hillingdon Civic Center (1977)

ARCHITECTS: Robert Matthew, Johnson Marshall, and Partners
LOCATION: Borough of Hillingdon, High Street, Uxbridge

A charming center designed in a traditional village manner. Warm brick, extensively employed for all of the units, is attractively massed. High-pitched roofs enhance the traditionalism. A strong brick base around the perimeter defines the large complex. Open plan offices welcome the visitor. A good example of vernacular housing applied to a large civic institution.

LONDON

Institute Of Education And Law Building (1973-78)

ARCHITECT: Denys Lasdun and Partners
LOCATION: University of London, Bedford Way WC1

Lasdun and Partners are known throughout the country for their innovative structures. For the design of the streamlined Institute, Lasdun employed a plan strongly expressing the triangular features. The texture of raw concrete contrasts effectively with tinted glass arranged in horizontal bands. Facilities include classrooms, offices, and lecture rooms. This structure is contemporary with Lasdun's highly successful National Theater.

Lloyd's (1928, 1981)

ARCHITECTS: Sir Edwin Cooper, original architect; Richard Rogers
LOCATION: 107 Leadenhall Street EC3

The previous Lloyd's first Exchange Building erected in 1928 by Sir Edwin Cooper was gutted to provide space for the extraordinary modern design by Richard Rogers. Rogers, best known for his Pompidou Center in Paris with Piano, has created a symphony of fascinating horizontal, vertical, and curving forms. Interior treatments carry out the design theme of the exterior treatment through the use of materials, form, and space. The impressive structure makes a striking addition to central London.

LONDON

Mosque (1978)

ARCHITECTS: Sir Frederick Gibberd and Partners
LOCATION: Park Road and Hanover Gate NW

The new Mosque is an interesting, if not odd, addition to London's Regent Park. The unique building with its soaring minaret was designed for London's growing Moslem population. Domes, arches, and other "Arabized" motifs and forms are reinterpreted in a contemporary approach. The unusual structure, although highly criticized as "unimaginative" and "uninventive," makes an interesting aesthetic impression.

LONDON

Museum Of London (1975)

ARCHITECTS: Powell and Moya
LOCATION: London Wall EC2, Barbican,
St. Pauls

This stark white building with horizontal emphasis is inconveniently located at a busy intersection. The exterior, executed in the International Style, provides a simple background for its function. Inside, a magnificent collection of Londonia is beautifully arranged. A history of the city is traced through three-dimensional models and reconstructions. A highlight is the Lord Mayor's coach.

LONDON

National Theater (1967-76)

ARCHITECTS: Denys Lasdun & Partners
LOCATION: South Bank SE1, of the Thames River

The internationally-appreciated National Theater is Lasdun's most important work to date. Strikingly situated on the banks of the Thames River, the structure is particularly beautiful when lighted at night. Both exterior and interior are of raw concrete. The structure features a series of terraces surrounding three auditoria on various levels. Space planning has been brilliantly handled throughout the complex. The National Theater was spearheaded by George Bernard Shaw and others interested in a center for the performing arts.

LONDON

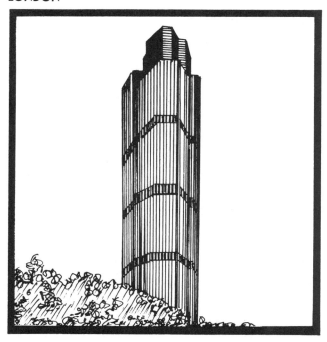

National Westminster Tower
(1981)

ARCHITECTS: Richard Seifert and Partners
LOCATION: 25 Old Broad Street EC2

The startling new "Nat West" Tower rises 600 feet and is England's tallest building and Europe's second tallest. The slender structure also has the distinction of being the world's tallest cantilevered building. Nineteen thousand square meters of stainless-steel curtain walling with ventilation louvres were employed for its construction, which give the complex a gleaming quality. The design of individual character conforms to a narrow site. The shape of the building displays the Bank's motif.

LONDON

New Zealand House (1960)

ARCHITECTS: Sir Robert Matthew, Johnson-Marshall
LOCATION: Haymarket and Pall Mall SW1

New Zealand House is one of England's finest examples of architecture based on prototypes developed by Le Corbusier and Mies van der Rohe. The "raised slabs-on-a-podium" approach remains a striking landmark although severely criticized as unsympathetic to the traditional surrounding buildings. The structure also has the distinction of being the first fully air-conditioned complex in England.

LONDON

Old Swan House (1876)

ARCHITECT: Richard Norman Shaw
LOCATION: 17 Chelsea Embankment SW3

Although not a member of the famous Arts and Crafts Movement, Shaw was sympathetic with its principles. The foremost architect of his day, he designed numerous structures, mostly residential, in England. The Old Swan House is his most "modern" work. This example of early modern design looks rather traditional by today's standards, with the Queen Anne detailing of its simple brick facade. Each of the five floors features a different design treatment. Interiors were executed by William Morris and the Arts and Crafts designers of the Morris, Marshall, & Faulkner Studio.

LONDON

Park Tower Hotel (1973)

ARCHITECT: Richard Seifert
LOCATION: Knightsbridge, London SW1

Known for his *PENTA HOTEL* (1972) and the soaring *CENTER POINT* (1961), Seifert is a master at designing efficient structures regardless of limitation. Park Tower is his most imaginative work. Here the architect wanted to avoid the typical flat facade. The Park Tower has been compared in its unusual shape to "stacked television sets," "corn on the cob," and "London's huge gasometer!" The interior features an interesting radiating sunburst motif.

LONDON

Polytechnic College Of Engineering And Science (1967-72)

ARCHITECTS: Lyons Israel Ellis Partnership
LOCATION: Clipstone Street W1

Constructed of concrete, glass, and tile, the Polytechnic building is set in a high density area of London in a mixed-use block. Contained within the well-planned space are facilities for lecture halls, communal areas, workshops, and parking. Bronze-toned glass harmonizes nicely with the other materials employed. The entire complex is expressive of its purpose and spirit.

LONDON

Post Office Tower (1960-65)

ARCHITECTS: Former Ministry of Public Buildings and Works
LOCATION: Cleveland Street Tower, Bloomsbury

The Post Office Tower was the tallest building in London at the time, rising to a height of 620 feet (including the mast). It was planned to be clear of other tall structures in order to accommodate London's telecommunications system. A revolving restaurant at the top of the structure provides a panoramic view of the city.

LONDON

Queen Elizabeth Hall, Purcell Room, And Hayward Gallery (1964)

ARCHITECTS: LCC/GLC Architects Department, Sir Hubert Bennett, and Jack Whittle
LOCATION: South Bank SE1, Near Waterloo Bridge

A part of the South Bank Arts Centre, these modern buildings comprise a complex devoted to music, theater, and art. Plans for this cultural arts center had been on the drawing boards since 1948. The design features terraces and walkways throughout the facilities to relieve the massive volumes of the concrete forms that house the various activities. Across the way and close by are the *ROYAL FESTIVAL HALL* and *THE NATIONAL THEATER.* The entire center has been severely criticized as cold, inconvenient and inhuman.

LONDON

Red House (1859)

ARCHITECT: Philip Webb
LOCATION: Red House Lane, Bexley Heath (SW London)

The Red House is one of the world's first examples of early modern residential design, often the first entry in textbooks on the subject. Owner and decorator of the Red House was William Morris, a founding member of the Arts and Crafts Movement in England. Philip Webb, also a member of the famous early modern design organization, was the leading architect of the group. Although at first glance the house may seem traditional, it features many ideas innovative for the period, including open planning, simplification of detail, structural design, and an emphasis on function.

Royal Festival Hall (1951, extended 1962)

ARCHITECTS: LCC Architects Department:
Robert Matthew, Leslie Martin, Edwin
Williams, and Peter Moro
LOCATION: South Bank SE1, near Waterloo
Bridge

Matthew is known in educational circles in
Great Britain as professor of architecture at
Edinburgh University. The superb Royal
Festival Hall was designed for the 1951
Festival of Britain and to replace the Queen's
Hall destroyed during World War II. Built of
reinforced concrete, the building is pleasantly
sited on the Thames River and surrounded by
a large terrace. A glass-walled restaurant with
a wonderful view of London caps the
complex. The concert hall seats 2,600
patrons.

LONDON

U.S. Chancellery (United States Embassy) (1955-60)

ARCHITECTS: Eero Saarinen Associates
(USA) with others
LOCATION: Grosvenor Square W1

Saarinen, the great American post-war
architect, also designed the TWA Terminal in
New York and the General Motors Research
Center in Michigan. Commissioned in 1955 by
the U.S. State Department to design a new
embassy, Saarinen intended to retain the
Georgian character of the structures in
Grosvenor Square. He employed a precast-
concrete design that he hoped would blacken
with pollution over time. Unfortunately the
stark stone texture and gold anodized-
aluminum trim still look garish enough to
generate harsh criticism.

LONDON

Whitechapel Art Gallery (1899)

ARCHITECT: Charles Harrison Townsend
LOCATION: 80 Whitechapel High Street

Townsend was influenced in his design of the Whitechapel Art Gallery by American architect Henry Hobson Richardson. Richardson, after studying at the Ecole des Beaux Arts in Paris, took the Grand Tour of Europe and became enamored with the medieval Romanesque style. His modern interpretation of the style in America earned him the title of the "Great Romanesque Revivalist." Townsend's Gallery has a low heavy arch, rusticated stone surfaces, and an emphasis on the horizontal form capturing the feeling of the Romanesque cathedral. The approach was considered modern at this time.

MITCHAM

Methodist Church (1959)

ARCHITECT: Edward D. Mills
LOCATION: Cricket Green, Mitcham, Surrey

Situated by a green cricket field, this modern church retains a quaint charm. Built close to the site of a church bombed during World War II, it salvaged the altar from the older church. The folded-concrete roof of the nave, designed by Ove Arup, is a focal point. An interesting feature, close to the altar, is a sunken area designed for the organ.

NORWICH

Friars Quay Housing (1972-75)

ARCHITECTS: Feilden and Mawson
LOCATION: Friars Quay section of Norwich

Architects in England have been concerned lately with planned community housing with special consideration for the human element. Friars Quay Housing combines city planning, restoration, and remodeling. The complex is set in a picturesque setting along the quays and takes full advantage of the site. The housing project combines a modern plan and architectural design, yet still retains a historical feeling.

NORWICH

Sainsbury Center For The Visual Arts (1974–78)

ARCHITECTS: Norman Foster Associates
LOCATION: University of East Anglia Campus

This extraordinary space-frame structure has been the object of much comment and comparison. Its emphasis on pure technology is a striking feature, a logical and effective background for its exhibits and function. Critics have called the Sainsbury Center "the airplane hangar," "the giant punch card," and the "giant cassette."

NORWICH

University Of East Anglia

(1962 - still in progress)

ARCHITECT: Sir Denys Lasdun
LOCATION: University of East Anglia
Campus, outskirts of Norwich

Harmoniously integrated with the
surrounding rolling countryside, the modern
buildings of this campus are effectively laid
out for optimum use of space. Lasdun, who is
particularly known for his successful National
Theater in London, has employed advanced
technology and materials to design a dramatic
series of buildings that have been both criticized and admired. The much-photographed
structures have had considerable impact on
university building in England.

NOTTINGHAM

Nottingham Playhouse (1961)

ARCHITECTS: Peter Moro and Partners
LOCATION: North on A60 from
Loughborough. Wellington Circus

The delightful Playhouse is especially dazzling
at night when artfully placed lighting
emphasizes the lines and forms of the
structure. A slatted-wall treatment is carried
throughout the interior and exterior, adding
an interesting decorative effect. The focal
point of the building is the huge central drum
that rises above the other facilities and houses
the cylindrical auditorium.

OXFORD

Florey Building (1968)

ARCHITECT: James Stirling
LOCATION: Oxford University Campus—
Queens College

Oxford boasts many admirable modern structures, but the Florey Building is one of the most imaginative. The structure of concrete and red brick has approximately seventy-four study bedrooms for undergraduates among its efficiently-planned facilities. Raised on bold structural supports, the entire curving building faces a central courtyard that in turn faces the river and Oxford to the north. Aluminum fabric privacy blinds add to the textural interest of the building. (Maps of Oxford's campus are available throughout the city.)

OXFORD

Law Libraries At Oxford University (1961–65)

ARCHITECT: Sir Leslie Martin
LOCATION: Oxford University Campus

Martin, a leading member of MARS (Modern Architectural Research Society) and professor of architecture at Cambridge, has designed numerous structures throughout England, particularly university buildings. The Libraries at Oxford feature strong horizontal forms with repeating window voids. Surrounding plazas, steps, and landscaping complement the clean design.

OXFORD

St. Catherine's College

(1959–60)

ARCHITECT: Arne Jacobsen (Denmark)
LOCATION: Oxford University Campus

Jacobsen, internationally famous both as an architect and furniture designer, designed two buildings in England before his death in 1974. (The other structure is the *DANISH EMBASSY* [completed after the architect's death] in London, located at 55 Sloane Street SW1.) St. Catherine's College is considered the finer design of the two buildings. For this complex Jacobsen incorporated ideas from work he had created in his homeland of Denmark. The orderly design, positioned on a flat riverside meadow, consists of three-story blocks housing numerous student facilities.

PERIVALE

Hoover Ltd. (Factory) (1932–35)

ARCHITECTS: Wallis Gilbert and Partners
LOCATION: Western Avenue WS (On A40 at Perivale)

Those who admire the Art Deco style of the 1930s appreciate this colorfully decorated hallmark of the period with its fan shape and sunburst motifs. The doorway decoration is particularly exciting; its Art Deco designers freely drew inspiration from sources including Egyptian, Aztec, African, and even the Russian Ballet. Art historian Sir Nicholas Pevsner describes the Hoover Building as "perhaps the most offensive of the modernistic atrocities along this road of typical bypass factories."

PORTSMOUTH

IBM Head Office (1971)

ARCHITECTS: Norman Foster Associates
LOCATION: IBM United Kingdom LTD,
Gosham, Hampshire

The striking new IBM Head Office creates the unusual illusion of "disappearing" as it is approached because of the reflective surface of the exterior. Surroundings seem to be part of the building, yet at second glance contrast immensely. Foster, known for his stunning Willis Faber Office in Ipswich (1975), is one of the most creative architects in England today, especially in his use of glass "skin" exteriors.

SUNDERLAND

Civic Center (1968)

ARCHITECT: Sir Basil Spence
LOCATION: Burdon Road, Tyner Wear,
10 miles ESE of Newcastle

Built in the southern section of this ship-building town on England's East Coast, the Civic Center is one of England's finest buildings of its type. Spence designed a cluster of hexagonal shapes for this large complex plan. Facilities include administrative offices, the civic suite, and parking spaces arranged on a triangular grid. The unusual hexagonal shapes create interesting roof terraces and connecting public plazas, courtyards, and steps.

SUSSEX COUNTY

SUSSEX UNIVERSITY

Gatwick Airport (1958)

ARCHITECT: Francis R. Stevens Yorke
LOCATION: Just south of Reigate in Horley,
Surrey

Yorke was one of the first British architects to
be influenced by the International Style and
establish modern ideas in England. Walter
Gropius, founder of the Bauhaus in Germany,
worked with Yorke while in England. The
efficient Gatwick Airport has many admirable
features, including an eight-hundred foot
viewing gallery. The Airport was designed to
conveniently accommodate air passengers.

Falmer House (1960)

ARCHITECT: Sir Basil Spence
LOCATION: Sussex University, near Brighton,
East Sussex

Buildings for the University are beautifully
located amid the two-hundred acre Stanmer
Park. With an interesting combination of brick
work with flattish arches, Falmer House is
considered one of the best designs on
campus. Quadrangles and water landscaping
design combine to enhance the structure.
Spence again employed his brick and
concrete arched approach with the design of
the Household Cavalry Regiment Buildings in
Knightsbridge, London.

SWINDON

Brunel Center (1970s)

ARCHITECTS: Douglas Stephen & Partners
LOCATION: Central Swindon, about 75 W of London

An inviting covered mall conveniently located in the town's center, Brunel Center is an influential urban renewal effort in England. Surrounded by plazas, seating, and landscaping, the structure was designed to harmonize with the existing buildings. The glass-and-steel structure features a large domed ceiling providing streams of light to flood the interior areas.

THAMESMEAD

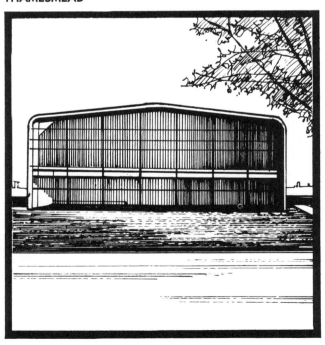

Modern Art Glass Ltd. (Warehouse and Showroom) (1973)

ARCHITECTS: Norman Foster Associates
LOCATION: Hailey Road, Thamesmead is located 11 miles E of Charing Cross, London

Dramatic use of glass as the principal building material highlights this structure by one of England's most imaginative current architects. Smaller in scale than Foster's overwhelming Willis Faber and Dumas offices in Ipswich, the Modern Art Glass Building features a similar reflective facade of glass. The frame of the building is a blue stove-enamelled corrugated steel sheet wrapped over a network of steel portal frames.

THAMESMEAD

Thamesmead (New Town)
(started 1972)

ARCHITECTS: Greater London Council, Sir Roger Walters
LOCATION: 11 miles E of Charring Cross, Abbey Wood SE2

Along with Cumbernauld and Milton Keynes, Thamesmead is the most important of England's "new towns." During the past two decades, the New Town Movement has evolved in response to growing housing problems in England. Thamesmead's high-rise and low-rise units, for sale or rent, have over fifty thousand inhabitants. The new town is not without problems, especially poor communications, but efforts are underway to solve these difficulties.

YORK

Hall At Bootham School (1964)

ARCHITECT: Trevor Dannatt
LOCATION: Bootham School, York

In a city that still looks almost totally medieval, with traditional buildings dating back centuries, the Assembly Hall at Bootham School is a fascinating contrast. The flat planes of the lower three-quarters of the building seem topped with a lid of glass skylights. Dannatt won the prestigious Architectural Award for the project. The architectural approach of the Hall at Bootham School has been compared to the work of the great Finnish designer, Alvar Aalto.

ADDITIONAL MODERN STRUCTURES OF INTEREST

BATH

Bath University Of Technology (1966)
ARCHITECTS: Robert Matthew,
Johnson-Marshall
LOCATION: Bath University Campus

BEAULIEU

National Motor Museum (1970–72)
ARCHITECTS: Leonard Manasach & Partners
LOCATION: On the Beaulieu estate,

A marvelous museum based on a cruciform
plan with glazed skylights running the length
of the building. Automobiles of all types are
effectively exhibited. A monorail runs
throughout the structure.

BIRKENHEAD

**Church of St. Michael and
All Angels** (1967)
ARCHITECTS: Richard O'Mahony & Partners
LOCATION: Just SE of Liverpool.
Woodchurch, Birkenhead

BIRMINGHAM

Birmingham Repertory Theatre (1972)
ARCHITECTS: Graham Winteringham
and others
LOCATION: Broad Street

National Exhibition Center (NEC) (1970s)
ARCHITECTS: Edward D. Mills & Partners
LOCATION: Eastern edge of town, green
belt between Birmingham and Solihull

Clad in ribbed-steel, this immense exhibition
center is one of the largest and finest in
Europe.

CAMBRIDGE

Churchill College (1968)
ARCHITECTS: Richard Sheppard, Robson, &
Partners
LOCATION: Cambridge University Campus

Downing College (1971)
ARCHITECTS: Howell, Killick, Partridge &
Amis
LOCATION: Cambridge University Campus

**Harvey Court, Gonville and Caius
College**
ARCHITECTS: Sir Leslie Martin and St. John
Wilson
LOCATION: Cambridge University Campus

Impington Village College (1936)
ARCHITECTS: Maxwell Fry with Walter
Gropius (USA)
LOCATION: Near Cambridge University
Campus

University Center (1964)
ARCHITECTS: Howell, Killick, Partridge,
& Amis
LOCATION: Cambridge University Campus

COVENTRY

Arts Center (1975)
ARCHITECTS: Renton Howard Wood Leven
Partnership
LOCATION: Gibbet Hill Road, University of
Warwick

DURHAM

Collingwood College (1974)
ARCHITECTS: Richard Sheppard, Robson,
& Partners
LOCATION: University of Durham

GRAVESEND

Civic Center (1964)
ARCHITECTS: H.T. Cadbury-Brown and
Partners with B. Richards
LOCATION: 22 miles E of London

HANLEY STOKE ON KENT

The City Museum & Art Gallery (1981)
LOCATION: 35 miles S of Manchester

This unique and functional structure contains one of the finest and largest ceramic collections in the world.

HORSHAM

Arts Center At Christ's Hospital (1975)
ARCHITECTS: Howell, Killick, Partridge, & Amis
LOCATION: 18 miles NNW of Brighton

KINGSTON-UPON-HULL

The Cecil Cinema (1955)
ARCHITECTS: J. P. Taylor and others
LOCATION: 157 miles N of London

LEEDS

Theater And Lecture Block, University of Leeds (1970s)
ARCHITECTS: Chamberlin, Powell, and Bon
LOCATION: University of Leeds campus, 1 mile from city center

A marvelous modern expansion to an existing plan.

LEICESTER

Library At Leicester University (1975)
ARCHITECTS: Castle Park Dean Hook
LOCATION: Leicester University campus

LIVERPOOL

Oriel Chambers (1864-65)
ARCHITECT: Peter Ellis
LOCATION: Water Street

An early example of modern office design in England.

LONDON

Annesley Lodge (1896)
ARCHITECT: Charles Francis Annesley Voysey
LOCATION: Platts Lane NW3

Called "the best house in London." Example of early modern design.

Arnos Grove Station (Piccadilly Line Underground Station) (1932)
ARCHITECT: Charles Holden
LOCATION: Arnos Grove, Outer London, Sudbury Town

Brunswick Center (1965–73)
ARCHITECT: Patrick Hodgkinson
LOCATION: Guilford Street WC1

A controversial housing development.

Battersea Power Station (1929–55)
ARCHITECTS: Halliday and Agate with Sir G. Gilbert Scott
LOCATION: Queenstown Road and Battersea Park Road SW8

An unusual design compared to "an upside-down table."

Broadcasting House (BBC Building) (1931)
ARCHITECTS: Val Myers and Watson-Hart
LOCATION: Portland Place W1

Faced with Portland stone, the tiered and rounded BBC building, in the Art Deco style, has been compared to "a ship coming at the onlooker."

Castrol House (Now Marathon House) (1960)
ARCHITECTS: Gollins, Melvin, Ward, and Partners
LOCATION: 174 Marylebone Road NW1

Cavalry Barracks At Knightbridge (1970)
ARCHITECT: Sir Basil Spence
LOCATION: South Carriage Drive, Hyde Park SW1

A modern facility planned to house the Queen's horses.

Center Point (1963–67)
ARCHITECTS: Richard Seifert and Partners
LOCATION: 101 New Oxford Street WC1

One of Seifert's best high-rise complexes.

College Of Architecture And Advanced Building Technology
ARCHITECTS: GLC Architects' Department
LOCATION: Marylebone Road and Luxborough Road

A powerfully-designed building with functions frankly expressed. The huge complex features overhanging studios.

Commercial Union Assurance Building (1968–69)
ARCHITECTS: Gollins Melvin Ward Partnership
LOCATION: Leadenhall Street and St. Mary's Axe EC3

Czechoslovak Embassy (1971)
ARCHITECTS: Sramek Bocan Stepanski/ Matthew Johnson-Marshall Part.
LOCATION: Kensington Palace Gardens

Danish Embassy (1977)
ARCHITECT: Arne Jacobsen, Dissing, and Weitling (Denmark)
LOCATION: 55 Sloane Street SW1

Elephant And Castle Development (1961)
ARCHITECT: Erno Goldfinger
LOCATION: Newington Causeway

A controversial commercial development.

Finsbury Health Center (1938)
ARCHITECTS: Lubetkin and Tecton
LOCATION: Pine Street EC1

An important work by this early modern architecture firm.

Flats At 26 St. James Place (1958)
ARCHITECT: Sir Denys Lasdun
LOCATION: 26 St. James's Place SW1

Hay's Wharf And St. Olvae House (1931–32)
ARCHITECT: H. S. Goodhart-Rendel
LOCATION: Tooley Street SE1

Interesting examples of the modern style.

Holland House (Now The National Employers' House) (1914)
ARCHITECT: Petrus Berlage (Holland)
LOCATION: 1-4 and 32 Bury Street EC3

An interesting work by Holland's "father of modern architecture."

Horniman Museum (1896)
ARCHITECT: Charles Harrison Townsend
LOCATION: 100 London Road SE23

One of the architect's greatest designs.

Highpoint 1 And 2 (1936–38)
ARCHITECTS: Lubetkin and Tecton
LOCATION: North Hill N7

A milestone in early modern housing in England.

IBM Industrial Park (1970)
ARCHITECTS: Richard Norman Foster Associates
LOCATION: Greenford Road, Greenford

Isokon Flats (1933)
ARCHITECT: Wells Coates
LOCATION: Lawn Road NW3

A well-known early modern housing development in England.

Joseph (1978)
ARCHITECTS: Norman Foster Associates
LOCATION: 6 Sloane Street SW1

A new modern fashion shop.

London Docklands Development Corporation Offices (1968–71)
ARCHITECTS: Norman Foster Associates
LOCATION: Millwall Dock E14

London Hilton (1963)
ARCHITECTS: Lewis Solomon Day
LOCATION: Park Lane W1

An early luxury hotel skyscraper in London.

London Wall (1963–82)
ARCHITECTS: City of London Planning Department
LOCATION: Between St. Martin-le Grand and Moorgate

Part of a vast modern redevelopment district in London.

Michelin House (1905–11)
ARCHITECT: F. Espinasse
LOCATION: 91 Fulham Road SW3

A strange little building faced with white faience. A fascinating example of craftsmanship and imagination.

New Victoria Cinema (1929–30)
ARCHITECT: E. Walmsley Lewis
LOCATION: Wilton Road SW1

A marvelous example of Art Deco in England. Lavish interiors.

New Zealand House (1960)
ARCHITECTS: Sir Robert Matthew, Johnson-Marshall
LOCATION: Haymarket and Pall Mall SW1

An important commercial building inspired by Le Corbusier.

Odeon Cinema (1937)
ARCHITECT: Harry Weedon
LOCATION: Finchley Road NW3

A fine example of the Art Deco Style.

Old Vic Theater Workshop (1958)
ARCHITECTS: Lyons Israel and Ellis with John Miller
LOCATION: 83-101 The Cut SE1

Early English Brutalism.

Paddington Station (1850–54)
ARCHITECTS: I. K. Brunel, Matthew Digby Wyatt, Owen Jones
LOCATION: Eastbourne Terrace and Praed Street W2

A monumental structure, like the Crystal Palace, demonstrating a remarkable system of iron and glass construction.

Palm House (1944–48)
ARCHITECTS: Decimus Burton, Richard Turner
LOCATION: Royal Botanical Gardens, Kew

Superb example of early iron and glass construction in England.

Penguin Pool (1935)
ARCHITECTS: Sir Ove Arup and Lubetkin and Tecton
LOCATION: London Zoo, Prince Albert Road NW1

A delightful concrete design. Other buildings at the London Zoo are interestingly designed including the *GORILLA HOUSE.*

Putney Swimming Pool And Dryburgh Hall (1969)
ARCHITECTS: Powell & Moya
LOCATION: Upper Richmond Road. SW

Public Library And Swimming Pool (1964)
ARCHITECTS: Sir Basil Spence, Bonnington, and Collins
LOCATION: Avenue Road NW3

Playboy Club (1963–65)
ARCHITECTS: C. Ballard and Blow with Walter Gropius, Benjamin Thompson, and Llewelyn Davies and Weeks
LOCATION: 45 Park Lane W1

A controversial work by the great early modern architect and Bauhaus director, Walter Gropius.

Richard Norman Shaw House (1874–76)
ARCHITECT: Richard Norman Shaw
LOCATION: 6 Ellerdale Road

Home of the early pioneer modern architect.

Royal College Of Art (1962–73)
ARCHITECTS: H. T. Cadbury-Brown, Sir Hugh Casson
LOCATION: Kensington Gore SW7

Royal College Of Surgeons (1960–64)
ARCHITECTS: Sir Denys Lasdun and Partners
LOCATION: Outer Circle and St. Andrew's Place, Regent's Park NW1

Roehampton Flats (Housing, Alton West Estate) (1955–59)
ARCHITECTS: London County Council
LOCATION: Roehampton Lane SW15

A highly acclaimed housing development based on Le Corbusier's ideas.

St. Katharine Dock House (1967)
ARCHITECTS: Renton, Howard Wood Associates
LOCATION: By Tower Bridge

St. Pancras Station (1866–68)
ARCHITECTS: W. H. Barlow and R. M. Ordish
LOCATION: Euston Road NW1

A superb example of early iron construction in Europe.

Senate House—University Of London
(started 1932)
ARCHITECT: Charles Holden
LOCATION: Malet Street and Montague Place WC1

Simpson's Department Store (1935)
ARCHITECT: Joseph Emberton
LOCATION: Piccadilly W1

A pioneering modern store design.

Studio House (1891)
ARCHITECT: Charles Francis Annesley Voysey
LOCATION: 17 St. Dunstan's Road W6

An interesting Arts and Crafts Movement project.

Sun House (1935)
ARCHITECT: E. Maxwell Fry
LOCATION: 9 Frognal Way NW3

One of the first modern International Style houses in England.

Tate Gallery Extension (1980–)
ARCHITECT: James Stirling
LOCATION: Millbank SW1, Extension to the north of Tate Gallery

A modern new addition to the original art gallery building of 1897. Houses the Turner collection (Clore Gallery).

Thorn House (1957–59)
ARCHITECTS: Sir Basil Spence and Partners
LOCATION: Upper St. Martin's Lane WC2

One of the earliest "tower on podium" designs in England.

TV-am (Breakfast Television Center) (1983)
ARCHITECTS: Terry Farrell Partnership
LOCATION: On the Regents Canal and Hawley Crescent, NW London (Camden Town)

A sensational home for England's new morning television show, the exciting post-modern building added to an existing 1930s and 1950s garage.

White House (1877)
ARCHITECT: Edward William Godwin
LOCATION: 96 Cheyne Walk (Original house destroyed)

Look for the blue plaque on the facade identifying the spot where the original, stark, modern white house stood. The private

residence was designed for the American painter James McNeill Whistler.

William Morris House (1860s)
LOCATION: 17 Red Lion Square

Townhouse of the great founder of the Arts and Crafts Movement.

Vickers Tower (Now Millbank Tower) (1963)
ARCHITECTS: Ronald Ward and Partners
LOCATION: Millbank SW1

An early glass skyscraper in England.

MAIDENHEAD

Library At Maidenhead (1970s)
ARCHITECTS: Ahrends, Burton, and Koralk
LOCATION: St. Iver's Road

A spectacular library featuring a network of space frames.

NEWCASTLE

Byker Community (1974)
ARCHITECT: Ralph Erskine
LOCATION: About 1 mile E of Newcastle city center

A much publicized housing development.

NEWCASTLE-UPON-TYNE

Newcastle-Upon-Tyne Shopping And Recreation Center (1973–76)
ARCHITECTS: Chapman Taylor Partners
LOCATION: Eldon Square

Built on an irregular site in the shape of the letter "F," this admirable complex features shops, cinemas, and recreation facilities.

NOTTINGHAM

Boots Head Office (1968)
ARCHITECTS: Skidmore, Owings, and Merrill
LOCATION: 1 Thayne Road, West Nottingham

Streamlined glass-and-steel commercial

complex by the United States' leading modern architectural firm.

Church Of The Good Shepherd (1966)
ARCHITECT: Gerald Goalen
LOCATION: Thackeray's Lane, Woodthrope, Nottingham

Nottingham University Library (1974)
ARCHITECT: Williamson, Faulkner, Brown, & Partners
LOCATION: University Park, on Library Road

OXFORD

Wolfson Block At St. Annes's College (1962)
ARCHITECTS: Killick, Partridge, & Amis
LOCATION: Oxford University Campus

READING

The Hexagon (1979)
ARCHITECTS: Robert Matthew, Johnson-Marshall, & Partners
LOCATION: 40 miles W of London, in middle of shopping & office center

This extraordinarily-designed music complex features superb acoustics.

RUNCORN

Town Center Housing (1976)
ARCHITECT: James Stirling
LOCATION: 10 miles ESE of Liverpool

An innovative housing project.

SAYER'S COMMON

Priory Of Our Lady Of Good Council (1980s)
ARCHITECT: Michael Blee
LOCATION: Approximately 10 miles N of Brighton

The unusual cone-shaped religious structure has been called a "Pop-Art Church."

SHEFFIELD

Crucible Theatre (1969–71)
ARCHITECTS: Renton Howard Wood Associates with others
LOCATION: Central Sheffield by town hall and Norfolk Street

A boldly-formed structure of white limestone aggregate and concrete blocks topped with bronze panels.

Park Hill Development (1966)
ARCHITECTS: Sheffield City Architects' Department
LOCATION: Park Hill section of Sheffield

A controversial modern housing project in England.

SOUTHAMPTON

University Of Southampton—Union (1970s)
ARCHITECTS: Sir Basil Spence, Bonnington, & Collins
LOCATION: University of Southampton Campus

SWINDEN

Wyvern Theater And Art Center (1972)
ARCHITECTS: Casson, Conder, & Partners
LOCATION: Prices Street

WARWICK

Arts Center (1971–74)
ARCHITECTS: Renton Howard Wood Levin Partnership
LOCATION: University of Warwick, off University ring road

A bold new facility that functions as the social, cultural, and theatrical center of the university.

Finland

FINLAND

• Rovaniemi

• Oulu

• Vaasa

• Seinajoki

• Ähtäri

• Jyväskylä
• Saynatsalo

• Noormarkku
Pori
• Tampere

Raisio
Vierumaki
• Lahti
Imatra
• Turku
Hyvinkää
Lappeenranta
• Salo Jarvenpaa
Kotka
Paimio
Espoo
Helsinki
Otaniemi
Hanko

MODERN ARCHITECTURE IN FINLAND

THE NATIONAL ROMANTIC MOVEMENT

Finland, although out of the mainstream of Europe, has piqued international interest because of the significant contribution made by her architects during recent decades. Finland's reputation for fine design and craftsmanship can be traced back to the National Romantic Movement, a counterpart to the Arts and Crafts Movement in England. The movement promoted handcrafted items designed after traditional Finnish motifs.

ELIEL SAARINEN

Saarinen is the pioneer modern architect in Finland. He, along with his partners Herman Gesellius and Armas Lindgren, received recognition with their Paris Exhibition in 1900. In 1902 they established their studio at Hvittrask outside Helsinki. Saarinen and his partners designed all the furnishings at Hvittrask to incorporate their National Romantic Movement philosophy.

ALVAR AALTO AND ERIK BRYGGMAN

Aalto is considered Finland's greatest modern architect, responsible for Finland's high reputation for the finest modern architectural and furniture design. Aalto worked with Erik Bryggman, another pioneer modern architect, for a short time, introducing the new European functionalism at the Jubilee Exhibition at Turku in 1929. The next year Aalto opened his own practice in Helsinki, developing a style that was a compromise between the International Style and Organic architecture. This architectural outlook influenced many other Scandinavian designers.

MODERN ARCHITECTURE AFTER WORLD WAR II

A remarkable number of modern structures have been built in Finland during recent decades, including the finest schools, offices, stores, museums, churches, sports facilities, and sanatoria. Finnish architects have also designed new forms of housing to meet growing needs. Larger outdoor areas for multi-story dwellings, terraced housing, housing units, and other housing solutions have been explored, always with a concern for human comfort and enjoyment. Leading modern Finnish architects today include Kaija and Heikki Siren, Timo and Tuomo Suomalainen, Lendegren and Jantti, Uno Ullberg, Viljo Rewell, and Erkki Huttunen.

ÄHTÄRI

Hotel Mesikammen (1973–76)

ARCHITECTS: Timo and Tuomo Suomalainen
LOCATION: Approximately 250 km NNW of
Helsinki

This inviting recreation and spa hotel, located
on a wooded slope, is especially designed to
complement the terrain and reflect its natural
beauty. The architects created a low structure
of only three floors to achieve the same
feeling as the environment. A highlight of the
wood structure is its rock floors—the actual
surface of the hill.

ESPOO

The Church Of
Espoonlahti (1976-80)

ARCHITECTS: Timo and Tuomo Suomalainen
LOCATION: In Kivenlahti, Kipparinkatu 8

This dynamic church, designed by Finland's
famous brother team, can accommodate up to
1,100 worshipers. The Suomalainens said of
the building, "It was our aim to create a
building combining a sense of a built space
with that of nature. ... It was our wish that
anyone who enters will find in this church
reverence, life, boldness, harmony, together
with an abundance of forms and colors." (Nov.
27, 1980)

ESPOO

Olarin Church And Multipurpose Facility (1976–81)

ARCHITECTS: Kapy and Simo Paavilainen
LOCATION: 10 miles W of Helsinki,
Olarinluoma 4

A clean and direct design of reinforced concrete with red brick facing, its massing of vertical forms and connecting sections complements the natural surrounding terrain. The interior is treated with white-painted walls, red-tile floors, and green-stained woodwork. The airy church has a capacity for five hundred persons. Excellent acoustics and attractive lighting—an interesting series of lamps hung on long white cords—provide a pleasant environment.

HANKO

Dance Pavilion At Hanko (1966)

ARCHITECT: Clas-Olof Lindqvist
LOCATION: Park at Hanko

This pavilion fifty miles SE of Turku is situated in a pleasantly landscaped park in the city enjoyed by the residents during the warmer summer months. A huge wooden platform supports the square dance hall. The most exciting feature of the building is the lofty cross-shaped ceiling windows that span the roof gap, supported by large laminated wood beams. An outdoor dancing area at the side is given privacy by means of a curving wood partition.

HANKO

Kudeneule Textile Factory (1958)

ARCHITECT: Viljo Rewell
LOCATION: Hanko, Hopearanta, (90 miles west of Helsinki)

Providing a pleasant and efficient working environment has been a major concern of Scandinavian architects for decades, following the commendable example set by Finland's great modern architect, Alvar Aalto. The Kudeneule Textile Factory complex, one of Finland's best, has been a prototype for similar structures. Two long wings flank a reflecting pool. A striking modern abstract sculpture on the terrace was created by Arni Tynys.

HELSINKI

Alppila Church (1957)

ARCHITECTS: Keijo Strom and Olavi Tuomisto
LOCATION: Viipurinkotu at Kotkankatu 2

A pristine white-painted brick structure greets the visitor to this religious facility in a poorer district of northern Helsinki. Both interior and exterior express simplicity and a humble atmosphere. The nave of the church is particularly interesting, enhanced by artfully placed window openings that wash the brick surfaces with sunlight.

HELSINKI

Finlandia Hall (1967–71)

ARCHITECT: Alvar Aalto
LOCATION: No. Mannerheimintie

At night, completely lit, this sparkling white marble structure glitters like a jewel in the heart of Helsinki. The massive concert hall, part of a plan for a large cultural center, was one of the last important works of Finland's greatest modern architect. The majestic structure is classically simple in design and form. Its white marble conveys the humanizing warmth associated with the philosophy of Aalto, who also designed many of the furnishings.

HELSINKI

House Of Culture (1958)

ARCHITECT: Alvar Aalto
LOCATION: Sturnenkatu (Sturegatan), Helsinki

Aalto, who loved brick, designed a special wedged-shaped brick for the House of Culture. The facade is a dramatic undulating form. The structure, which functions as a meeting place for Finnish Communists, boasts facilities including a fifteen-hundred-seat auditorium, a cinema, a restaurant, and parking. The charming interior features among its unique innovations a flexible stage design.

HELSINKI

Hvitträsk (1902)

ARCHITECTS: Eliel Saarinen, with Hermann
Gesellius and Armas Lindgren
LOCATION: Approximately 25 kilometers W
of city. Follow Jorvas motorway, turn off at
Kivenlahti exit, follow signs to Kauklahti,
then follow signs to Hvittrask

Eliel Saarinen is known as the "father of
modern architecture in Finland." At the turn of
the century, a leader of the National Romantic
Movement, he designed the *NATIONAL
MUSEUM*. Saarinen and his partners built
Hvitträsk as the firm's joint house and studio.
Open to the public, this imaginative complex
has both Art Nouveau and English Arts and
Crafts Movement influence in its furnishings
and details.

HELSINKI

Kallio Church (Kallion Kirkko) (1912)

ARCHITECT: Lars Sonck
LOCATION: Itainen Papinkatu 2

Considered one of Finland's architectural
treasures, the stately Kallio Church is a fine
example of the Finnish Romantic Style—an
early modern movement popular at the turn
of the century. Commanding a hilltop
location, the huge granite tower of the church
can be seen looming above the city. A
wooden altar relief by Hannes Autere called
"Come unto me, all ye that labor," is a focal
point in the vast congregational space.

HELSINKI

Kannelmaen Kirkko
(Kannelmaki Church) (1968)

ARCHITECTS: Marjatta and Martti Jaatinen
LOCATION: Vanhaistentie 6

Nicely sited in a quiet suburban area of
Helsinki, the powerfully formed Kannelmaki
Church greatly contrasts, and yet complements,
its surroundings. Tiered steps lead up to a
triangular entry adding to the drama of the
structure. The soaring altar wall is the focal
point highlighted with an infill of colorful
stained glass. The art is the work of Hilkka
Toivola Karpukka entitled, "Chiesa Nuova"
(New Church).

HELSINKI

Marimekko Factory (1974)

ARCHITECTS: Erkki Kairamo and Reijo
Lahtinen
LOCATION: Vanha Talvitie 3

Marimekko textiles have delighted the world
with colorful and fanciful abstract stylized
designs. Many tourists flock to see not only
how the fabrics are created, but also the
fascinating building where they are
manufactured. A pure example of
Constructivism, an artistic movement that
stressed simple harmonic proportions and the
beauty inherent in a structure, Marimekko
Factory makes a stunning impression.

HELSINKI

Municipal Theater (City Theater In Helsinki) (1964–67)

ARCHITECT: T. Penttila
LOCATION: No. Helsinki on Elaintarhantie

The irregular outline of the Municipal Theater presents an unusual and inviting atmosphere. Penttila is one of many architects of the new generation that seek significant expressions for contemporary living. The splendid Municipal Theater, featuring the latest building technology and materials, is an excellent prototype for numerous similar structures being built in Finland today.

HELSINKI

National Opera House (1980-)

ARCHITECTS: Hyvamaki-Karbunen-Parkkinen
LOCATION: Corner of Tonnrotinkatu and Katu

The National Opera House represents the finest of Finnish building over the past decades. The structure, a cultural companion to Alvar Aalto's famous Finlandia House close by, features a series of interesting intersecting planes and window bands. The breathtaking interior matches the spirit of the exterior design.

HELSINKI

National Pensions Institute (1953–56)

ARCHITECT: Alvar Aalto
LOCATION: Mannerheimvagen at Nordenskioldinkatu

Many devotees of Aalto make a pilgrimage to see his National Pensions Institute, an inviting building of red brick and copper arranged around a garden and pool. Aalto's sensitive use of natural materials in pure surfaces can be observed in the design of this structure. Furniture for the interior was designed by the architect.

HELSINKI

Railway Station At Helsinki (1910–14)

ARCHITECT: Eliel Saarinen
LOCATION: On Simonkatu Kavok off Mannerheimintie

The Railway Station in Helsinki is Eliel Saarinen's masterpiece and one of the first modern structures in Scandinavia to receive world-wide attention. It features reinforced concrete vaults unusual for this period and a spectacular glass and steel roof. Saarinen later migrated to the USA, where he became involved with the prestigious Cranbrook Academy of Design in Bloomfield, Michigan.

HELSINKI

Rautatalo Office Building
(1953)

ARCHITECT: Alvar Aalto
LOCATION: Keskuskatu 3 (Centralgatan 3)

Aalto has been ranked with Mies van der Rohe, Le Corbusier, and Frank Lloyd Wright as a titan of modern architecture. His great concern for the individual has earned him the label of the "humanist architect." The Rautatalo Office Building, Aalto's first project in Helsinki, is a sedate eight-story structure that adjoins Saarinen's early Romantic Style building. The Artek Studio is located on the corner of the Rautatalo Building.

HELSINKI

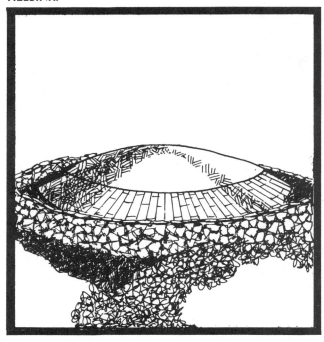

Taivallahti Church (Temppeliaukio) (1969)

ARCHITECTS: Timo and Tuomo Suomalainen
LOCATION: Sutherinkatu 3

Taivallahti, "a piece of nature in the midst of a city," is one of the world's most spectacular architectural creations. The structure is literally "architecture by removal," since the existing rock has been left as intact as possible. The architects have combined dramatic building materials of copper, wood, brick, and glass to contrast with the natural outcropping of stone. The copper dome seems to hang suspended over the church, creating a broad ring of supporting windows that reflect the light from within.

HELSINKI

Theater Restaurant Wing Extension (1968–78)

ARCHITECT: E.O. Hansson OY
LOCATION: Behind the City Theater,
Mannerheiminti & Esplanadi

This delightful and airy environment was created to provide a year-round garden atmosphere. Its billowing curved glass roof and walls were inspired by greenhouse plans. The new modern wing is an extension of the theater and nicely blends with the architectural design of the older wing. Various restaurants, including an outdoor patio eating area, are facilitated by the engaging glass extension.

HYVINKÄÄ

Hyvinkää Church (1961)

ARCHITECT: Professor Aarno Ruusuvuori
LOCATION: Hyvinge, 30 miles N of Helsinki

Respected as an educator and designer, Professor Ruusuvuori has created one of Finland's great hallmarks of modern church design. Constructed of glass, steel, and concrete, the church is set in a lovely wooded area just north of Helsinki. The gleaming concrete-and-glass texture is arranged in a striking triangular shape. The triangular motif is carried throughout the interiors.

IMATRA

Cemetery Chapel At Imatra
(1961–62)

ARCHITECTS: Jaakko Kontio and Kalle Raike
LOCATION: 20 miles NNE of Lappeenranta

Nestled among tall pines, the Cemetery Chapel is constructed of lime-washed brick masonry, with a copper roof and a concrete bell tower. The outstanding focal point is a huge diagonal glass skylight that casts light directly over the altar. An inner courtyard introduces mourners into the serene interior chapel. The complex makes a stunning contrast with the natural setting.

IMATRA

Vuoksenniska Church (1957–59)

ARCHITECT: Alvar Aalto
LOCATION: 166 miles ENE of Helsinki, near the Russian border

Vuoksenniska Church is one of Aalto's best-known early religious structures. The most prominent feature is a dramatically soaring bell tower that hovers over the irregular forms of the church itself. Massive concrete sliding doors between the three sections allow simultaneous functions. Colorful tile work complements the pure white surfaces, adding to the spacious effect of the complex.

JARVENPAA

Cemetery Chapel (1957)

ARCHITECTS: Tarja and Esko Toiviainen
LOCATION: 22 miles N of Helsinki

Natural materials are simply incorporated into the design of the Cemetery Chapel. Many of the walls are of large plate glass, providing a sweeping view of the surrounding grounds. Inside, an interesting tapestry by Laila Karttumen hangs behind the catafalque.

JYVÄSKYLÄ

Alvar Aalto Museum (Taidemuseo) (1973)

ARCHITECT: Alvar Aalto
LOCATION: 182 miles N of Helsinki

Alvar Aalto Museum, with the exception of its restrooms, has no rectangular space. The structure burrows impressively into the hillside. The museum was named in honor of the famous architect and furniture designer, who was embarrassed by the honor. Inside the museum there is organization as the interior design moves from space to space. The gallery is located to receive a flood of light from the ceiling.

JYVÄSKYLÄ

University And Teacher's College (1953)

ARCHITECT: Alvar Aalto
LOCATION: 182 miles N of Helsinki

Aalto was born and schooled close to Jyvaskyla. Intending to incorporate the lovely surrounding trees into the design of the structure, he created unique interior supportive columns representing the feeling of a tree. The architectural plan has provoked much interest and some criticism. The high quality of educational facilities in Finland today was inspired in large part by Aalto.

LAHTI

Church Of The Cross (Ristin Kirkko) (1970–78)

ARCHITECT: Alvar Aalto & Co.
LOCATION: 60 miles NNE of Helsinki, on Kirkkokatu 4

Actual construction on the church began ten months after the great architect's death in May 1976. The impressive Ristin Kirkko terminated the north-south axis plan begun by another important Finnish architect, Eliel Saarinen, who designed the town hall in 1912. The massive brick church by Aalto creates a magnificent culmination of the efforts of these two world-famous designers. The church features fifty-two windows that form a cross on the front facade surmounted by a concrete bell tower. Steps leading up to the church, landscaping, and the building's placement on the site complement the structures.

LAHTI

Lahti Theater (Lahden Teatteri) (1973–82)

ARCHITECTS: Pekka Salminen Ky and others
LOCATION: 60 miles NNE of Helsinki, on Kirkkokatu 14

This fascinating arrangement of forms and lines is created through the use of concrete modules set in a concrete frame. The system sets up a lacy, airy atmosphere. Latest advancements in technical design and lighting are employed, making this the finest theater in Finland today. The four-story complex has an orchestra pit that is hydraulically operated so it can double as part of the audience seating. The seating arrangement for 765 people is flexible with unique rearranging when needed.

NOORMARKU

Villa Mairea (1938)

ARCHITECT: Alvar Aalto
LOCATION: Privately owned (8 miles NNE of Pori)

The Villa Mairea ranks as one of the most important early modern residential efforts in the world. It was built for Aalto's lifelong patron and friend, Mairea Gullishsen. Built of wood, tile, and whitewashed brick, the home is designed around an outdoor swimming pool, sauna, and garden court. The interior design of fresh white-patinated walls, wood panelling, tile floors, and other simple materials became a prototype for Scandinavian interior treatments.

OTANIEMI

Chapel Of The Technical University (1957)

ARCHITECTS: Kaija and Keikki Siren
LOCATION: 6 miles W of Helsinki

This husband-and-wife architectural team has designed the Chapel of the Technical University in a manner that embodies the philosophy of many Finns—structure that becomes a part of nature. The chapel is surrounded by beautiful trees. Spacious windows provide a lovely view and flood the building with light. A series of slender wood rounds enhances the chapel and entry courtyard.

OTANIEMI

Dipoli Students' Activity And Congress Center (1964–66)

ARCHITECTS: Raili Paatelainen and Reima Pietila
LOCATION: Technical University 6 miles W of Helsinki

The architects were careful to preserve this natural setting dramatically located on a rocky knoll in a wooded area. Following the perimeter of the terrain and capturing its spirit, the plan is massed into two large zones, administrative and public. Raw concrete combined with wood is frankly exposed throughout the complex. The exterior is sheathed with copper.

OTANIEMI

Technical University Center At Otaniemi (1962–65)

ARCHITECTS: Elissa and Alvar Aalto
LOCATION: Technical University 6 miles W of Helsinki

Situated on a choice hill site in the center of the campus, the main buildings are the auditorium halls. A dramatic staircase leads up to the sweeping fan-shaped structure, and a curved window facade carries out the design theme. Materials include dark red brick, black granite, and copper. An entrance hall extending the full length of the structure channels traffic to the impressive lecture rooms and auditorium.

OULU

St. Thomas Church (1975)

ARCHITECT: Juha Leiviska
LOCATION: Puolivalinkangas, Oulu (280 miles N of Helsinki)

The church is built in the midst of a majestic fir forest, the trees preserved around the site. The architect hoped to create a timeless environment with the wide disconnected appearance. The front and back are clearly separated for privacy. The principal exterior building material is red brick. A light and spacious feeling has been accomplished inside the main chapel through the use of white-painted walls and woodwork, with streams of natural and artificial light filling the space.

PAIMIO

Tuberculosis Sanatorium (1929–33)

ARCHITECT: Alvar Aalto
LOCATION: 14 miles E of Turku

This building brought Aalto international attention. Reinforced concrete and plate glass combined with a sensitive floor plan made the TB Sanatorium a much-copied prototype for similar structures. Known as the "humanist architect," Aalto incorporated features that would contribute to the well-being of the patients—uplifting color schemes, a balcony on each floor, fresh air and sunlight, areas for patient congregation, and other pleasant facilities.

SALO

Cemetery Chapel At Salo (1964)

ARCHITECT: Eero Eerikainen
LOCATION: 30 Miles E of Turku

The unique triangular plan won the first prize in an extensive competition held in 1963. White concrete walls support a glass-and-tubular-steel space frame ceiling that allows shafts of bright sunlight into the chapel area. Clean white walls and geometric forms are softened by plants growing along the sides of the pews. The bell tower is disconnected from the main chapel and lined by garden walls.

SAYNATSALO

Town Hall (Kunnantalo) (1950)

ARCHITECT: Alvar Aalto
LOCATION: 8 miles SE of Jyvaskyla

With the design of this town hall, Aalto completely broke the confines of the modern idiom popular throughout Europe and America at the time. The beauty of this much-admired complex results from imaginative use of space, form, and materials. An inviting stepped approach leads to the central garden court with adjoining buildings on a series of levels. Constructed of warm-colored brick, the Town Hall is nicely placed with respect for the natural setting of this small island town.

SEINÄJOKI

Town Hall (1953–67)

and **Library** (1963–65)
ARCHITECT: Alvar Aalto
LOCATION: c. 50 miles SE of Vaasa

Interesting fan and wedge shapes employed for the design of the Town Hall and Library reflect Aalto's work later in his architectural career. A high roof soars above the Town Hall covering the council chamber and creating a focus for the building. Bold concave and convex exterior walls of the Library create visual excitement and functional space within. Aalto's work combines a nice compromise of the International and Organic Styles.

TAMPERE

Cathedral At Tampere

(1902–07)

ARCHITECT: Lars Sonck
LOCATION: 100 miles NNW of Helsinki,
Tuomiokirko Katu 1

Lars Sonck, along with Eliel Saarinen, was the foremost exponent of National Romanticism in Finland, and Tampere Cathedral is Sonck's most representative work. The Cathedral is prominently situated on a hillside. Its granite stone contrasts with the charming red-tile roofs and spires. The interior is a fascinating mixture of Gothic, Byzantine, and Art Nouveau decoration—superb craftsmanship.

TAMPERE

Kaleva Church (1964-6)

ARCHITECTS: Paatelainen and Pietila
LOCATION: Liisanpuisto

Striking vertical curved slabs characterize this much-photographed church. Built on a grassy mound on a triangular site, the church contrasts with the natural surroundings. Curving exterior planes are sheathed with cream-colored tile, providing glowing texture. A small cruciform bell tower floats above the sculptured structure. The interior has magnificent soaring space. Concrete, wood, and glass are impressively combined and exquisitely finished.

TAMPERE

Recreation And Congregational Center (Hervannan Vapaa-Aika) (1978)

ARCHITECTS: Raili and Reima Pietila
LOCATION: Lindforsinkatu 5

To provide a feeling "close to the earth and friendly" was the objective of the architects. The figure of the tree is suggested by red brick walls and projecting columns. Distinctive rounded corners soften the lines of the heavy structure. The brick column is repeated, enlarged, to create a soaring bell tower topped with a cross. The front axis of the multi-purpose building contains space for church services.

TAMPERE

Sara Hildén Art Museum (Sara Hildénin Taidemuseo) (1979)

ARCHITECTS: The Pekka Ilveskoski Firm
LOCATION: On the shore of Lake Nasijarvi beside Särkänniemi Recreation Center (Tampere's popular tourist attraction)

Tiered down a sloping site overlooking Lake Nasijarvi, the Taidemuseo is one of Tampere's newest modern buildings. The Art Museum primarily exhibits a collection of works donated by Sara Hilden, a well-known businesswoman and art collector. Today, the main focus is on classic foreign and Finnish modern art. Simplicity and clarity of architectural forms provide an ideal background for the displays.

TAMPERE

Vatiala Cemetery Chapel
(1960–61)

ARCHITECT: Viljo Rewell
LOCATION: Vatiala Cemetery, E of Tampere

Designed a few years before the architect's
death in 1964, the stunning church features an
imaginative parabolic roof faced with copper.
A smaller chapel is linked to the larger
structure by a central entrance hall. Tall trees
surround the structures, enhancing the visual
image of simplicity of materials and form.
Rewell was one of Aalto's most famous
students, the church one of Rewell's best-
known works.

TAPIOLA

Tapiola Garden City (1956–62)

ARCHITECTS: Original scheme by Aarne
Ervi (numerous architects)
LOCATION: 5 miles W of Helsinki

Situated in a beautiful setting of small lakes
and wooded areas, Tapiola is an administrative,
business, and cultural center for
approximately fifty thousand inhabitants.
Residents are able to communicate with
nature, free from the noise and traffic of the
city, within easy reach of downtown
Helsinki—buses leave every fifteen minutes.
Other noteworthy public structures include:
ADMINISTRATIVE AND SHOPPING CENTER
(1959) by Aarne Ervi, SWIMMING STADIUM
(1964) by Aarne Ervi, CHURCH AT TAPIOLA
(1964) by Aarno Ruusuvvuori, and TOWER
BLOCKS OF FLATS (1959) by Viljo Rewell.

TURKU

Resurrection Chapel (Ylosnousemuskappeli)

(1938–41)

ARCHITECT: Erik Bryggman
LOCATION: Turun hautausmaa (Turku Cemetery)

Considered Bryggman's most important work, the chapel features a pure rational approach. Inside, a single row of simple structural columns in updated classical manner borders a large aisle that looks out into a lovely garden. An exciting nave sensitively employs natural light as an architectural element. Subtle light washes the sanctuary wall, adding to the charm of the chapel.

TURKU

Theater At Turku (Kaupunginteatteri) (1960–63)

ARCHITECTS: Risto-Veikko Luukkonen & Helmer Stenros
LOCATION: Itainen Rantakatu 14

Located on the banks of the river, the theater at Turku commands a prominent position. The elevated stage tower, situated between workshops and office spaces, is the focal point of the complex. The building is partly clad in ceramic tile and copper, with uniform strips of window bands on the lower elevations. An interesting stepped plan lends a sculptural quality to the vertical and horizontal massing.

ADDITIONAL MODERN STRUCTURES OF INTEREST

ESPOO

AMFI Housing Area (1980–)
LOCATION: Kivenlahti, (the new town project of Asuntosaatio)

A beautifully-located housing development interestingly arranged in a tiered and circular composition.

Espoo Fine Arts Center (Espoon Kulttuurikeskus (1980–87)
ARCHITECT: Arto Sipinen
LOCATION: Tapiola center, approximately 10 miles W of Helsinki

Even though the architect has employed prefabricated modular sections in the construction of the new Fine Arts Center, he has attempted to create a style of oneness with the surrounding wilderness.

The Chapel Of Soukka (1975–78)
ARCHITECT: Veijo Martikaihen
LOCATION: On a rocky hillside in Soukka

"In planning and building the Chapel in the rocky landscape of Soukka, man was the starting point and the measure from the chapel courtyard, continuing through all the facilities into the sanctuary." (Veijo Martikainen, Aug. 20, 1978.)

HELSINKI

Lauttasaaren Kirkko (Lauttassari Church) (1957–59)
ARCHITECT: Keijo Petaja
LOCATION: SW Helsinki, Myllykallionrinne 1

The approach to the Church and Parish Center is impressively terraced. A lofty tower provides a focal point. Especially interesting is the deeply-glazed east side.

Malmin Kirkko (Malmi Church) (1981)
ARCHITECT: Kristian Gullichsen
LOCATION: Central Helsinki, Kunnantie

One of Finland's newest churches, the Malmi Church "looks like a church"—a goal of the designer. Constructed of warm brick.

Maunulan Kirkko (Maunula Church) (1980)
ARCHITECT: Ahti Korhonen
LOCATION: Metsapurontie 15, West Central Helsinki

A small and lightly scaled white church designed to blend into an unpretentious neighborhood.

Meilahden Kirkko (Meilahti Church) (Post World War II)
ARCHITECT: Markus Tavio
LOCATION: Pihlajatie 16

A flexible and inviting church—the first modern religious structure built after the war.

Mikael Agricolan Kirkko (Mikael Agricola Church) (1935)
ARCHITECT: Lars Sonck
LOCATION: Tehtaankatu 23, SW Helsinki

Named after Finland's reformer, the Mikael Agricola church is a powerful example of Sonck's work—designed after his famous Kallio Church.

National Museum (1901–12)
ARCHITECT: Eliel Saarinen
LOCATION: Mannerheimintie 34

In the design of this museum can be seen the strong architectural elements and bold use of materials influenced by the Arts and Crafts Movement in England.

Paragon House (1970s)
ARCHITECT: Aarno Ruusuvuori
LOCATION: Makelankatu 84

An excellent example of functional office design in Finland.

Parliament House Extension (1978)
ARCHITECT: Laiho Pitkanen-Raunio
LOCATION: Aurorankatu 6 and Mannerheimintie 30

A stately modern addition to the front of the old building. Built of cast-in-place concrete.

Teollesuuskeskus (1952)
ARCHITECT: Viljo Rewell
LOCATION: Etelaranta 10

A splendid large multi-purpose center on the waterfront.

Tower At Helsinki Stadium (1936–52)
ARCHITECTS: Y. Lindegren and T. Jantti
LOCATION: Olympia Stadium Paavon Nurmenkatu 1 A

A soaring vertical tower and sports facility, for years one of Helsinki's most important modern landmarks.

Enso-Gutzeit (1959–62)
ARCHITECT: Alvar Aalto
LOCATION: Kanavaranta 1

Strong mullions of marble dominate the design of this administrative headquarters for a large paper and cellulose concern.

JYVASKYLA

New Theater (1983)
ARCHITECT: Original plan by Alvar Aalto, completed by others
LOCATION: Town Center, 182 miles N of Helsinki

This admirable New Theater is one of the master architect's original designs completed after his death in 1976.

LAHTI

Kansallis-Osake-Pankki Building (1964)
ARCHITECT: Viljo Rewell
LOCATION: Aleksanterinkatu 10

An admired banking facility with numerous conveniences for the customer and employee.

Town Hall (1912)
ARCHITECT: Eliel Saarinen
LOCATION: Puistokatu 2

One of the great Finnish architect's first important modern structures.

OULU

Oulu University (1973–78)
ARCHITECTS: Various architects
LOCATION: Linnaniaa, Oulu

Sensitive modern planning for a student body of 5,000 students.

Pyhan Tuomaan Church (1975)
ARCHITECT: Juha Leiviska
LOCATION: Puolivalinkangas

A clean and structural brick and glass church located in a pleasant wooded area.

RAISIO

Raisio City Hall (1981)
ARCHITECT: Arto Sipinen
LOCATION: Just outside Turku

A beautiful city hall of red brick walls with visible steel supports.

ROVANIEMI

Civic And Cultural Center (1963–68)
ARCHITECT: Alvar Aalto
LOCATION: Approximately 125 miles N of Oulu

This ambitious building program includes a *LIBRARY* featuring clerestory windows. The center shows Aalto's masterful use of natural materials and sensitive combinations of mass and space.

HYVINKÄÄ

Rantasipi Hyvinkaa (1970s)
ARCHITECT: Martti and Anna-Maija Jaatinen (Interior Designer)
LOCATION: Rantasipi Hyvinkaa, approximately 30 miles N of Helsinki

A popular modern recreation center for tourists.

TAMPERE

Hervanta Shopping Center (1979)
ARCHITECTS: Reima & Raili Pietila
LOCATION: Einkaufszentrum Hervanta

Tampere is becoming a city of works by the well-known modern designers, Reima and Raili Pietila. This center with its undulating facade of arches is impressive.

SUNILA

Sunila Sulphatecellulose Plant (1936)
ARCHITECT: Alvar Aalto
LOCATION: Above Kotka, 86 miles E of
Helsinki

Sunila Plant's marvelous industrial complex
design has been compared to Frank Lloyd
Wright's well-planned Johnson Wax Factory in
Racine, Wisconsin.

Hotel Rosendahl (1972–77)
ARCHITECTS: Jaakko & Kaarina Laapotti/
Martti Kukkonen
LOCATION: Pyynikintie 13

The cleverest feature of this delightful hotel
complex is its sensitivity to its natural
surroundings, both beach and forest. In order
to preserve the natural beauty, the architect
kept the structure low, almost hidden in
nature. An exterior facade of glass reflects the
beauty of the environment. Supportive
reinforced concrete employed throughout
adds an aesthetic touch as well.

Tampere Workers' Theater (1985)
ARCHITECTS: Marjatta and Martti Jaatinen
LOCATION: Hameenpuisto 32

This new theater will provide facilities for
one of the oldest professional theaters in the
country.

TURKU

Agricultural House (Maalaistentalo) (1927–28)
ARCHITECT: Alvar Aalto
LOCATION: Humalistonkatu—Puutarhakatu 8

Aalto, who worked for a short period with
Bryggman, also designed the *APARTMENT
BUILDING (ASULNATALO)* (1927–28) at
Lantinen Pitkakatu 20 and *TURUN SANOMAT
PRESS (TURUN SANOMIEN TAKO)* (1927–29)
at Kaupplaskatu 5.

Hotelli Hospits Betel (Hospits Betal Hotel) (1928)
ARCHITECT: Erik Bryggman
LOCATION: Yliopistonkatu 29

One of Bryggman's best-known works. Turku
boasts a number of works by this important
early modern architect. (Bryggman's offices
were in Turku.) Other works include:
APARTMENT BUILDING (1927) at
Yliopistonkatu 27, *ABO AKADEMIN
KIRJASTON KIRJATORNI "BOOK TOWER" OF
ABO AKADEMI LIBRARY* (1935) at
Tuomiokirkkokatu 2-4.

Pyhan Ristin Kappeli (Chapel Of The Holy Cross) (1967)
ARCHITECT: Pekka Pitkanen
LOCATION: Turku Cemetery

Sibelius Museum (Sibelius-Museo) (1967)
ARCHITECT: Woldemar Baeckman
LOCATION: Plispankatu 17

State Offices (Valtion Virastotalo) (1969)
ARCHITECTS: Helmer Stenros and
Risto-Veikko Luukkonen
LOCATION: Itsenaisyydenaukio 2

Waino Aaltonen Museum (1967)
ARCHITECTS: Irma ja Matti Aaltonen
LOCATION: Itainen Rantakatu 38

VAASA

Sandpiper Hotel At Vassa (1970s)
DESIGNER: Yuro Kukkapuro
LOCATION: Approximatley 220 miles NW
of Helsinki

A ground-hugging contemporary arrangement
of forms with interiors and furnishings
designed by one of Finland's leading
designers. A popular resort hotel.

VIERUMAKI

Sports Institute (1933–36)
ARCHITECT: Erik Bryggman
LOCATION: 12 miles NE of Hahti, South
Finland

One of Finland's first important modern
buildings designed for sports activities.

France

FRANCE

Lille •

• Amiens

• Le Havre

• Rouen Roissy-en-France

Poissy • • Le Raincy Nancy •

Saint-Quentin • • Paris Fontaines-les-Gres • Strasbourg

Nemours • • Troyes Baccarat

Ronchamp •

Audincourt

Quimper •

Evan-les-Bains

Nantes • Flaine

Eveux-sur-l'Arbresle • • Lyon

Firminy •

Royan • Grenoble

Bordeaux •

Vence

St. Paul • Nice

La Gaude

Marseilles • Hyèrers

La Grande Motte • Cap Benet

Bayonne •

Lourdes • Perpignan

Le Boulou

MODERN ARCHITECTURE IN FRANCE

EARLY USE OF IRON CONSTRUCTION

The Industrial Revolution and the technical development of iron had a great impact on architecture in France. Labrouste's libraries, constructed of iron, are usually considered the first modern buildings in France. The roof over the Theatre-Francais was an engineering wonder for the eighteenth century. The Eiffel Tower, designed in 1889, amazed the world and further demonstrated the potential of iron construction.

ART NOUVEAU

Paris became the center for the popular Art Nouveau style from 1890 to 1910. Samuel Bing opened his *Maison l 'Art Nouveau* shop in 1895, featuring furniture and accessories of many important Art Nouveau designers. Art Nouveau, derived from nature, employed motifs based on plant forms, animals, insects, and organic lines. The great Parisian actress, Sarah Bernhardt, patronized this style and became an Art Nouveau motif, as did Loie Fuller, the American-born Parisian dancer at the Folies Bergere. Hector Guimard was the leading architect of this period; his Art Nouveau entrances to the Metro have become delightful landmarks in Paris. Many restaurants (like Maxim's), apartment houses, and private homes show Art Nouveau influence.

REINFORCED CONCRETE

Reinforced concrete was developed and perfected by the Parisian architect Auguste Perret in 1901. This development had a great influence on many early modern architects, providing means for an entirely new approach to architecture. Perret's house at 25 bis Rue de Franklin is thought to be the world's first building employing reinforced concrete.

LE CORBUSIER AND THE INTERNATIONAL STYLE

The Swiss-born French architect, Le Corbusier, is internationally recognized as one of the most important influences on modern architecture. After training with Perret in Paris and Peter Behrens in Berlin, Le Corbusier established his own practice at 22 Rue des Sevres in Paris. His creations were received with great hostility by Parisians, but others throughout the world appreciated his work. The International Style (officially named at an exhibit at The Museum of Modern Art in New York City in 1932) was developed by Le Corbusier, the Bauhaus in Germany, and other European modern architects during the 1920s and 1930s.

ART DECO

The decorative arts between the world wars utilized sleek geometric modernism. Art Deco, a total style encompassing all branches of the arts, reached its peak in France during the Paris World Fair of 1925, officially launching the new modernism.

ARCHITECTURE AFTER WORLD WAR II

Modern architecture was gradually accepted after the war. The influence of Le Corbusier and the International Style continued. State-supported housing projects were imaginative, but often were poorly constructed with inferior materials and workmanship. Outstanding contributions have been made through the efforts of such prominent designers as Jean Prouve, Bernard Zehrfuss, Paul Andreu, Louis Arretche, Charles Pivot, Maurince Novarina, Guillaume Gillet, Nicolas Kazis, Michel Marot, Jean Balladur, Pierre Vago, Francois Deslaugiers, and a few avante garde firms. The influence of international architects, such as Marcel Breuer (USA), Pier Luigi (Italy), Ricardo Bofill (Spain), Harry Seidler (Australia), and Oscar Niemeyer (Brazil), has also been strong.

AUDINCOURT

Church Of The Sacred Heart (Eglise Du Sacre Coeur) (1950)

ARCHITECT: Maurice Novarina
LOCATION: (11 miles S of Belfort) Route de Seloncourt, Audincourt

Many art enthusiasts come to the Church of the Sacred Heart not for the architecture, but rather to see the colorful band of seventeen windows designed by Fernand Leger. In Paris at the turn of the century, Leger, along with Picasso and Braque, helped create abstract painting. Leger's stained-glass work illustrates the Passions of the Lord. The simply-designed architecture is a perfect background for displaying the colorful work. The Baptistry features lovely abstract stained-glass designs by Jean Bazaine.

BACCARAT

St. Remy (1957)

ARCHITECT: Nicolas Kazis
LOCATION: Avenue de Lachapelle 33 miles SE of Nancy

Famed Baccarat crystal has been made in this town for over two hundred years. The bold concrete forms of the church of St. Remy in this historic town seem austere and forbidding, but the interior is softened by exquisite colored windows designed to wash the walls with light. The windows are deeply and irregularly set, increasing their aesthetic appeal.

BAYONNE

Satellite Town (1963–69)

ARCHITECT: Marcel Breuer (USA)
LOCATION: Outskirts of Bayonne

This immense project was a unique challenge for the internationally renowned architect. Satellite Town is an important example of modern city planning, with functionally designed structural buildings situated around a large open plaza. The town is located near the famous Biarritz Beach on France's Atlantic Coast.

BORDEAUX

Laboratories Sarget, Corporate Hdqrs. & Pharmaceutical (1965–68)

ARCHITECT: Marcel Breuer and Robert G. Gatje
LOCATION: Avenue Fitzgerald Kennedy, 33700 MERIGNAC

Breuer, the world-famous German-American architect, carefully separated the functional areas of this huge complex. Administrative offices are housed in a crescent-shaped wing easily seen from the highway. Bridges connect the other blocks. The entire structure is of pre-cast concrete.

CAP BENET

Boissonnas House II (1964)

ARCHITECT: Philip Johnson (USA)
LOCATION: (Privately owned) The hills of
Cap Benet, overlooking the Mediterranean
Sea

Johnson, one of America's foremost modern
architects, is an early follower of Ludwig Mies
van der Rohe. After designing his famous
glass house in New Canaan, Connecticut in
1949, Johnson designed the Boissonnas home
in New Canaan. This second private home for
the Boissonnas family features a massive
floating concrete roof over an outside atrium.

EVIAN-LES-BAINS

Spa Pavilion (1957)

ARCHITECT: Jean Prouve, M. Novarina, and
S. Ketoff
LOCATION: Quai P. Leger, Evian-les-Bains,
Lake Geneva

Jean Prouve is France's most admired
contemporary engineer-architect, known
throughout Europe for his brilliant designs
utilizing advanced technology. The Spa
Pavilion is located in a park overlooking
lovely Lake Geneva. Interior T-shaped steel
structural supports and large expanses of
glass give the building an airy feeling,
capturing the spirit of its function—fun and
relaxation. The Spa's famous mineral water is
found in the bar room.

EVREUX-SUR L'ARBESLE

Le Couvent Sainte Marie De La Tourette (1954–59)

ARCHITECT: Le Corbusier
LOCATION: 16 miles NW of Lyons

La tourette is a complex and intriguing structure designed as a monastery for the Dominicans. The raw concrete exterior is stark, with only a bell turret and repeating window voids providing interest. Evoking the spirit of its purpose, the structure, perched on a gently sloping hillside, contrasts dramatically with its natural surroundings.

FIRMINY

The Youth Center And House Of Culture (1960–65)

ARCHITECT: Le Corbusier
LOCATION: Firminy-Vert

Plans for expansion of Firminy-Vert are still in progress, although Le Corbusier died in a tragic swimming accident in 1965. With sixteen spans intersected by two expansion joints, this structure is constructed of raw concrete with primary and secondary color used for accents—a feature often employed by the great architect. Le Corbusier's *UNITE DE HABITATION* is also close by.

FLAINE

Mountain Resort Of Flaine (1960–69)

ARCHITECT: Marcel Breuer (USA)
LOCATION: Mountain Resort of Flaine in Haute Savoie E France

After this internationally famous architect left Nazi Germany to settle in America, he received numerous commissions from European countries. This bold concrete four-star resort hotel, perched on a slope in a breathtakingly beautiful mountain setting, has a brutalistic textural finish—a good example of Breuer's individualistic break from Bauhaus principles. Sensitively oriented to its site, the hotel's interior treatment throughout is similar to the exterior design.

FONTAINES-LES GRES

St. Agnes (1956)

ARCHITECT: Michel Marot
LOCATION: 12 miles NW of Troyes

Interestingly located in a small village, this modern church has an unusual entrance of various textures and forms introducing an impressive interior. All wall surfaces are irregularly shaped and covered with wood strips. On the altar wall hangs a simple stylized statue of Christ dramatized by the play of sunlight streaming through soft gray, white, and yellow windows.

LA GAUDE

IBM Complex (1960–66)

ARCHITECT: Marcel Breuer (USA)
LOCATION: Isolated countryside a few
miles NE of Nice

This sprawling research center for one of the
world's largest corporations is located close to
the French Riviera. The design stresses a Y-
shaped theme, including Y-shaped elevated
concrete supports similar to those employed
by Breuer for his famous UNESCO Building
in Paris. The entire surface treatment is raw
concrete.

LA GRANDE MOTTE

La Grande Motte
Pyramid (1963–75)

ARCHITECT: Jean Balladur
LOCATION: Riviera coastline of Languedoc
& Rousillon, Hirault

Built along the beautiful hundred-mile
coastline of the Mediterranean Sea, La Grande
Motte Pyramid commands a striking position.
The massive housing complex, built to
accommodate the heavy tourist traffic, is
distinguished by its bold, unusual pyramid
and rounded shapes. Apartment complexes
afford a lovely view and incorporate a balcony
that is arranged in an overall tiered
composition.

LE BOULOU

Le Parc De La Marca Hispania (1977)

ARCHITECTS: Taller de Arquitectura (Spain)
LOCATION: Franco-Spanish border, approximately 20 km S of Perpignan

Le Parc de la Marca Hispania or "Homage to Catalonia France" was commissioned in 1974 by the Societe des Autoroutes du Sud. Taller de Arquitectura, led by Ricardo Bofill, is located in Barcelona. The intriguing structure includes temple-topped pyramid forms symbolizing the spirit of the location and the people of Catalonia. A series of steps lead up the hillside to the structure dramatizing the design on the horizon.

LE HAVRE

Maison De La Culture (House Of Culture) (1983)

ARCHITECT: Oscar Niemeyer (Brazil)
LOCATION: La Place Carnot, on the waterfront

The spectacular new Maison de la Culture, with its bold swirling concrete forms, fulfills the destiny of Auguste Perret's original plans for Le Havre. The bold concrete composition seems a fitting culmination for the city, planned by the architect who pioneered reinforced concrete. Brazil's internationally famous architect, Niemeyer, is known for his imaginative use of concrete, especially after designing the entire modern city of Brasilia. The meandering walkways of Niemeyer's Maison de la Culture entice the visitor throughout the dramatic spaces.

LE HAVRE

St. Joseph's Church (1959)

ARCHITECT: Auguste Perret
LOCATION: Boulevard Francois I

St. Joseph's Church is the last work of the great French architect who developed and refined the use of reinforced concrete at the turn of the century. The soaring octagonal tower of the church, looming 350 feet into the air, can be seen for miles. Perret's masterful use of reinforced concrete has created an immense interior recalling the awesome effect of medieval Gothic cathedrals. Superb stained-glass windows by Margaret Hure contrast with the raw concrete texture.

LE RAINCY

Church Of Notre Dame (1922–23)

ARCHITECT: Auguste Perret
LOCATION: 40, allee du Jardin anglais (Seine-Saint-Denis), a few miles ENE of Paris, Place de l'Eglise

Known as "the father of modern architecture in France" for his innovative use of material and form, Perret designed this church that has become one of his most visited works. The engaging building is constructed of reinforced concrete, with windows of colorful stained glass in a modern design. Perret did not attempt to conceal the concrete—unusual for the time.

LOURDES

St. Pius X Basilica (1958)

ARCHITECT: Eugene Freyssinet, engineer;
Pierre Vago, architect
LOCATION: Cite Religieuse, Lourdes

Freyssinet, a prominent pioneer of modern design in France, collaborated with Vago to create a religious shelter for the 22,000 pilgrims who visit the famous Grotto of Saint Bernadette annually. The huge concrete basilica is underground and covered with lawn so as not to overwhelm the little traditional church close by. The structure is generally used only during unpleasant weather conditions.

MARSEILLES

Unité D'Habitation (1938)

ARCHITECT: Le Corbusier
LOCATION: Boulevard Michelet

This apartment complex, astounding for its time, evoked much criticism in France, including a lawsuit for creating a blight on the countryside. Le Corbusier used a modular design throughout the structure based on "human dimensions." The uniform box-like design with a series of supports on the open ground floor has become a prototype for similar buildings around the world. Parts of the building are open to the public.

NANCY

Villa Louis Majorelle (c. 1900)

ARCHITECT: Henri Sauvage
LOCATION: 1 rue Majorelle

At the turn of the century Nancy was an important design center for the popular Art Nouveau style. Louis Majorelle, one of the leading furniture designers during this period, produced exquisitely carved pieces featuring motifs from nature. Majorelle's house by Sauvage is an excellent example of Art Nouveau architecture in France, with typical use of organic forms and flowing lines.

NANTES

Unité D'Habitation (1955)

ARCHITECT: Le Corbusier
LOCATION: Nantes-Reze (Southwest of Nantes)

Built a few years after Le Corbusier's world famous Unité d'Habitation in Marseilles, this Unité features a "shoe-box" system of construction: Each apartment is an independent box of pre-stressed concrete having no connection with the adjoining apartment except two bands of lead. The whole complex "floats" on slender piers with a uniform design of windows and balconies.

NEMOURS

Centre Regional D'Informatique (1975–79)

ARCHITECT: Francois Deslaugiers
LOCATION: approximately 70 km. SSE of Paris

A unique glass-and-metal "clip together industrial system" designed for the Department of Income Tax. Deslaugiers, one of France's most imaginative modern architects, had difficulty convincing the organization to accept this innovative architectural approach. The avante garde complex provides delightful contrast to the traditional surroundings.

PARIS

Art Nouveau House On Avenue Rapp (1900)

ARCHITECT: Jules Lavirotte
LOCATION: 29 Avenue Rapp, east of the Eiffel Tower

French architects were known at the turn of the century for their flamboyant interpretation of Art Nouveau Style. Twisting serpents, plant and animal forms, and women with flowing hair have been dramatically integrated into the design of this house, attracting tourists and architectural students from all over the world. The house is considered one of the finest examples of domestic Art Nouveau architecture in France from the 1890–1910 period.

PARIS

Bibliothèque Nationale (1855)

ARCHITECT: Henri Labrouste
LOCATION: Rue de richelieu

Although its date would indicate a Victorian structure, the Library is an excellent example of the early use of iron construction. This second great library design brought Labrouste world-wide attention. To provide the needed light for reading, he planned unusually large areas of glass for this period of time. Frankly exposed interior iron supports, although in part decorative, were unique in the 1850s.

PARIS

Castel Béranger (1895–97)

ARCHITECT: Hector Guimard
LOCATION: 14 Rue La Fontaine

Guimard was the nation's foremost exponent of Art Nouveau design, particularly admired for his delightful entrances to the Metro. Considered one of Guimard's most important architectural contributions, Castel Beranger boasts sweeping Art Nouveau carvings around the doorway. All details bear the architect's distinctive stamp, even the grills covering the air vents.

PARIS

Eiffel Tower (1889)

ENGINEER: Gustave Eiffel
LOCATION: Left Bank of Seine, between Avenue de Suffren and Avenue de la Bourdonnais

This extraordinary tower of iron was the symbol for the Paris Exposition of 1889. The tallest structure in the world at the time, it paved the way for further development of iron as a construction material. It was denounced by many as a disgrace to France; and others thought the tower unsafe. It was intended to stand for only twenty years, but through the years has become so popular that it is universally recognized as a symbol of Paris. The tower's iron Art Nouveau organic filigree was stripped off for munitions during World War I.

PARIS

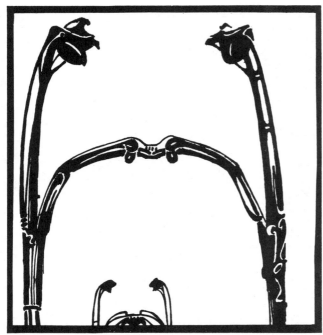

Entrances To The Metro (c. 1900)

ARCHITECT: Hector Guimard
LOCATION: A few remain throughout the city—one just east of the Louvre, one on the Cité

Art Nouveau designer Guimard's most famous works are undoubtedly these delightful entrances to the Paris Metro (subway). The iron structures were designed to simulate growing plants clustered around the steps leading down into the Metro area. Unfortunately many have been removed, but dozens remain.

PARIS

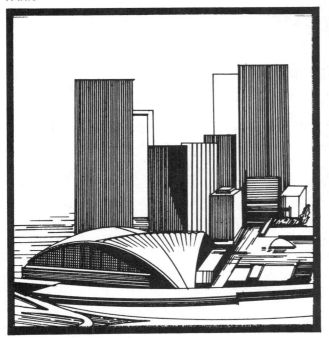

Exhibition Hall C.N.I.T. La Défense Development (1958–)

ARCHITECTS: R. Camelot, J. de Mailly, B. Zehrfuss, Pier Luigi Nervi, and Jean Prouve. LOCATION: Rond-point de la Défense, Paris-Puteaux

The huge inverted concrete shell CNIT (National Center for Industry and Technology) Exhibition Hall rests on three supports, providing a "floating" space. Close by is the grand *FIAT TOWER* of polished granite, its forty-five stories making it the tallest building in the development. The tinted glass windows are enlarged near the top to insure uniform appearance. Among the many buildings of interest is the pink mirror-clad *MANHATTAN TOWER*.

PARIS

"Front De Seine Complex" (1970s)

LOCATION: Across the Seine from Radio-France House

Construction on this immense housing development took place during the past decade. It includes sixteen modern residential and office towers with added facilities for cultural and sports activities. A garden and shopping plaza are supported on an eighteen-foot concrete podium above the traffic.

PARIS

Halles Centrales (1854–66)

(Now Destroyed)

ARCHITECT: Victor Baltard
LOCATION: The Halles Quarter (Les Halles)
was built on the old site (see page 139)

Baltard built a series of huge iron, glass, and
wood structures to accommodate the bustling
market trade. The Halles Centrales was
recently destroyed to make way for an
immense modern facility that will house
numerous contemporary functions. The old
structure was a world masterpiece of iron
construction.

PARIS

House At 25 Bis Rue Franklin (1901)

ARCHITECT: Auguste Perret
LOCATION: 25 Bis Rue Franklin

Perret, one of the great pioneers among
modern architects in Europe, has often been
referred to as "the father of modern
architecture in France." This much-publicized
building is credited as one of the world's first
structures to use reinforced concrete. This
method allowed for a light and airy facade
with thin wall supports and large expanses of
window.

PARIS

Les Halles I (1974–)

ARCHITECTS: Vasconi and Pencreac'h
LOCATION: The Halles Quarter (nearly
90 acres)

This controversial project, spearheaded by
Major Jacques Chirac, will cover a twenty-five-
acre site left vacant after Victor Baltard's
immense cast iron and glass pavilions were
razed in 1971. The projected modern
development will cost $1.1 billion and will
feature an underground pedestrian network, a
forum, a hotel, a commercial center, a cultural
complex, and other public facilities.

PARIS

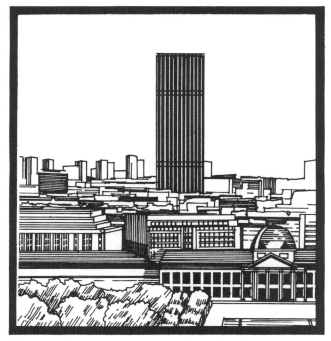

Maine-Montparnasse Tower (1970s)

ARCHITECTS: French Architectural Group
LOCATION: Place du 18-Juin-1940

Looming above the skyline, the spectacular
tower with its fifty-eight floors is the tallest
office building in Europe. The exterior
curtain wall is sheathed with bronze-tinted
glass reflecting the surrounding neighborhood.
The fifty-sixth floor observatory commands a
magnificent panoramic view of Paris.

PARIS

Notre Dame Du Travail (1901)

ARCHITECT: Jules Astruc
LOCATION: 59, Rue Vercingetorix

A jewel of early modern design, this little church is tucked in a busy section of the city. Instead of employing the traditional stone-and-brick building materials for religious architecture, visionary architect Jules Astruc designed a church of iron. The structural supports are not covered with decoration but are frankly exposed, adding a new dimension to the space.

PARIS

Pompidou Centre (National Center Of Art & Culture)

(1971)

ARCHITECTS: Richard Rogers and Renzo Piano
LOCATION: Hotel de Ville Quarter at Beaubourg Plateau

Outrageous, stunning, ridiculous, delightful, weird, fantastic—no adjectives adequately describe the Pompidou Center. The controversial structure is both a museum and display complex made of gigantic steel trusses. The bold high-technical design is interrupted by primary colors of red, blue, and yellow, as well as an exterior escalator. Pompidou Center's startling contrast with its traditional surroundings has triggered much criticism.

PARIS

Radio-France House (1963)

ARCHITECT: Henry Bernard
LOCATION: 116 Avenue de President Kennedy

This imposing structure, pleasantly situated along the Seine River, is interestingly viewed from the Eiffel Tower. The complex consists of one huge concentric building with a 230-foot tower. The massive building is the largest single construction in France. Tours are available.

PARIS

The Salvation Army Building (Cite De Refuge) (1932–33)

ARCHITECT: Le Corbusier
LOCATION: 12 rue Cantagrel

The Salvation Army Building was built during Le Corbusier's "barren" years, when he was writing on his philosophies of design and city planning. The building features a box design, employing simple surfaces and large areas of glass block. The entire building has recently been restored and presented in a number of periodicals and books.

Swiss Pavilion (1925)

ARCHITECT: Le Corbusier
LOCATION: Left Bank, by Montsouris Park,
Cité Universitaire

Designed as a student dormitory for the Cité
Universitaire, the Swiss Pavilion became a
prototype for residential flats throughout
Europe. Like most of Le Corbusier's work, the
building was highly criticized by traditionalists.
Le Corbusier, with the Bauhaus designers in
Germany and other pioneer modern
architects, helped to establish design
principles that came to be known as "the
International Style"—a term coined by
American architect Philip Johnson in 1932.

PARIS

St. Geneviève Library (1843–50)

ARCHITECT: Henri Labrouste
LOCATION: Rue Valette

Most textbooks on modern architecture begin
with the design of this library. Under the
traditional neo-Renaissance facade is an iron
structure, one of the first of its kind. The iron
construction is frankly exposed throughout
the library interior.

PARIS

The Australian Embassy (1978)

ARCHITECTS: Harry Seidler (Australia) with others
LOCATION: 4 rue Jean Rey

One of the most dynamic buildings in Paris, the impressive Australian Embassy creates a bold image in its urban setting. Two huge curving wedge-shaped structural forms are connected by a two-story glass enclosure and bridge. The juxtaposition of form and space throughout the complex achieves a sense of surprise without sacrificing unity and integrity.

PARIS

Unesco Building (1953–58)

ARCHITECTS: Marcel Breuer in collaboration with Nervi and Zehrfuss.
LOCATION: Place de Fontenoy (Left Bank, near Ecole Militaire)

This famous Y-shaped structure was designed by world-renowned architects, reflecting the international purpose of the building. The complex consists of three buildings for US cultural and educational headquarters. Prominent among these is the eight-story Y-shaped secretariat with curving facade, tapered supportive columns, and large windows with sun shields. Henry Moore created the sculpture in front of the building.

POISSY

Villa Savoye (1930)

ARCHITECT: Le Corbusier
LOCATION: A field by the Ecole
Le Corbusier

Considered Le Corbusier's residential masterpiece, the white reinforced concrete house floats on slender columns. The Villa Savoye exemplifies many of Le Corbusier's architectural concepts—open plan, free facades, and roof garden. The home was occupied by both German and Allied soldiers during World War II. This early modern structure has been restored in response to numerous requests from around the world to save the house. Check at the gate for admittance.

ROISSY-EN-FRANCE

Charles De Gaulle Airport (1969–76)

ARCHITECT: Paul Andreu
LOCATION: A few miles NE of Paris off the freeway (follow the signs)

Strikingly stark modern design characterizes this efficient airport plan that covers an area a third the size of Paris. Passengers enjoy mobile floor strips and glass tubes for easy transport from check-in stations to the airplane. The center atrium, a bold focal point in the complex, features a series of large fountains and passenger escalator tubes.

RONCHAMP

Notre Dame Du Haut (1950–55)

ARCHITECT: Le Corbusier
LOCATION: Ronchamp, Vosges (13 miles W of Belfort)

A popular pilgrimage church was built on the site of this church destroyed during World War II. The massive curved concrete structure with its white-textured surface, one of the great monuments of modern ecclesiastical architecture, has been compared to "a nun's hat," "inverted praying hands," and "St. Peter's boat." The abstractly painted access doors and stained glass windows were also designed by the architect. The principal entrance was made difficult to locate as a symbol of man's search for the kingdom of heaven.

ROUEN

Church Of St. Joan Of Arc (1979)

ARCHITECT: Louis Arretche
LOCATION: The Old Market Place

Tourists flock to this old Market Place to see where Joan of Arc was martyred at the stake. Sweeping high above the roof-tops surrounding the Old Market Place, the boldly formed Church with its roof resembling the tail of a huge fish (symbolic of Christianity) provides striking contrast with the traditional architecture. The church was built to commemorate the patron saint of France. The stained glass windows were removed from St. Vincent's Church for protection during World War II before St. Vincent's was destroyed. A stylistic statue of St. Joan guards the entrance, and a few steps away a slender bronze cross marks the exact spot where she died.

ROYAN

Church Of Notre Dame En Son Immaculee Conception (1954–59)

ARCHITECT: Guillaume Gillet
LOCATION: Rue du Chateau d'Eau at Rue de Foncillon

Large and striking, this church is built on an oval plan. It is constructed entirely of reinforced concrete except for a focal point of light shining through stained glass behind the altar, a true offspring of Perret's earlier church at Le Raincy (page 131). Gillet has interestingly integrated traditional effects into this dramatic contemporary rendition.

SAINT PAUL-EN VENCE

Maeght Foundation (1968)

ARCHITECT: Josef Luis Sert (Spain, then USA)
LOCATION: c. 19 miles NW of Nice, 3 miles from Venice

The dazzling white museum, designed by the famous Spanish architect, Luis Sert, features dramatic upswept curving roofs. The engaging complex is considered one of the most important modern museums in Europe. A striking Alexander Calder sculpture in the garden introduces the fascinating displays inside. Beautifully situated in the hills, the museum is composed of courtyards, umbrellas on the higher terrace, a cloister section, and concrete roof shells that admit light into the rooms.

SAINT-QUENTIN

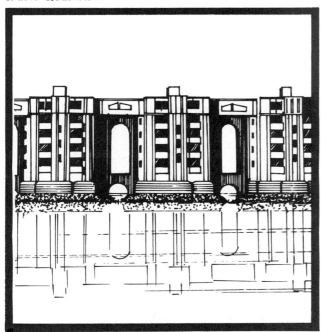

Les Arcades Du Lac And Le Viaduc (1981)

ARCHITECTS: Ricardo Bofill of Taller de Arquitectura (Spain)
LOCATION: A few miles WSW of Paris

An intriguing "viaduct" structure designed by Barcelona-based architect Ricardo Bofill, known for his creative building projects throughout Europe. This unique housing development outside of Paris has been called "A Wage Earner's Versailles." Le Viaduc's traversing arches are reflected in an artificial lake. Bofill attempted to create the imagery of palaces and boulevards for this new city.

VENCE

Matisse Chapel (Chapel of the Rosary)

ARTIST: Henri Matisse
LOCATION: 13 miles NW of Nice

A simple building with whitewashed walls, a tiled roof, and a forty-foot crescent-shaped cross houses some delightful works of painter Henri Matisse. Here the artist felt that he had created his masterpiece, "the culmination of a whole life dedicated to the search for truth." The colorful stained glass, exquisitely carved door, and walls of black-and-white line drawings fired on white tiles were all created by the artist. A private chapel used by Dominican nuns, it is open to visitors a few days each week.

ADDITIONAL MODERN STRUCTURES OF INTEREST

AMIENS

Railway Station And Office Tower (1943)
ARCHITECT: Auguste Perret
LOCATION: Place Alphonse Flouet by Gare

One of the last important works by Perret, "the father of modern architecture in France." Also of interest is *MAISON DE LA CULTURE* (1965) by Pierre Sonrel by Place Leon Gontier

CLICHY

The Maison Du Peuple (1938–39)
ARCHITECT: Jean Prouve
LOCATION: N. Paris, off Blvd. Clichy

An excellent example, even today, of advanced technical achievement in the use of sheet steel construction by France's great engineer/designer.

EVRY

Evry New Town (1970s)
ARCHITECTS: Various architects
LOCATION: about 25 kilometers S of Paris

Evry is one of the most unique new towns in France. It is based on an X shape. Unusual pyramidal residential units are spectacular.

GRENOBLE

"Ile Verte" (1969)
ARCHITECT: Charles Pivot
LOCATION: Avenue du Marechal Le Clerc

An attractive housing scheme that has achieved both functional and pleasing design.

LILLE

Ceramique Coilliot (1897)
ARCHITECT: Hector Guimard
LOCATION: 14 Rue de Fleurus

An interesting commercial design in the Art Nouveau style.

LYON

Abattoirs De La Mouche Et Marche Aux Bestiaux (1909–28)
ARCHITECT: Tony Garnier
LOCATION: 236, rue Marcel-Merieux

Tony Garnier was one of France's important early modern architects whose innovative designs, devoid of ornamentation, were instrumental in the development of modern architecture. Unfortunately only the market of this huge iron and glass work exists today.

Church Of Notre-Dame-De-Balmont (1964)
ARCHITECT: Pierre Genton
LOCATION: Inquire, Place Bellecour, Lyons

This religious structure expressively combines form, materials, and light.

Credit Lyonnais Tower (1977)
ARCHITECTS: Cossutta & Associates
LOCATION: La Part-Dieu area of Lyon across the Rhone River

Surrounded by many box-like modern structures, this soaring cylindrical tower looms over the skyline. Constructed of precast concrete polished to a high gloss finish, the forty-two-story structure functions as a banking facility. A pyramid skylight tops the structure.

Vacherie Municipale (1903–06)
ARCHITECT: Tony Garnier
LOCATION: Parc de la Tete d'Or

This building was Garnier's first significant project and received wide support from the townspeople of Lyon. The large structural complex incorporated a sensitivity to environmental problems—unusual for this period.

MARLY-LE-ROI

Marly-Les-Grandes-Terres (1958)
ARCHITECTS: Marcel Lods and J.J. Honneger

LOCATION: 10 miles W of Paris

One of the best "new towns" in France after World War II.

MARSEILLES

Cité Radieuse, Toulon
ARCHITECT: Le Corbusier
LOCATION: South Marseilles, close to Rue de Rome

Le Corbusier's most famous example of town planning, Cite Radieuse expresses the master modern architect's philosophy of design.

MONACO

Monte-Carlo Congress Centre (Les Spelugues) (1978)
LOCATION: Stradles Boulevard Louis-II

This mammoth complex, arranged in a hexagonal plan, comprises apartment units and a luxury hotel.

MONTMAGNY

Church Of St. Therese (1926)
ARCHITECT: Auguste Perret
LOCATION: 242, rue Epinay (Val d'Oise), N Paris suburb, just S of Montmorency

A remarkable structure for the time, this church features an exposed concrete frame with strong geometric patterns.

NICE

Chagall Museum (1970s)
LOCATION: Corner of Boulevard de Cimiez and Avenue du Docteur Menard in the hills of Cimiez above Nice

The first museum built by France to exhibit the works of a single artist, the Chagall Museum features a display of 450 works by the famous Russian-born artist.

NOISIEL-SUR MARNE

Chocolate Factory (1871–72)
ARCHITECT: Jules Saulnier

LOCATION: 13 miles E of Paris, left bank of Marne River

This fanciful and colorful structure of geometrical design is regarded as one of the first multi-story, metal-framed structures in the world.

PARIS

Additional Works In The Art Nouveau Style (Turn of the Century)
ARCHITECT: Hector Guimard

The ROSZÉ BLOCK, 34 Rue Boileau
STUDIO BUILDING FOR MME. CARPEAUX, 39 Blvd. Exelmans
LYCÉE SACRÉ-COEUR, 9 Avenue de la Frillière
VILLA, 8 Grande Ave. de la Villa-de-la-Reunion
RESIDENCE, 11 Rue Francois-Millet
HOTEL MEZZARA, 60 Rue La Fontaine
APARTMENT BUILDINGS, 8 and 10 Rue Agar
APARTMENT BUILDINGS, 17-21 Rue La Fontaine
APARTMENT BUILDINGS, 43 Rue Gros
RESIDENCE, 41 Rue Chardon-Lagache

Brazilian Students' Hostel (1956–59)
ARCHITECT: Le Corbusier
LOCATION: Cité Universitaire, Av. de la Porte Gentilly

Raised on pilotis (stilts), the unified facade of this hostel has a precise arrangement of windows and rough-cast concrete.

Building At 51 Rue Raynouard
ARCHITECT: Auguste Perret
LOCATION: 51 Rue Raynouard

An early modern work in France with precast concrete units—even the bath and washbasin on the top floor are of concrete.

Céramic-Hotel (Turn of the Century)
ARCHITECT: Jules Lavirotte with Alexandre Bigot
LOCATION: 34 Avenue de Wagram

A lavish example of Art Nouveau architecture

Coco Chanel's Home
LOCATION: Rue de Cambon behind the Hotel Ritz

Although the exterior of this structure is not modern, its mirrored staircase in the Art Deco style has been much publicized. Now a perfume shop, the building was the home of the legendary Coco Chanel.

Communist Party Headquarters (1971)
ARCHITECT: Oscar Niemeyer (Brazil)
LOCATION: Boulevard de la Villette

This stunning glass-walled building by South America's most illustrious modern architect, meanders in a snake-like fashion.

Conseil Economique (1937)
ARCHITECT: Auguste Perret
LOCATION: Place d'Iena

Delicate reverse-tapered columns without the classical treatment are employed in this work by the architect who developed reinforced concrete.

Cubistic Houses On Rue Mallet-Stevens (1927)
ARCHITECT: Robert Mallet-Stevens
LOCATION: Rue Mallet-Stevens, a short dead end street off Rue du Docteur Blanche, 16th Arr.

This unique street features stark cubistic houses designed for composers, architects, film directors, painters, and others involved in the arts. The austere lines and forms of the houses, all concentrated on this one street, and all created by one architect, has earned it the reputation of being one of the most unusual streets in Paris.

Gare Du Nord (1864)
ARCHITECT: J.I. Hittorff
LOCATION: off the Rue du Faubourg

This train station is an excellent example of early iron construction in France. Also of interest is the Gare de l'Est close by off the Rue de Magenta.

Guimard House (1909)
ARCHITECT: Hector Guimard
LOCATION: 122 Rue Mozart

A delightful Art Nouveau work and home of the designer.

La Roche-Jeanneret House (1923)
ARCHITECT: Le Corbusier
LOCATION: 10 square de Docteur Blanche

Now the Foundation Le Corbusier, two houses join together featuring a curving double-height wall. The complex is used as a gallery for Raoul La Roche's cubist paintings.

La Samaritaine Department Store (Turn of the Century)
ARCHITECT: Frantz Jourdain
LOCATION: Rue de Pont Neuf between Rue de Rivoli & Quai du Louvre

A flamboyant Art Nouveau work featuring an exposed metal frame with a myriad of added floral motifs.

Lycée Italien (Turn of the Century)
ARCHITECT: Jules Lavirotte
LOCATION: 12 Rue Sédillot

One of Lavirotte's most flamboyant works in the Art Nouveau style.

Maison On Rue Belliard (1913)
ARCHITECT: H. Deneux
LOCATION: Rue Belliard

A creative exterior composition of geometric mosaics unusual for the period.

Museum Of Modern Art
ARCHITECTS: J.C. Dondel, A. Aubert with others
LOCATION: By the Palais Chaillot, Avenue du President Wilson

Early example of modern neo-classical architecture. Houses an excellent collection of modern art.

New Entrance And Underground Facilities For The Louvre (work in progress)
ARCHITECT: I.M. Pei (USA)
LOCATION: Courtyard in front of Louvre Museum

Pei, America's distinguished modern architect, used a computer system to analyze this new addition and entrance to one of the world's most famous art museums. He selected a glass pyramid structure that will top an underground network of parking space, restaurants and shops.

Newspaper Office Of "Le Parisien" (1903)
ARCHITECT: G. Chedanne
LOCATION: Rue de Reaumur

Outstanding early example of a frankly exposed iron facade.

Ozenfant Studio (1922–23)
ARCHITECT: Le Corbusier
LOCATION: 15 Avenue Reille

An elegant four-story house built for the artist Ozenfant. Designed in the International Style promoted by Le Corbusier.

Palais Des Congres And Centre International De Paris (1970s)
ARCHITECTS: Various architects
LOCATION: Near the Bois de Boulogne on Champs-Elysees-Defense axis

An admirable modern cluster of buildings including the unique Palais des Congres (home of the Paris Symphony Orcheestra), the 42 story *CONCORDE-LA FAYETTE* hotel, and business and recreational facilities.

Residence At 142 Avenue De Versailles (Turn of Century)
ARCHITECT: Hector Guimard
LOCATION: 142 Avenue de Versailles

An early Art Nouveau project by France's foremost designer in this style at the turn of the century.

Roche (1900)
LOCATION: No. 52 Rue de Dantzig

A fascinating "modern" building that was a part of the great Paris Exhibition of 1900, the Roche (Beehive) was reconstructed after the Exhibition to its present location. It has been a favorite meeting place for scores of famous painters, politicians, writers, actors, and poets.

Rue Des Hautes-Formes (1975–79)
ARCHITECTS: Georgia Benamo and Christian de Portzamparc
LOCATION: Rue des Hautes-Formes

Large modernistic slab blocks with a variety of window designs and hanging arches make a striking impression.

Saint-Jean-De-Montmartre "Brick St. John" (1894–1904)
ARCHITECTS: Anatole de Baudot and Paul Cottacin
LOCATION: Place des Abbesses, Montmartre

This gem of an early modern church employed an advanced building system for the day employing reinforced concrete. The stylized motifs throughout are creatively interpreted.

Synogogue (1913)
ARCHITECT: Hector Guimard
LOCATION: 10 Rue Pavee

A romantic and expressive Art Nouveau religious building.

Theatre Champs Elysees (1911–13)
ARCHITECTS: Auguste Perret and Henri van de Velde
LOCATION: Avenue de Montaigne (leads from the Champs Elysees)

This innovative little theater is not located on the famous Champs-Elysees as the name suggests. The building was originally designed by the great Belgian Art Nouveau architect Henri van de Velde. Later it was renovated in a more "modern" manner by Perret, who combined a contemporary feeling with simple classical detailing.

Tristan Tzara House (1926)
ARCHITECT: Adolf Loos (Austria)
LOCATION: Avenue Junot

An interesting work by the famous Secessionist member from Austria who taught at the Sorbonne.

PARIS

(NEUILLY SUR SEINE)

Maison Jaoul
ARCHITECT: Le Corbusier
LOCATION: 81 rue de Longchamp, Neuilly sur Seine

A duplex design attached by an entrance court, the Maison Jaoul is constructed of concrete and rough brick—a departure in use of materials for Le Corbusier.

QUIMPER

Fleetguard Factory (1977)
ARCHITECTS: Richard Rogers & Partners
LOCATION: W Brittany

A startling factory design with a network of bright red space frames rising above the roofline. A work by the architect who designed the Pompidou Center in Paris.

STRASBOURG

Cafe "Aubette" (1926)
ARCHITECT: Theo van Doesburg (Holland)
LOCATION: At Place Kleber

This important work by the founder of the De Stijl design group in Holland has been extensively remodeled and restored. The establishment, now called *"FLUNCH"* functions as an eating facility.

Palais De La Musique Et Des Congrès
LOCATION: N of town on the Avenue Herrenschmidt

A stately and well-planned facility for concerts and meetings.

"Palais De L'Europe" (1972–77)
ARCHITECT: Mr. Henry Bernard
LOCATION: Boulevard de la Dordogne, NE Strasbourg

An interestingly designed building that functions as a meeting facility for various European institutions.

VILLEMOISON

Castel Orgeval (1905)
ARCHITECT: Hector Guimard
LOCATION: Villemoison, a suburb of Paris

One of the finest examples of a private residential work in the Art Nouveau style in the world.

Germany

GERMANY

Fehmarn

Lübeck

Hamburg

Bremerhaven

Berlin
Potsdam
Hanover
Hildesheim
Wolfsburg
Dessau
Emmerich
Münster
Bottrop
Bocholt
Hagen
Marl
Rheinberg
Gelsenkirchen
Paderborn
Essen
Dortmund
Kassel
Krefeld
Bochum
Düsseldorf
Neviges
Bergisch-Gladsbach
Duren
Leverkusen
Weimar
Monchen-
Gladbach
Bonn
Bensburg
Cologne
Karl Marxstadt
(Chemnitz)

Alfeld-en-der-Leine

Hoechst
Frankfurt-am-Main
Mainz
Darmstadt
Hasloch-am-Main

Kaiserslautern
Mannheim
Ludwigshafen
Würzburg
Saarbrücken
Nuremberg

Karlsruhe
Pforzheim
Stuttgart
Wildbad
Sindelfingen

Freiburg
Ulm
Dachau
Neu-Ulm
Munich
Lörrock
Lake Starnberg
Badenweiler

THE MODERN MOVEMENT IN GERMANY

EARLIEST MODERN BUILDINGS IN GERMANY

Many of Germany's first modern structures were commissioned to leading architects from other European countries, including Josef Maria Olbrich from Austria, J. L. Mathieu Lauweriks from Holland, and Henri van de Velde from Belgium. These architects helped to spread new building concepts throughout Germany.

DEUTSCHER WERKBUND

This group founded by architect Herman Muthesius in 1907 was a counterpart to the Arts and Crafts Movement in England— Muthesius had come under the influence of William Morris while in England. But the Werkbund differed from Morris's philosophy in a willingness to work with the machine and industry. The Werkbund held impressive exhibitions of architecture, industrial art, and furnishings demonstrating cooperation of the designer with the machine. Notable Werkbund exhibitions were held in Cologne in 1914, Stuttgart in 1927, and Paris in 1930. The leading member of the Werkbund was Peter Behrens who has been called "the father of modern architecture" in Germany.

THE BAUHAUS

The Bauhaus is the single most important influence in promoting the new modernism. This experimental design school was founded by Berlin architect Walter Gropius in 1919 in Weimar. Gropius, who felt that creative design could work hand in hand with technology, helped to unite art and industry. He brought together a distinguished faculty including Paul Klee, Wassily Kandinsky, Josef and Annie Albers, Maholy Nagy, Lionel Feininger, and Marcel Breuer, and had an artist and a craftsman to train each student. Mies van der Rohe, one of the giants of modern architecture, was the director at the school from 1930 until Hitler's stormtroopers closed the Bauhaus in 1933. Many of the faculty were offered positions in the United States, where they spread the concepts of the Bauhaus and further developed modern design concepts.

GERMAN EXPRESSIONISM

The work of the Expressionist architects is distinguished by the use of bold lines, forms, and textures. This expressive architecture is among the world's most imaginative and exciting. The style, which arose around 1910 after the death of Jugendstil (German Art Nouveau), was developed by such architects as Bruno Taut, Eric Mendelsohn, Hans Poelzig, Rudolf Steiner, and some of the Bauhaus designers. For more extensive reference see Wolfgang Pehnt's *Expressionistic Architecture*.

ARCHITECTURE AFTER WORLD WAR II

After World War II the need to rebuild Germany provided opportunity for modernistic to develop their ideas. The Bauhaus influence continued, and a new generation of architects, including Frei Otto, Egon Eiermann, and Hans Scharoun has gained world recognition with its individualistic modern structures.

ALFELD-EN-DER LEINE

Fagus Shoe Factory (1911–13)

ARCHITECT: Walter Gropius
LOCATION: 12 miles SW of Hildesheim

Gropius, the German-American architect, writer, and educator, was a key figure in the development of modern architecture. He opened his own office in 1910 in Berlin, and a year later designed this hallmark of modern factory design. Constructed of glass and steel, the functional structure embodied many innovative design ideas that would later be incorporated into the philosophies of the Bauhaus school, founded by Gropius in Weimar in 1919.

BADENWEILER

Kurhaus At Badenweiler (1962–65)

ARCHITECT: Klaus Humpert
LOCATION: West slope of Black Forest, 13 miles N of Lörrock

Spectacularly situated at the base of an old castle ruin, this original complex has a myriad of paths that wind intriguingly through the various facilities geared for recreational activities, including a small concert hall, a cafe, reading rooms, and a gallery. The network of walkways conforms to the hillside; the large glass structure contrasts with the surroundings.

BENSBERG

Bensberg Town Hall (1967)

ARCHITECT: Gottfried Bohm
LOCATION: 9 miles E of Cologne

Bohm, son of the well-known Expressionist architect, Dominikus Bohm, is respected for his expressive use of free-form concrete. The Bensberg Town Hall is situated boldly at the top of a hill in the town. Bohm designed a structure that would harmonize with traditional surroundings, including an old castle. The blend of old and new makes a striking impression.

BERGISCH-GLADSBACH

Community Center (1983)

ARCHITECTS: Professor Gottfried Bohm and Hans Linder
LOCATION: c. 12 miles ENE of Cologne (Koln) in city center

Situated on a large busy market square, the striking new Community Center makes a vivid contrast with its surroundings. Bohm, known for his numerous bold concrete structures, has ingeniously incorporated imaginative design with an existing theater and restaurant/hotel. The new structural design actually emphasizes and enhances the decorative theater. The colorful modern complex is constructed of steel, tile, and glass materials. The interior treatment and lighting are particularly stunning.

BERLIN

AEG Turbine Factory (Turbinen-Halle) (Technisches Museum) (1909)

ARCHITECT: Peter Behrens
LOCATION: Hutten Strasse/Corner Berlichingen Strasse

Because of his important contribution to the modern movement, Behrens has been called "the father of modern architecture in Germany." Behrens was one of the first designers to work with industry and the machine. The much praised AEG Factory, built for a large electrical organization, is Behrens' first major work and Germany's first major modern building. In his Berlin office, Behrens trained three giants of modern architecture—Le Corbusier, Mies van der Rohe, and Walter Gropius.

BERLIN

Grosse Schauspielhaus (today "Friedrichstadt-Palast") (1919)

ARCHITECT: Hans Poelzig
LOCATION: Friedrich Strasse, East Berlin

One of the most remarkable early modern buildings in the world, the Grosse Schauspielhaus is Hans Poelzig's most famous work. Known as a professor as well as an architect, Poelzig was one of the chief inventors of the German Expressionist Style. This highly innovative structure with its "dripping stalactite" forms is a superb example of this architectural approach. The large theater was conceived as a work of art, concerned more with character than harmony. The building has been extensively altered.

BERLIN

International Congress Centrum Berlin (1979)

ARCHITECTS: Rolf Schüller and Ursulina Schüler-Witte
LOCATION: At Messedamm

The remarkable ICC, constructed at a cost of nearly one billion marks, has already become an important landmark in Germany. The huge complex is symbolic of the new spirit of growth, prosperity, and well-being in Berlin today. The facility houses space for a myriad of functions, including exhibitions, fairs, and conventions. Flanking the street and situated on a slight incline, the ICC is composed of a variety of expressive horizontal, vertical, and diagonal forms arranged at different levels. Flags from many nations provide a colorful accent against the structural complex.

BERLIN

Kaiser Wilhelm Memorial Church (1963)

ARCHITECT: Egon Eiermann
LOCATION: Breitscheidplatz

Standing symbolically next to the ruined tower of a neo-Romanesque church, the stunning new "Emperor William Memorial Church" makes a significant impression. The octagonal structure with its flat roof was born out of the war-torn rubble of the previous church. Eiermann combined black steel and concrete pierced with brilliantly colored glass designed by Gabriel Loire from Chartres, France. The building is a keen reminder of the destruction of war incorporated into a spirit of regrowth.

BERLIN

New National Gallery (National Galerie) (1962–68)

ARCHITECT: Ludwig Mies van der Rohe (Germany and USA)
LOCATION: Potsdamer Strasse 50

Mies, the famed director of the Bauhaus from 1930 until its closing in 1933, came to America where he became the Director of Architecture at Illinois Institute of Technology. After the war he was invited back to Berlin to design this modernistic steel and glass structure. The simplicity of the New National Gallery expresses Mies' philosophy of "Less of More." The structure is an appropriate background for a diverse collection of 19th and 20th century art.

BERLIN

Philharmonic Hall (1963)

ARCHITECT: Hans Scharoun
LOCATION: Kemperplatz

A spectacular example of the neo-Expressionist style of architecture, the Philharmonic Hall is Scharoun's most notable work. The architect is known for employing acute angles, rounded corners, circular forms, and irregular groupings. The interior treatment is as stunning as the exterior design and the acoustics are superb. The Berliners, known for their sense of humor, have nicknamed the Philharmonic Hall "Karajani's Circus."

BERLIN

The Church Of The Maria Regina Martyrum (1962)

ARCHITECTS: Hans Schadel and
Friedrich Ebert
LOCATION: On Hecker Damm 230/232

This modernistic church was built as a tribute to the Catholic martyrs who died from 1933 to 1945. A soaring brutalistic bell tower functions as an entry gate and symbol of this tragedy of war. A vast interior courtyard, devoid of landscaping, links the tower to the church beyond. A plain austere block building is tempered by abstract sculpture by the entrance and attached to the facade. The interior space carries out the same theme.

BOCHUM

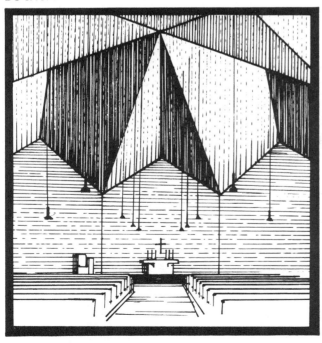

Christ Church (1959)

ARCHITECT: Dieter Oesterlen
LOCATION: Am Rathaus

The architect has sympathetically preserved the old church tower that survived the bombings of World War II. Many churches were partially destroyed throughout Germany, and architects have been challenged with new design problems in their attempt to incorporate precious ruins into a new structure. Christ's Church, with its diamond shapes, is one of Germany's finest successes.

BOTTROP

Holy Cross Church (1957)

ARCHITECT: Rudolf Schwartz
LOCATION: Scharnholzstrasse, Bottrop,
NW of Essen

The facade of Holy Cross Church immediately impresses the visitor. An enormous abstract stained-glass design by George Meistermann dominates one entire wall. Bold use of rough concrete and brick is strongly supportive of the colorful stained-glass composition. The realistic "all-seeing eye of God" in the nave provides a jarring note in the otherwise restful building.

BREMERHAVEN

Maritime Museum (Deutsches Schiffahrtsmuseum) (1969–75)

ARCHITECT: Hans Scharoun
LOCATION: Old Port Basin, 33 miles N of
Bermen Vanronzelstr. 235

Pleasantly located by a sea-wall promenade, the German Maritime Museum is one of Scharoun's most brilliantly designed structures. It is as simple, clean, and direct as the exhibits housed inside. The structure expresses its function perfectly, giving an impression of ships and the sea. Known for his more eccentrically designed Philharmonic Hall in Berlin, Scharoun demonstrates his versatility with the Maritime Museum.

CARTROP RAUXEL

New City Centre (1966–76)

ARCHITECTS: Arne Jacobsen (Denmark) with Otto Weitling—after Jacobsen's death in 1971, Weitling & Dissing
LOCATION: c. 10 miles NW of Dortmund

Handsomely surrounded by landscaping, pools, plazas, and seating, the northern wing of the complex houses the town hall, with the southern wing functioning as a Stadhall with facilities for a theater, an opera house, a restaurant, and a sports hall. A boldly upswept roof enclosed with glass introduces the imaginative City Centre. The repeating form is harmoniously employed throughout the complex.

COLOGNE-MARIENBURG

St. Maria Konigin (1956)

ARCHITECT: Dominikus Bohm
LOCATION: Goeghestrasse at Leyboldstrasse

Bohm was a pioneer of modern church design in Germany, responsible for many religious structures in the country. St. Maria Konigin is one of his last important works. The simple box-shaped church features magnificent stained-glass windows on the south side. The highly abstract gray-green glass captures the lines, shapes, and spirit of the lovely wooded area close by. The building functions as a supportive backdrop for this artistic work.

DACHAU

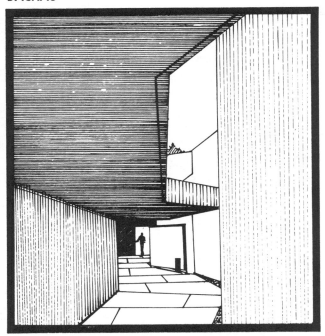

Church Of The Atonement (Protestant Church Of Reconciliation) (1965–67)

ARCHITECT: Helmut Striffler
LOCATION: On Dachau Concentration Camp Memorial Grounds

The horrors of war and the struggle and persecution of the Jews are expressed in the strong design of the Church of the Atonement. The long, low building was constructed in the "Brutalistic manner"—a term coined in 1954 to describe frankly exposed concrete in its roughest form. The gray texture of the raw material seems a suitable background to convey the function of the religious complex.

DARMSTADT

Wedding Tower (Hochzeitsturm) (1905–08)

ARCHITECT: Josef Maria Olbrich (Austria)
LOCATION: E of Darmstadt in the Mathildenhöhe

Olbrich, the famous Austrian designer, was a founding member of the Secession in Vienna—an avante-garde group of young artists who broke with traditional artistic expressions. He was invited by the Grand Duke Ernst Ludwig of Darmstadt to design the Hochzeitsturm as part of an exhibition to commemorate the Duke's marriage. The Expressionist tower features such innovative ideas as corner window treatments and a billowing roof form that influenced architects around Europe.

DESSAU (EAST GERMANY)

The Bauhaus (1925–26)

ARCHITECT: Walter Gropius (Germany
and USA)
LOCATION: 71 miles SW of Berlin

Gropius gained international recognition
when he organized the Bauhaus, an
experimental design school at Weimar in
1919. Forced to leave Weimar, a community
hostile to new design concepts, the faculty
and student body moved to receptive Dessau
close by. The Bauhaus building was totally
inventive, designed and executed by Gropius
and Bauhaus students. Many architectural
concepts expressed in this landmark building
became a basis for the International Style.
The important hallmark of architecture was
restored after extensive damage during World
War II.

DUREN

St. Anna (1956)

ARCHITECT: Rudolf Schwartz
LOCATION: Annaplatz, Duren, 17 miles E of
Aachen

The strong yet spiritual design of St. Anna is
admired throughout Europe. Surrounded on
two sides by bold walls made of raw concrete
and war rubble, the rough texture of the
church is highlighted by glass brick. The
height of the nave is awesome. From massive
criss-cross beams hang shimmering strings of
metallic lights.

BIELEFELD

Kunsthalle-Richard Kaselowksy Museum (1966-68)

ARCHITECT: Philip Johnson (USA) with Professor Casar F. Pinnau
LOCATION: In Artur-Ladebeck-Strasse in old town

Massive and stately, this impressive museum of art was designed by America's famous modern architect, Philip Johnson, in collaboration with German architect, Professor Casar F. Pinnau. The concrete structure is sheathed with granite block accented by slender entry projections and tinted glass doorway. Rodin's "The Thinker" is effectively placed to the right, creating a main focus for the exterior facade. Exhibit areas are interestingly arranged and well lit. A garden wall encloses an outdoor space that links the museum to the park.

DÜSSELDORF

Rheinhalle (1924–26)

ARCHITECT: Wilhelm Kreis, restored by Hentrich & Petschnigg
LOCATION: In the Hofgarten by Oberkasseler Bridge and Heinrich-Heine Allee

This structure is an excellent example of imaginative use of form during the early period of modern design in Germany. The Rheinhalle features a bold round form punctuated with a series of slender, vertical fenestrations. Rheinhalle, considered Kreis' most important work, is a highly praised manifestation of the Expressionist style in Germany. Close by is Kries' *LANDESMUSEUM VOLK UN WIRTSCHAFT* (People and Economy).

DÜSSELDORF

St. Rochus (1955)

ARCHITECT: Paul Schneider-Esleben
LOCATION: Rochusmarkt

St. Rochus is one of the best of the modern churches built around bombed ruins left after World War II. The old Romanesque Revival tower was built in the late nineteenth century. Rather than build a matching church, the architect designed an elliptical shape that actually plays up the old tower by contrast of materials and form. The blend of old and new makes a unique impression.

DÜSSELDORF

Thyssen House (Phonix-Rheinrohr) (1957–60)

ARCHITECTS: H. Hentrich and H. Petschnigg
LOCATION: By crossroads at Berliner Allee & Hofgarten Strasse on August-Thyssen-Str. 1

Because the government of the Third Reich did not encourage modern architecture, most of Germany's great architects left the country. After the war, however, large building programs were promoted and funded in Germany. The sleek and functional Thyssen House skyscraper is one of the finest examples of its type built during this period. With its three huge monoliths sandwiched together, the people of Dusseldorf call the office building the Dreischeilbenhaus (three-slice house).

EMMERICH

The Church Of The Holy Ghost (1965–66)

ARCHITECT: Dieter Baumewerd
LOCATION: 16 miles W of Bocholt

A concrete church of changing planes and angles, this structure can best be appreciated from an aerial view. The interior is equally intriguing, with concrete columns topped by spreading lotus forms which in turn open up into the roof. Effective lighting highlights interior walls that are clad with colorful abstract glass. The strong and symbolic altar cross is of blood-red warped war materials.

ESSEN-ALTSTADT OST

Auferstehungskirche (Church Of The Resurrection) (1929)

ARCHITECT: Otto Bartning
LOCATION: Essen-Altstadt Ose, suburb of Essen

The remarkable Auferstenhungskirche, destroyed in World War II, was rebuilt because of its architectural importance as an early example of religious design. Breaking with traditional building concepts, Bartning felt that a church should embody new technology, form, and materials that are employed in the Church of the Resurrection, reflecting the architect's philosophy.

FRANKFURT-AM-MAIN

Museum Of Modern Art
(work in progress)

ARCHITECT: Hans Hollein (Austria)
LOCATION: "The Riverbank of Museums" between Old Town Hall and Cathedral

Built on a pie-shaped lot, Austria's imaginative architect has created a spectacular modern museum fashioned to its triangular site near the riverfront. Because of its unusual form, the complex has been likened to a "mammoth triangular ship." The focal point of the building is the remarkable projecting point or "prow." A series of huge skylights add drama to the interior spaces and prove effective lighting for the exhibit areas. The entrance is closest to the Old City, thereby providing a welcoming and convenient link between the old and the new.

FRANKFURT-AM-MAIN

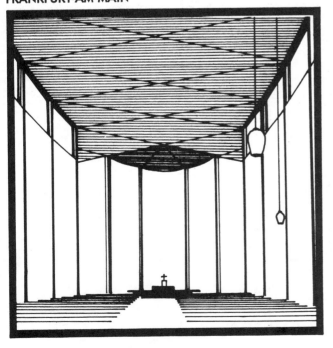

St. Michael (1954)

ARCHITECT: Rudolf Schwartz
LOCATION: Rotlintstrasse at Gellertstrasse

The austere exterior of St. Michael gives the illusion of a formidable fortress closed to the outside world. The interior projects the same seclusion. Soaring stark panels are interspersed with wood supports topped with clerestory windows, conveying an atmosphere of calm. The strong design of the building is one of extreme simplicity.

FRANKFURT-AM-MAIN

Kunsthandwerk Museum (Decorative Arts) (1983–85)

ARCHITECT: Richard Meier (USA)
LOCATION: Riverbank Museum Area, Schaumainkia 15

Richard Meier's dazzling white museum on Frankfurt's riverfront makes a stunning impression. Meier, who is well known in the United States, has designed this museum in a similar manner to his Atheneum in New Harmony, Indiana, the High Museum in Atlanta, Georgia, and his Seminary Building in Hartford, Connecticut. White modular units are employed throughout the complex, complemented by fascinating lighting and interior detailing. The clean, simple background is a perfect foil for the displays.

FRIELINGSDORF

Parish Church (1926–27)

ARCHITECT: Dominikus Bohm
LOCATION: Frielingsdorf, near Cologne

A highly admired example of Expressionist architecture in Germany, the Parish Church features bold vaults cast in concrete and painted white. These large vaults reflect the light unevenly, heightening the aesthetic effect throughout the interior space. The structure is one of Bohm's best known churches.

GELSENKIRCHEN

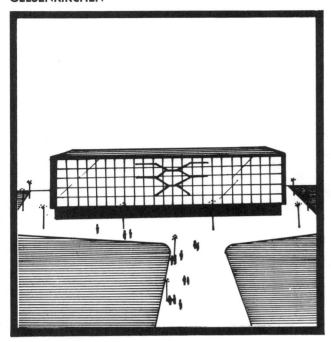

Theater At Gelsenkirchen (1960)

ARCHITECTS: Werner Ruhnau, Ortwin Rave, & Max von Hausen
LOCATION: Ebertplatz

Like a brilliant jewel set in the midst of a rather gray industrial area, the inviting rectangular theater boasts two-and-one-half stories of glass windows. The U-shaped auditorium, with its 1,050 seats, is also surrounded by glass. The theater, one of the finest structures of its kind in Germany, has incorporated the latest advances in theater design.

HAMBURG

Chilehaus (1923)

ARCHITECT: Fritz Högar
LOCATION: On the Burchard Platz at Fischertwiete 2

One of Germany's most unique buildings of the early modern period, the Chilehaus is a great example of Expressionist architecture. The exaggerated stepped brick design, a complete departure from traditional building forms at the time, influenced modern architects as far away as America. Höger's dramatic *SPRINKENHOF BUILDING* and *ANZEIGER BUILDINGS* close by are also notable for their Expressionist design.

HANOVER

St. Martins (1957)

ARCHITECT: Dieter Oesternlen
LOCATION: Badenstedter Strasse

Most of the original church was destroyed by bombs during World War II, but the old tower survived, and has been nostalgically incorporated into the new design. The juxtaposition of old and new structures adds to St. Martin's design interest. Particularly unique is the treatment of concrete blocks with glass and stained glass. Light filtering through these windows washes the walls with soft illumination.

HASLOCH-AM-MAIN

St. Joseph (1958)

ARCHITECT: Hans Schadel
LOCATION: Hasloch-am-Main,
just W of Wurzburg

Travellers enjoy a look at the interior of this engaging church, with its clean, simple design. An impressive focal point inside is a superb statue on the altar wall created by Julius Bausenwin. Indirect natural lighting softens the area, complementing the modern sculpture. An atmosphere of meditative calm pervades the structure.

HOECHST

Hoechst AG Farbwerke For IG Farben Co. (1924)

ARCHITECT: Peter Behrens
LOCATION: Frankfurt's farthest western suburb, 6230 Frankfurt a.m.

Behrens has been called "the father of modern architecture in Germany." As a leading member of the Deutscher Werkbund his influence was great. Germany's first industrial designer, he trained Le Corbusier, Mies van der Rohe, and Walter Gropius. The Hochst Farbwerke (Textiles Factory) is one of his most remarkable works and designed at the end of the great architect's career. A unique design of interior brick "stalactites" creates a colorful kaleidoscope effect. The superbly treated lighting contributes to the powerful mood.

**KARL MARXSTADT (FORMERLY CHEMNITZ)
EAST GERMANY**

Schocken Department Store (1928–29)

ARCHITECT: Eric Mendelsohn (Germany and USA)
LOCATION: Downtown, Karl Marxstadt

After the creation of his Einstein Laboratory, Mendelsohn is known for his department store designs in Germany. Most notable are the Schocken stores in Chemnitz and Stuttgart. Strong shadow-casting cornices cap bold curvilinear horizontal forms. Wide bands of glass further highlight this commerical structure.

KREFELD

Hermann Lange House (Museum Haus Lange & Haus Esters) (1928)

ARCHITECT: Ludwig Mies van der Rohe (Germany and USA)
LOCATION: 12 miles NW of Dusseldorf, Wilhelmschofalle 91-97

With the clean structural design of Hermann Lange House, Mies began to develop his ideas on modern residential design. The house makes the most of the form and texture of brick. One of the world's giants of modern architecture, Mies was appointed Bauhaus director from 1930 until 1933, when Nazi stormtroopers closed the school's doors forever. In the late 1930s Mies migrated to Chicago, where he developed his famous steel-and-glass skyscrapers.

LAKE STARNBERG

Training Center For Siemens AF (1970s)

ARCHITECTS: Friis & Moltke (Denmark)
LOCATION: By Lake Starnberger See, S of Munich

The popular architectural firm of Friis & Moltke in Denmark won the competition for this project. The Training Center is beautifully located on a sloping wooded area by the lake. The large complex, which harmonizes effectively with the site, features three terraced areas with a separate building housing eighty resident guests.

LEVERKUSEN-BURIG

Christ Church (1958)

ARCHITECTS: Hentrich and Petschnigg
LOCATION: Stresemannplatz at
Erzbergerstrasse

One of the most striking expressions of
church design in Germany, Christ Church
achieves interest by its huge triangular
windows set atop blue glazed brick walls.
Long slender cords with lamps at varying
levels plunge into the interior space of the
nave from a remarkable geometrically trussed
ceiling. The versatile architectural team of
Hentrich and Petschnigg is responsible for
many of Germany's most interesting and
innovative structures.

MAINZ

City Hall At Mainz (1970s)

ARCHITECT: Arne Jacobsen (Denmark)
LOCATION: On the Rheinstrasse,
downtown Mainz

Strikingly situated in a spacious plaza
overlooking the Rhein River, the new City Hall
makes a stunning impression. Designed by
Denmark's foremost modern architect, this
modern building was one of the last works by
Jacobsen and completed after his death. A
unique geometric design is punctuated by
contrasting dark tinted glass windows
emphasized by the dazzling white concrete.
Large abstract light posts in the plaza lead up
to the entrance enhancing the design theme.

MANNHEIM

National Theater (1957)

ARCHITECT: Gerhard Weber
LOCATION: Goetheplatz

When Mannheim was badly damaged during Allied bombing, the centuries-old National Theater was one of the buildings completely destroyed. The new National Theater, though nicely situated in a spacious park, had to be built above an existing bomb shelter. Glass has been generously used throughout the building, which contains theaters, shops, offices, and other facilities. The festive structural complex is one of Europe's best theater arrangements.

MANNHEIM

The New Modern Art Gallery (Kunsthalle Mannheim) (1980s)

ARCHITECTS: Lange-Mitzlaff-Bohm-Muller
LOCATION: Entrance on Moltkestrasse 9 and from Friedrichsplatz

Adjoining the earlier Art Gallery designed by Hermann Billing in 1907, the new wing of the Modern Art Gallery is an admirable example of incorporating the old and new. Situated in a nicely landscaped setting, the two structures, constructed of red sandstone, make a compatible impression. The vertical line is dominant on both structures, yet interpreted in a fresh contemporary approach on the new wing. The interior of the new wing is light and airy, topped with a series of skylights. Clean white surfaces provide an effective background for an important collection of modern art.

MONCHEN-GLADBACH

The Stadtisches Museum Abteiberg (1983)

ARCHITECT: Hans Hollein (Austria)
LOCATION: c. 16 miles WSW of Dusseldorf

Known for his spectacular office and shop creations in Vienna, Hollein has designed this museum that has already become a popular tourist attraction and a national landmark. Drama mounts as the visitor ascends a serpentine arrangement of steps that lead up to clusters of structural buildings on the hilltop. Exhibit spaces, positioned at various angles, are centered around open courtyards. The building designs have been compared to the approaches of a number of past great modern architects, including Alvar Aalto of Finland, Carlo Scarpa of Italy, Louis Kahn of the United States, and Isozaki of Japan. Hollein's new museum, however, achieves a fascinating identity of its own.

MUNICH

BMW Headquarters and Museum (1973)

ARCHITECT: Carl Schwanzer (Austria)
LOCATION: In Olympic Park, just E of Olympic Village

Schwanzer, noted Austrian architect and teacher, has designed spectacular exhibition buildings and Austrian embassies throughout the world. The BMW headquarters is one of his most interesting and unusual projects. The complex features a large quadrifoil tower of four connected cylinders. The peculiar museum, in the form of a teacup and completely windowless, sharply contrasts with the office complex.

MUNICH

Neue Pinakothek (1981)

ARCHITECT: Alexander von Branca
LOCATION: N of Alte Pinakothek on
Theresien Strasse—Entrance on Arcis
Strasse

Measuring one kilometer around the
complex, the Neue Pinakothek replaces the
Pinakothek destroyed in World War II and is
one of Germany's largest museum buildings.
The mammoth steel, concrete, and tinted
glass structure features modern oriels and
turrets that recall the medieval castle. The
impressive new art fortress consists of 25,000
cubic meters of concrete and 2,500 tons of
steel. Housed inside is a marvelous collection
of historic and modern German paintings. An
arrangement of plazas, steps, and reflecting
pools enhances the large complex.

MUNICH

Olympic Stadium (1972)

ARCHITECT: Frei Otto
LOCATION: Olympic Park, c. 5 kilometers
NW of Munich city center

The Olympic Stadium is Otto's masterpiece—
a supreme example of his unique steel cable-
and-mast construction. The huge stadium,
built for the 1972 Olympics, seats 8,000
people and boasts the largest roof in the
world. Approximately 90,000 square yards of
tinted acrylic glass were used in the
construction. This brilliantly planned
architectural approach is ideal for enclosing
large spaces inexpensively and effectively.
Otto has received many commissions for
similar structures, including the building for
the German Exhibition at Montreal's World
Fair of 1967.

MUNICH

The Munich Hypobank (1980)

ARCHITECTS: Walter & Bea Betz
LOCATION: Between Denninger-Strasse &
Richard-Strauss-Strasse

An extraordinary and dazzling design of metal
and glass, the new Hypobank makes a
powerful impression in its downtown setting.
The most commanding feature of the
complex is the massive supportive cylinders
that rise skyward the full length of the
building. The vertical emphasis is tempered
by low-rise wings that thread throughout the
raised sections of the towers. Horizontal
window banding further counters the
powerful vertical cylinders.

MÜNSTER

City Theater (1956)

ARCHITECTS: Harald Deilmann, Max von
Gausen, Ortwin Rave, and Werner Ruhnau
LOCATION: Neubruckenstrasse

An innovative structure that seats over 900
theater-goers, City Theater is one of Europe's
most interesting buildings. Adding to the
fascinating swirling form of the design is the
integration of the new building with the
existing ruined walls of the former
Romberger Hof, which was bombed during
the war. Natural and artificial lighting
throughout the building is spectacular.

NEVIGES

Pilgrimage Church (1972)

ARCHITECT: Gottfried Bohm
LOCATION: 21 miles NE of Düsseldorf

A bold church that gains interest through powerfully sculptured forms, the Pilgrimage Church is a supreme example of the potential of concrete as a building material. The church's brutalistic reinforced concrete framework, columns, and folded plates all suggest metaphoric expressions. The exterior has been compared to a rigorous mountain range with its massive peaks of concrete.

POTSDAM

Einstein Tower And Laboratory (1919)

ARCHITECT: Eric Mendelsohn
LOCATION: 17 miles SW of Berlin

Mendelsohn, an influential modern architect practicing in Berlin after World War I, was especially interested in the sculptural possibilities of architecture. This fascinating monolithic tower served as a laboratory for Albert Einstein, where he later developed his Theory of Relativity. The interior was designed to combine a telescope and all the essential facilities for this special structure. The imaginative design of punched-out walls, angular window frames, and rounded corners has been compared to a "sphinx, with paws ready to spring."

RHEINBERG

New Town Hall (Stadthalle) (1980s)

ARCHITECT: Gottfried Bohm
LOCATION: c. 25 miles W of Bottrop

Surrounded by baroque houses, shops, offices, and a 12th century church, the new Town Hall is an ambitious building program that sets up a functional unification of an existing town hall of 1449 flanking a picturesque market square. The main public entrance features an airy glass and steel "butterfly-shaped" roof covering an inner courtyard. The real excitement unfolds in the vast "interior public square." Five layered levels look onto the atrium that is covered with a modular lighting system. Functions include offices, banquet spaces, shops, meeting rooms, a public restaurant, and major civic areas.

SAARBRÜCKEN

The Church Of Mary The Queen (Katholische Kirche Maria Konigin) (1956)

ARCHITECT: Rudolf Schwartz
LOCATION: Kohlweg, 5500 Saarbrücken-Rotenbuhl, Zweibrücker Strasse

After World War II, architects of the new generation developed individualistic styles breaking with the severity of rectangular forms. Bauhaus principles of the International Style continued during the post-war period, but structures like the Church of Mary the Queen were a dramatic break. Unique rhythmic cut-away forms expose colorful stained-glass windows.

SAARBRÜCKEN

St. Albert (1957)

ARCHITECT: Gottfried Bohm
LOCATION: Jagersfreuder Strasse

Because the church has one of the most unusual and spectacular modern naves in Europe, some critics feel that the complicated design of St. Albert is perhaps a little overdone. A contemporary version of the medieval Gothic flying buttress is expressed in concrete supports that surround the church, adding to the total design image. Close by, the tower and baptistry construction carry out the creative theme of this admirable church.

STUTTGART

Liederhalle (1956)

ARCHITECTS: Adolf Abel and Rolf Gutbrod
LOCATION: Berlinerplatz

The impressive Liederhalle is a large complex consisting of three auditoriums. Constructed of concrete, glass, and glazed brick, the structure is situated in a downtown setting surrounded by older contrasting buildings. A series of steps leads up to the Liederhalle, adding to the drama of the building's design and setting. Ultra-modern design treatment is executed throughout the facility. Because of perfectly planned acoustics, it is possible to stage three concerts simultaneously.

STUTTGART

Railroad Station (Hauptbahnhof) (1914–27)

ARCHITECTS: Paul Bonatz and F. R. Scholer
LOCATION: On Arnulf-Klett-Platz

Considered one of Germany's finest early modern train stations, the enormous stone Hauptbahnhof makes a strong silhouette in central Stuttgart. Moving toward more expressive structural forms, the architects have created this functional building without the decorative details commonly employed during past decades. Interestingly, the building suggests Romanesque classicism reduced to its basic design. Bonatz helped to bridge the gap between nineteenth century Eclecticism and early modern Functionalism.

STUTTGART

Sports Hall (Hanns-Martin-Schleyer-Halle) (1981–83)

ARCHITECTS: Siegel, Wonneberg, and Partner
LOCATION: Mercedesstrasse 69 (NE Stuttgart in Bad Cannstadt)

Hailed as Europe's newest and finest modern sports facilities, the Hanns-Martin-Schleyer-Halle makes a vivid impact in its setting. Mammoth projecting forms and a striking sawtooth roofline contribute to the unusual design concept. The huge flexible complex can accommodate many various sports activities and boasts the highest level of technology for human enjoyment and convenience.

STUTTGART

Staatsgalerie Wurttembergische (1979–83)

ARCHITECT: James Stirling (Great Britain)
LOCATION: Konrad-Adenauer Strasse 32

Stirling, the distinguished English modern architect, has received numerous honors and awards for his many creative and impressive works, including the prestigious international Pritzker Architecture Prize. His design for this new addition to Stuttgart's famed National Museum has already drawn international attention—both praise and criticism. The huge undulating glass facade is the focal point and entrance to the new structure. To the far right of the enormous complex is Stirling's KAMMERTHEATER. Both structures are treated in a distinctive horizontal banding of alternating sandstone and travertine.

STUTTGART

Television Tower (Fernsehturm) (1956)

ARCHITECT: Fritz Leonhardt
LOCATION: S Stuttgart off Rt. 3 at Degerloch, Hoher Bopser

This dramatic 712-foot tower was considered revolutionary in 1956. Today many soaring television towers are found throughout Germany. Still, the tower at Stuttgart is considered a landmark design. The tapering concrete tower is topped by an exciting revolving restaurant. Above it, an observation deck affording a panoramic view of Stuttgart is well worth the visit.

WOLFSBURG

Cultural Center And Parish Church (1960–62)

ARCHITECT: Alvar Aalto (Finland)
LOCATION: Cultural Center: downtown; Church: on Klieversberg

Fascinating wedge-shaped elements combine to create an interesting and unusual cultural center. The world-famous Finnish architect was known for his humanistic approach to architecture that is reflected in both the Cultural and Civic Center and the Parish Church—Church of the Holy Ghost. The church features simple flowing forms highlighted by a rounded bell tower. Aalto's work interestingly combines elements of the International Style with those of the organic philosophy. These building complexes in Wolfsburg are considered a great contribution to Germany's hallmarks of modern architecture.

WOLFSBURG

Cultural Center Complex Theater (1970s)

ARCHITECT: Hans Scharoun
LOCATION: Downtown cultural center, am Klierersburg

This Cultural Center is one of the last important works by Germany's illustrious modern architect. Internationally known for his Philharmonic Hall in Berlin, Scharoun's architectural approach is one of great imagination combined with advanced building technology. Beautifully nestled on a wooded site, the Cultural Center is more conservatively designed than Scharoun's other projects.

ADDITIONAL MODERN STRUCTURES OF INTEREST

AACHEN

Central Museum Of Art (work in progress, 1980s)
ARCHITECTS: Wilhelm Kucker with Winfried Golling
LOCATION: In the Kurpark. Inquire: Markt 39-41

The new Central Museum of Art will take years to complete. It is beautifully planned to enhance its wooded parkland setting and will be one of the finest modern museums in Germany.

AACHEN (AIX-LA-CHAPELLE)

Faculty Of Medicine (1982)
ARCHITECTS: Weber, Brand & Partner
LOCATION: 40 miles W of Cologne (Köln)

This extraordinary new facility features strong colorful forms beautifully contrasting with its natural surroundings. The large complex is one of the finest of its kind in Europe.

BERLIN

Bauhaus Archives/Museum For Architecture And Structural Design
ARCHITECTS: Walter Gropius and TAC.
LOCATION: Klingelhofer Strasse 13-14

The last important work of the master architect and Bauhaus founder. Early modern German art collection featuring many works of the Bauhaus faculty and students.

Congress Hall (1957)
ARCHITECT: Hugh Stubbins, Jr. (USA)
LOCATION: Tiergarten, close to the Berlin wall

The huge flowing concrete roof seems to symbolically welcome the visitor. The expressive form of the huge curving roof has been compared to a giant megaphone proclaiming freedom of speech.

Europa Center (1963–65)
LOCATION: E of the Breitscheidplatz

A large shopping and business complex centered around a 22-story tower. The center includes modern shops, restaurants, an ice rink and a casino.

Flats (1955)
ARCHITECT: Alvar Aalto
LOCATION: Tiergarten

Part of an urban development program in the Tiergarten. Many international architects were invited to participate in this endeavor.

Free University Of Berlin (1963–present)
ARCHITECT: Candilis, Josic and Woods
LOCATION: Altensteinstrasse 40

A plan based on the idea of a "web." Designers have tried to symbolize free and open society.

Japanese Culture Center (1983)
ARCHITECT: Kisho Kurokawa (Japan)
LOCATION: Inquire at Verkenhrsampt, Europa Center

This is a strong example of the "structure and power" of Post-Structurism—a new architectural development in Japan inspired by avante-garde French architects Gilles Deleuze, Jacques Derrida, and Jean Baudrillard.

Kirche AM Hohenzollerndamm (1931–33)
ARCHITECT: Friz Hoger
LOCATION: Hohenzollerndamm 202/203

An impressive work by the designer of the famous Chilehaus in Hamburg.

Kreuzkirche (1930)
ARCHITECT: Gunther Paulus
LOCATION: Hohenzollerndamm 130

An interesting example of German Expressionism constructed of brick with a sculptural porch faced with purple ceramic.

Kurferstendamm Complex (Former Universum-Kino Cinema) (1928)
ARCHITECT: Eric Mendelsohn
LOCATION: at Lehniner Platz, Kurfurstendamm 153

This large complex includes one of Mendelsohn's most imaginative designs—a cinema building. (Mendelsohn fled Germany before World War II and set up his practice in San Francisco.)

National Library (1976)
ARCHITECT: Hans Scharoun
LOCATION: Potsdamer Strasse 33

Considerably larger than Scharoun's famous Philharmonic Hall nearby, the dramatically designed library is the architect's last work.

St. Norbert-Kirche (1961–62)
ARCHITECTS: Hermann Fehling and Damel Gogel
LOCATION: Dominicusstrasse 196

Suhne Christi Church (1962–64)
ARCHITECT: Hanrudolph Plarre
LOCATION: Siedmensstadt-West

Criss-crossing metal spheres create a striking roof topping an octagonal plan.

Unité D'Habitation (1957)
ARCHITECT: Le Corbusier
LOCATION: Reichssportfeld, Off Heer Strasse

The internationally renowned architect's Unité in Berlin combines the ingenuity and mastery of space planning similar to his more famous Unité Marseilles, France. As part of the Interbau, the Berlin International Building Exhibition of 1957, this finely designed Unité features 557 apartments overlooking the old Olympic grounds. Raised off the ground by pilotis (stilts), the raw concrete structure is punctuated with a variety of colorful panels, a favorite design treatment of the architect.

BONN

Beethoven Halle (1959)
ARCHITECT: Wolske
LOCATION: Wachsbleiche 17 D-5300

An example of new German architecture after World War II not based on the severity of rectangular forms.

Bundeshaus And Government Quarter (1933–1949)
ARCHITECT: Witte in 1933, Schwippert in 1949

LOCATION: Bundeskanzlerplatz to Gorresstrasse

Impressive modern architecture designed for function. Beautifully located by the Rhine River.

Municipal Theater (1963–65)
ARCHITECT: Gessler u. Beck of Stuttgart
LOCATION: Am Boeselagerhof 1 D-53

BRUHL

D.O.M. Headquarters (1980)
ARCHITECT: Robert Stern
LOCATION: 7 miles South of Cologne

The boldly formed D.O.M. Headquarters is a unique example in Germany of Postmodern architecture.

COLOGNE (see KÖLN)
COLOGNE-RIEHL

St. Engelbert (1931–33)
ARCHITECT: Dominikus Bohm
LOCATION: Suburb of Cologne, c. 4 km. N from the Cathedral on Riehler Gurtel 50

One of Bohm's most admired works in the German Expressionist Style.

DARMSTADT

Mathildenhöhe (1900)
ARCHITECTS: Works by various artists
LOCATION: Just E of town on Alexanderstr. to Dieburger Str.

At the turn of the century, the Grand Duke of Darmstadt held an exhibition. Many Jugendstil buildings from this event still remain. Noteworthy is the *ERNST LUDWIG HOUSE* by Josef Maria Olbrich and *BEHRENS HOUSE* by Peter Behrens.

DÜSSELDORF

Kunstmuseum (1925–26)
ARCHITECT: Wilhelm Kreis
LOCATION: Kunstpalast, Ehrenhof Orangeriestr. 6

A building conveying the power of the Third Reich with massive structural design. Kreis was one of Hitler's favorite architects.

Mannesmannrohren-Werke (Mannesmann Tubes) (1911–12)
ARCHITECT: Peter Behrens
LOCATION: On the Berger Allee (Mannesmannufer 2-3)

As a leading member of the Deutscher Werkbund founded in 1907, Behren's work influenced a new modern direction in architecture and design. He accepted the tremendous potential and challenge of the machine and working with industry. His title, "the father of modern architecture in Germany," is well respected. The Mannesmann Building, still occupied by the same company, is an excellent example of Behren's practical and functional approach. Numerous innovative ideas were incorporated into the exterior and space planning designs.

Theater At Dusseldorf (Schauspielhaus) (1967–69)
ARCHITECT: Bernhard Pfau
LOCATION: Gustav-Grundgens-Platz

With a curving exterior, this theater is an example of architecture not expressed with rigid rectangular forms.

Tietz Department Store (Now Kaufhof Store) (1906–08)
ARCHITECT: Josef Maria Olbrich (Austria)
LOCATION: An der Ko

An interesting work by the famous Secessionist member who tried to free himself of traditionalism in his design approach.

FEHMARN

Holiday Center (1970s)
ARCHITECT: Arne Jacobsen (Denmark)
LOCATION: NW Germany on Baltic Island

A fascinating structure of gables, recesses, and balconies with a fiberglass finish by Denmark's master architect.

FRANKFURT

IG-Garbenindustrie Corporation (Now U.S.A. Offices) (1928)
ARCHITECT: Hans Poelzig

LOCATION: Reuterweg

This administrative office building for a United States corporation is an early important work by the famous German Expressionist architect.

Museum of German Architecture (1984)
ARCHITECT: Oswald Mathias Ungers
LOCATION: South bank of Main River

The new museum has already created excitement in architectural circles around the world. The reinforced concrete structure encloses an existing 18th-century villa incorporating its Ionic columns into the new design.

New Town Section Of Frankfurt (post World War II)

A number of outstanding modern buildings are found in this new town section including the BAYER-HAUS by Professor Blattner (1952) located on Am Eschenheimer Turm, the ZURICH-HAUS designed by Udo von Schauroth and Werner Stuckeli (1959–63) located on Bockenheimer Landstrasse, and the POST OFFICE TELECOMMUNICATIONS CENTER (FERNMELDETURM) (1977), located 1 km. N of the Palmengarten.

Olivetti Building (1970)
ARCHITECT: Egon Eiermann
LOCATION: Lyoner Strasse

The sleek Olivetti building is one of the last important works by Germany's famous modern architect.

FREIBURG

Schneider Store (1975)
ARCHITECT: Heinz Mohl
LOCATION: Corner of the Munsterplatz

Good modern design sympathetically integrated into its traditional environment. (The magnificent Munster is close by.)

HAGEN

The Folkwang Museum (Note: This museum may have another name now)

ARCHITECTS: Henri van de Velde, Peter Behrens, and Karl Gerard
LOCATION: c. 50 miles NE of Cologne

Simplification of structure and brick detailing inside are beautifully expressed in this early modern building by Germany's famous pioneer modern architects.

HAMBURG

Canadian Pacific Hamburg Plaza Hotel
LOCATION: Planten un Blomen Park

Congress Center (1973)
LOCATION: By the Planten un Blomen Park

The Hanse Quarter Arcade (Late 1970's)
ARCHITECTS: Various architects
LOCATION: Entrance on corner of Poststrasse & Gross Bleichen

The Hanse Quarter is part of a fascinating network of shopping arcades in downtown Hamburg. A huge glass and steel cupola lights the angled interior spaces.

Heinrich Hertz Telecommunications Tower (Fernmeldeturm) (1968)
LOCATION: Outside the West entrance to Planten un Blomen

Known as "Tele-Michel" by Hamburgers. Features a revolving restaurant at the top of the tower.

Sprinkenhof (1926–28)
ARCHITECT: Fritz Höger & Gerson
LOCATION: On the Burchardplatz

Just across the street from Hogar's spectacular Chilehaus, the Sprinkenhof building has a surface covered with vitrified bricks— some of them with gold plate.

State Opera House (1955)
LOCATION: W of the Neuer Jungferstieg— on Dammtorstrasse

KAISERSLAUTERN

New Town Hall (Rathaus) (1968)
ARCHITECT: Roland Ostertag
LOCATION: On the Rathausplatz

Germany's and Europe's tallest town hall.

KARLSRUHE

Baden State Theater (1970–75)
LOCATION: Just SE of the Ettlinger Tor.

A brilliant new theater design incorporated with the latest technical developments.

KÖLN (COLOGNE)

Dance Pavilion (1957)
(Terrassenschirme) (1971)
ARCHITECT: Frei Otto with others
LOCATION: Rheinpark, Deutz

An unusual architectural technique utilizing a mast-and-cable support system. (See Munich Olympic Stadium.)

Dischhaus (1929)
ARCHITECTS: Bruno Paul with Franz Weber

An interesting curved commercial structure wrapping a corner by Germany's important early modern architect.

Ehemalige Villa Deichmann (Private House) (1903–04)
ARCHITECT: Josef Maria Olbrich (Austria)
LOCATION: Theodor-Heuss-Ring 9

An interesting private house in the Art Nouveau style by the internationally famous Austrian modern architect at the turn of the century.

Evangelische Kirche (1967–68)
ARCHITECTS: Georg Rasch and Winfried Wolsky
LOCATION: Buchforst, Kopernikusstrasse (near Köln)

Gurzenich (1952–55)
ARCHITECTS: Karl Bank, Rudolf Schwarz
LOCATION: Martinstrs/Quatermarkt

Municipal Theater (Opernhaus) (1959–62)
ARCHITECT: Wilhelm Riphahn with Hans Menne
LOCATION: Offenbachplatz

A modernistically-styled opera house that has been admired throughout Germany.

Rathaus (City Hall) (1966–72)
ARCHITECTS: Karl Bank with Eugen Weiler
LOCATION: Alter Markt/Rathausplatz

School For Music (Staatl, Hochschule Fur Musik) (1973–76)
ARCHITECTS: Werkgruppe 7 und Bauturm
LOCATION: Dagobertstrasse

Brilliant red forms outline the design components of this stunning complex.

St. Alban The New
ARCHITECT: Hans Schilling
LOCATION: On the Kyotostrasse

A unique vertical brick construction in an austere treatment.

St. Gertrud (1964–65)
ARCHITECT: Gottfried Bohm
LOCATION: Krefelder Strasse 45-57

A soaring structural tower hovers over smaller towers for the design of this bold modern church.

Verwaltungsgebaude Des Tuv Rheinland (1972–74)
ARCHITECTS: Helmut Nentrich and Hubert Petschnigg
LOCATION: Poll, Am grauen Stein (near Koln)

An impressive multi-story complex by one of Germany's most famous architectural teams.

LÜBECK

Cowshed Gut Garkau Farm (1924–25)
ARCHITECT: Hugo Haring
LOCATION: am Ponitzer See Gemeinde Scharbeutz

Although Haring built few structures, his influence was great, teaching his theory of functional organic architecture. This cow shed gained him international recognition. (Owner: D. Roders.)

LUDWIGSHAFEN

Friedrich-Ebert-Halle (1965)
ARCHITECT: Roland Rainer (Austria)

LOCATION: W Bank of Rhine, opposite Mannheim in Ebertpark

A dynamic structure of brutalistic concrete that splays outward in various directions bringing a powerful rhythmic quality to the design. Functions as a multi-purpose center.

Wilhelm-Hack Museum (Joan Miro Facade)
LOCATION: Downtown Ludwigshafen, close to Marktplatz

A colorful red, blue, green, and yellow facade on the museum by Joan Miro makes a spectacular impact.

MANNHEIM

Friedrichsplatz (1901)
ARCHITECT: Bruno Schmitz
LOCATION: Friedrichsplatz

This architectural masterpiece is designed in the Jugendstil (Art Nouveau Style).

Rosengarten Conference Center (1899/1903/1974)
ARCHITECTS: Bruno Schmitz and others
LOCATION: Rosengartenplatz 2

An elegant new addition to the original structure, the complex features an impressive concert hall. The building of 1903 is a good example of the Judendstil.

Telecommunications Tower (1975)
LOCATION: E of theater in the Luisenpark

A soaring tower with a revolving restaurant at the top.

Trinity Church (1959)
ARCHITECT: Helmut Striffler
LOCATION: G4 Block

The most appealing aspect of this unique church is its innovative use of small panels of colored glass and concrete. (Stained glass created by famed Gabriel Loire of France.)

MARL

Marl Town Hall (1964–69)
ARCHITECTS: Van den Broek and Bakema (Holland)

LOCATION: c. 25 miles NW of Dortmund

A "cluster" city made up of many centers of intensity rather than the traditional main center. The town and town hall were designed by The Netherlands' famous architectural and town planning team.

MUNICH

Maxburg Rebuilding (1957)
ARCHITECTS: Theo Pabst and Sepp Ruf.
LOCATION: At Lenbachplatz

Gleaming modern architecture interestingly harmonizes with traditional buildings and integrates with the tower of the Graf Maxburg fort that survived World War II bombings.

NEU-ULM

St. Johannes Baptist Church (1921–26)
ARCHITECT: Dominikus Bohm
LOCATION: Inquire: Verkehrsburo, Munsterplatz 51 in Ulm

Completely breaking with traditionalism at the time, this church, with its massive and bold design, is a good example of German Expressionism.

NUREMBURG

Grandstand On The Zeppelinfeld (Zeppelintribune) (1934–37)
ARCHITECT: Albert Speer
LOCATION: On the Zeppelinfeld, Zeppelinstrasse/Beuthener Strasse

A massive and strong structural building that expressed the spirit of the Third Reich. Designed by Hitler's favorite architect and designer.

Meistersingerhalle (1963)
ARCHITECTS: Harald Loebermann with Prof. Puchner
LOCATION: In the Luitpoldhain, SE of town, Munchener Strasse 21

New Municipal Library (1953–54)
ARCHITECT: Fritz u. Walter Mayer
LOCATION: Egidienplatz 32

New Town Hall (Rathaus Nurnberg) (1954)
ARCHITECT: K. Schneckendorf
LOCATION: Side of the Hauptmarkt, Hochbauamt der Stadt Nurnberg

PADERBORN

Diocesan Museum (1969–1975)
ARCHITECT: Gottfried Bohm
LOCATION: Markt 17, c. 100 miles NE of Koln. Inquire at Marienplatz 2a for directions

This building of complex spaces and unusual form creates an intriguing background for exhibits. Construction is principally of glass and metal.

PFORZHEIM

Church Of St. Matthew (1953)
ARCHITECT: Egon Eiermann
LOCATION: Western district Arlinger, 5½ km. S of Pforzheim

An expressive tent-shaped church featuring colored glass fenestration that contrasts dramatically with the concrete of the bomb-rubble structure.

SINDELFINGEN

Sports Hall (1976–77)
ARCHITECTS: Gunter Behnisch & Partners
LOCATION: 9 miles SW of Stuttgart on Hohenzollernstrasse

An exceptional modern arrangement of tubular steel frames that carry a roof covering the stadium.

STUTTGART

Calwer Passage (1974–78)
ARCHITECTS: H. Kammerer, W. Belz, & Partner
LOCATION: Calwer Strasse 42-64

A delightful steel-and-glass-roofed shopping passage with modernized shops displaying stylized logos over the doorways—an old German custom.

GERMANY

City Hall (1956) (1978–80)
ARCHITECTS: H. Jassoy and J. Vollmer
LOCATION: On the Markt-Platzflugel

A simple and well articulated City Hall and focal point in the old traditional marketplace in downtown Stuttgart.

Kleines Haus (1960–62)
ARCHITECTS: H. Volkar, K. Placking, and B. Perlia
LOCATION: N of Neues Schloss by Schlossgarten Park

An avant-garde hexagonal theater designed for drama and comedy productions—replacing a traditional theater.

Landtag (1960–61)
ARCHITECTS: R. Zinsmeister with G. Scheffler
LOCATION: NE Stuttgart in Schlossgarten Park, K. Adenauer Strs. 3

A cubic design of glass that functions as the state parliament of Waden-Wurttemburg.

The Planetarium (1970–77)
ARCHITECTS: W. Beck-Erlang and Partner
LOCATION: Neckarstrasse 47

An unusual ziggurat-shaped roof is featured for the design composition of the new Planetarium with supportive steel trusses at the edges.

Romeo And Juliet Flats (1954–59)
ARCHITECT: Hans Scharoun
LOCATION: Stuttgart-Zuffenhauser, Rot, Schozacher Strasse 40

A housing complex utilizing an unusual nine-directions plan by Germany's great neo-Expressionist architect.

Weissenhofsiedlung Housing (Exhibition) (1927)
ARCHITECTS: Mies van der Rohe, Le Corbusier, J.J.P. Oud, Walter Gropius, Hans Poelzig, Mart Stam, Hans Scharoun, Peter Behrens, M. and B. Taut, and others.
LOCATION: At Am Weissenhof and Friedrich-Ebert Strasse

A housing and exhibition project that brought Mies (architect in charge) and others

international attention. Seventeen well-known modern architects were invited to participate. Especially interesting is Le Corbusier's *CITROHAN HOUSE*. The entire exhibition was denounced by Hitler. Maps can be obtained to identify each work.

ULM

Church Of The Holy Spirit (Heilig-Geist-Kirche)
LOCATION: SW section of Ulm by the Romerstrasse

A dominating site above the town with a unique campanile in the shape of a human finger.

School Of Design (Hochscule Fur Gestaltung)
ARCHITECT: Max Bill
LOCATION: Near Fort Oberer Kuhberg (off Fremmelfinger Weg)

A spartan and efficient complex. Functions as a modern school of design. Considered an offspring of the famous Bauhaus.

WILDBAD

Thermalbad (Treatment Center) (1977) **(Treatment Center**
LOCATION: In the Kurplatz behind Graf Eberhard Baths 12 miles SW of Pforzheim

A modern facility in one of Germany's most popular spas.

192

Ireland

IRELAND

Creeslough

Burt

Londonderry

Belfast

Cultra

Donegal

Garrison

Dundalk

Collinstown

Dublin

MODERN ARCHITECTURE IN IRELAND

EARLY DEVELOPMENTS

Due to problems of poverty and political struggle during the 19th and early 20th centuries, Ireland's modern architectural progress was slow. Additionally, like many other European nations, Ireland's design direction was uncertain. Gothic, Romanesque, Georgian, and other traditional approaches were often revived.

PIONEER EFFORTS

A selected number of buildings by R.M. Butler showed an awareness and sensitivity to new techniques and styles, although his work was still primarily traditional. It was a beginning. Desmond FitzGerald was one of the first Irish architects to introduce ideas of the "modern movement" on the continent to his country. This is especially demonstrated in his airport terminal building of 1943 at Collinstown.

CONTRIBUTION OF MICHAEL SCOTT

Michael Scott is Ireland's best known modern architect and the first to gain international recognition. His innovative Dublin Bus Station of 1950 was Scott's first important work. (He has since formed the partnership of Scott, Tallon, and Walker.) Other notable contributions made to promoting modern architecture in Ireland have been made by Raymond McGrath, Liam McCormick, and a number of excellent architectural firms.

PRESENT CONDITIONS

Today public acceptance and support of contemporary architecture are evident throughout Ireland, and many cities possess fine examples of modern design. Contemporary construction today is primarily structural modern design featuring clean, simple forms. Progressive architects are keenly aware of new building problems, techniques, and solutions.

BURT

County Donegal Church At Burt

ARCHITECTS: Liam McCormick and Partners
LOCATION: A parish 6 miles NW of Londonderry

It was not until the third quarter of the present century that a vital break with traditional churches occurred in Ireland. The modern church designs of Liam McCormick are especially noteworthy throughout the country. The swirling roof treatment harmonizes with the surrounding grassy countryside setting. The bold form of the roof culminates in a sharply pointed spire that creates a focal point for the structure.

CULTRA

The Ulster Folk And Transport Museum (1983)

ARCHITECTS: Ferguson & McIlveen
LOCATION: A few miles NE of Belfast, on shoreline

Situated in a rolling wooded terrain, the architects were charged to create three distinct exhibit spaces. Three pitched roofs with glazed gabled ends—the only natural light sources—connect four enclosures of green enameled steel. Temperature and humidity control were worked into the plan to provide a suitable environment for the exhibits. The award-winning museum has been highly praised as a building of character, strength, and aesthetic appeal.

DUBLIN

Bus Terminus (1950)

ARCHITECT: Michael Scott
LOCATION: Amiens Street

Regarded as one of Ireland's most important pioneer modern architects, Scott was the first to be recognized outside of Ireland. The Bus Terminus, with its striking undulating roof, makes an impressive site in downtown Dublin. Rounded forms are repeated with a soaring, slanted window band that wraps around the second floor of the structure. The unusually designed Bus Terminus is Scott's best-known work.

DUBLIN

Fitzwilliam Lawn Tennis Club

ARCHITECTS: Stephenson, Gibney, and Associates
LOCATION: Inquire: Visitor Ctr., 14 Upper O'Connell St.

An outstanding example of modern Irish architecture, the Fitzwilliam Lawn Tennis Club features bold brick masonry construction. The exterior facade is punctuated with random projecting glass window openings that give the building an unusual identity. Planned for maximum efficiency of space, the Tennis Club captures the spirit of its function.

DUBLIN

Irish Life Building

ARCHITECTS: Robinson, Keeffe, and Devane
LOCATION: Inquire: Tourist Ctr., 14 Upper
O'Connell St.

Modern architecture had a relatively slow beginning in Ireland, traditionally oriented for many centuries. But most buildings designed in Ireland today are in the modern style. The Irish Life Building, with its series of arched pillar supports, represents a current trend in innovative contemporary design and is considered one of the country's finest modern buildings.

DUBLIN

New Abbey Theatre (1966)

ARCHITECT: Michael Scott and Partners
LOCATION: Corner of Abbey Street and
Marlborough Street

Influenced by Le Corbusier, the Bauhaus, and the International Style, Scott was one of the first Irish architects to introduce these design philosophies to Ireland. The New Abbey Theatre expresses a strong design that reflects the architects' individualistic approach. The plain massive facade and exterior walls of masonry are topped with a band of glass windows that follow the perimeter of the structure.

DUBLIN

The United States Embassy (1964)

ARCHITECT: John Johansen (USA)
LOCATION: Inquire: Tourist Ctr., 14 Upper O'Connell St.

Johansen, a prominent modern American architect, was selected to build this unique structure for the United States. The circular building is symbolic of early Celtic Christian design. The structure fits nicely on a busy corner site, welcoming the visitor from all vantage points. The three-storied building features unusual twisting supports framing the windows in an alternating reverse system.

DUNDALK

Carroll's Tobacco Factory

ARCHITECTS: Michael Scott, Tallon, and Walker
LOCATION: On Dundalk Bay near mouth of Castle River On main Dublin-Belfast road, 2 miles S of Dundalk

A streamlined and stunning structure, the Carroll's Tobacco Factory is beautifully situated in a country setting, surrounded by a large reflecting pond that mirrors the building. The long, low complex is built primarily of dark tinted glass with slender steel supports. An interesting network of trusses and lighting integrates the interior spaces.

ADDITIONAL MODERN STRUCTURES OF INTEREST

COLLINSTOWN

Airport Terminal Building (1943)
ARCHITECT: Desmond FitzGerald
LOCATION: Air Terminal, a few miles N of Dublin's city center

One of the first buildings in Ireland to show the influence of the modern movement.

CREESLOUGH

Church At Creeslough, St. Michael's (1972)
ARCHITECT: Liam McCormick
LOCATION: Donegal County, NW Ireland, a few miles outside Creeslough

One of McCormick's most notable designs.

DUBLIN

Architects' Offices (1980s)
ARCHITECTS: Stephenson, Gibney, and Associates
LOCATION: On Bride Street

An inviting modern complex of brick and bronzed windows, these attractive offices are built around an angled open courtyard.

Arts Faculty, Trinity College (Late 1970s)
ARCHITECTS: Ahrends, Burton & Koralek
LOCATION: Trinity College campus

An ambitious complex of reinforced concrete and glass arranged in horizontal levels.

Bank In Dublin
ARCHITECTS: Stephenson Associates (Late 1970s)
LOCATION: Corner of Trinity Street by Half Penny Bridge

An assertive structure with bold horizontal forms.

Headquarters For The Bank Of Ireland (1973)
ARCHITECTS: Michael Scott and Partners
LOCATION: On Baggot Street

An impressive facility featuring the latest developments in technology and design suitable for its function.

Headquarters Of The Irish Broadcasting Services (1967)
ARCHITECTS: Michael Scott and Partners
LOCATION: Inquire: Tourist Ctr., 14 Upper O'Connell St.

Holy Trinity Church (1980s)
ARCHITECTS: A and D Wejchert
LOCATION: Grangemore in north Dublin

Dynamic diagonal forms and lines combine in the design of this church to create a bold silhouette on the countryside

New Library (1967)
ARCHITECT: Paul Koralek
LOCATION: Between Fellows Park and the Old Library

A clean and simply designed building that contrasts with its surroundings.

GARRISON

Church At Garrison
ARCHITECT: Liam McCormick
LOCATION: W Northern Ireland, c. 90 miles WSW of Belfast

McCormick is particularly known for his unique religious structures. This church is one of his best.

KILL

R. J. Goff & Company Pavilion (1975)
ARCHITECTS: Scott Tallon Walker
LOCATION: c. 15 miles SW of Dublin

This huge pavilion was designed to function as a bloodstock sales complex. The glass and concrete structure features a circular building for horse sales.

LONDONDERRY

Church At Steelstown
ARCHITECT: Liam McCormick
LOCATION: Steelstown, a suburb of
Londonderry

Space and strong forms are interestingly
treated for the design of this church.

NEWTON

Our Lady Of The Nativity Church (1970s)
ARCHITECT: Tyndall Hogan Hurley
LOCATION: A few miles off Dublin-Gatway

The design of this bold religious structure
features heavy textured white walls both
inside and outside.

Italy

ITALY

Fagnano Olona
Aosta
Ivrea
Como
Busto Arsizio
Milan
Sauze d'Oulx
Turin
Udine
Pordenone
Gorizia
Redipuglia
Treviso
Venice
Trieste
Padua
Genoa
Bologna
Pescia
Florence
Sienna
Chianciano
Pescara
Francavilla
Rome
San Felice
Terracina
Naples
Torre del Greco
Vietri-sul-Mare
Salerno
Matera
Taranto
Lecce

MODERN ARCHITECTURE IN ITALY

IRON STRUCTURES

The first structure in Italy to be considered modern is Mengoni's remarkable iron roof spanning the Galeria Vittorio Emanuele II in Milan.

FUTURISM

This short-lived movement from 1910 to 1916 issued a manifesto that violently rejected the past and glorified the beauty of the machine. Although primarily an artistic movement, the philosophy inspired architects like Sant'Elia, whose writings influenced early modern architects in Italy.

ART NOUVEAU

A number of Italian architects and designers became involved with this decorative style popular throughout Europe at the turn of the century. The style, employing organic lines and plant forms inspired from nature, was considered a complete break with the past.

GRUPPO 7

This architects' cooperative of 1926 was made up of leading avant-garde architects who tried to come to terms with the machine and new engineering advances from the unique perspective of their own country. Terragni was the leading member of the group.

PIER LUIGI NERVI AND GIO PONTI

Nervi and Ponti are the most important early modern architects in Italy. Nervi's exhibition halls and Ponti's Pirelli Building have influenced architects throughout the world. Ponti founded *Domus* magazine, an international design periodical, in 1926, and was editor until his death.

THE MILAN TRIENNALE

Gio Ponti helped establish this world-renowned competition exhibit. Since 1933 it has been held every three years with only a few interruptions. International designers are invited as well as Italian designers, providing an excellent opportunity for introducing to the world the latest techniques, materials, and designs.

THE PERIOD AFTER WORLD WAR II

After the war Italy emerged as a world leader of modern design, especially in the field of furnishings. Italian architects are known for their innovative approach to solving design problems. Many Italian architects have received international acclaim for their work. The 1980 Venice Biennale Exhibition demonstrated the Italian's creativity in modern design featuring spectacular examples of Postmodern architecture.

BOLOGNA

Pavillion De L'Esprit Nouveau
(Reconstruction 1977)

ARCHITECT: Andre Wogensky, architect in charge
LOCATION: Adjacent to Museum of Modern Art

Located on the International Exposition grounds of Bologna, the clean white modular building is a faithful reconstruction of Le Corbusier's famous pavilion for the 1925 International Exposition in Paris. (At the Exposition, the officials put Le Corbusier's house in a far corner where it could not easily be seen!) The architectural treasure demonstrates the master modern architect's philosophy of design, employing his five points of architecture.

BUSTO ARSIZO

Technical College (1963–64)
ARCHITECT: Enrico Castiglioni
LOCATION: Busto Arsizo, 19 miles NW of Milan

This building's almost alarming form is direct and strong in expression. The raw concrete structure is technically daring, appropriately symbolic for its function. Castiglioni is one of Italy's most imaginative contemporary designers; the Technical College has brought him international recognition.

CHIANCIANO TERME

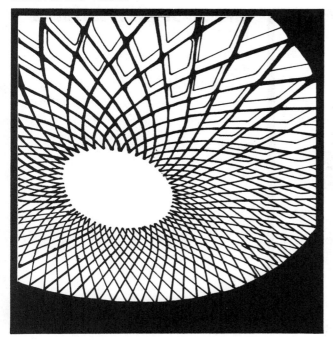

Spa And Casino (1952)

ARCHITECTS: Pier Luigi Nervi with other architects
LOCATION: Viale Baccelli, Chianciano Terms—47 miles SE of Siena

Designed a number of years before Nervi's famous Pallazzo dello Sport for the 1960 Olympic games in Rome, the Spa and Casino is equally interesting. The structure is situated in a town boasting one of Italy's finest natural mineral springs. The casino has a spectacular lacy concrete ceiling that dominates the interior space—another incredible engineering feat by Italy's master engineer.

COMO

Casa Del Popolo (Formerly Casa Del Fascio) (1938)

ARCHITECT: Giuseppe Terragni
LOCATION: 25 miles N of Milan, near the Swiss border, at NW end of Via Dante

The Casa del Popolo was one of the first important pre-war structures built in Italy and one of the first to receive world-wide attention. Terragni helped to establish ideas of Italian Rationalism; clean, clear, and direct, the Casa del Popolo became a prototype for similar buildings throughout Italy. The office building, featuring an exposed structural frame, is built around an open courtyard in the back.

FLORENCE

Church Of The Autostrada De Sole (1961)

ARCHITECT: Giovanni Michelucci
LOCATION: S. Giovanni Battista, Raccordo Autostrada del Sole (Prato) in Florence

This fascinating structure of twisting flowing forms blends dome and walls into one huge mass. Coarse rubble block expressively arranged provides an impressive memorial to the men who lost their lives during the construction of Italy's Autostrada (freeway).

FRANCAVILLA AL MARE

San Franco (1959)

ARCHITECT: Ludovico Quaroni
LOCATION: Piazza San Franco, 5 miles SE of Pescara

With a bell tower that soars majestically above the small seaside town on Italy's eastern coast, this modern church is an interesting focal point on the horizon. San Franco blends with the traditional forms of the old buildings of the town. The hot Italian sun streams through four windows located under the enormous roof—a highlight of the church's design.

LECCE

New Town Cemetery (1982)

ARCHITECTS: Alessando Anselmi with
GRAU (Gruppo Romano Architetti,
Urbanistici)
LOCATION: At Lecce, 50 miles SE of
Taranto

This ancient town is situated on the "heel" of
Italy's boot-shaped peninsula. Anselmi, with
GRAU, an architectural organization formed in
the 1960s, consisting of fourteen architects,
has created an awesome cemetery from the
local sandstone that has been used for the
magnificent Baroque buildings in Lecce for
centuries. The guiding force of the design is a
variety of bold geometric forms.

MILAN

City Hall, Segrate (1962)

ARCHITECTS: Michele Achilli and others
LOCATION: Viale XXV Aprile in Milan

Italian architects of the past few decades have
earned a reputation for extraordinary design.
The City Hall at Segrate in Milan is an
example of their employment of flamboyant
form. Heavy columns are tightly massed
between curving tiered floor slabs. The effect
beckons the visitor into the interior spaces.

MILAN

Galeria Vittorio Emmanuel II (1865–67)

ARCHITECT: Guiseppe Mengoni
LOCATION: Between the Opera House and Cathedral Piazza

This enormous complex, with a dome forty-eight meters high, was the largest shopping arcade in Europe when it was built. Mengoni was one of the first architects to create a massive iron roof covering a large enclosed space. Structures of this type were offspring of Joseph Paxton's spectacular Crystal Palace designed in London for the 1851 exposition. Mengoni fell to his death while supervising this project.

MILAN

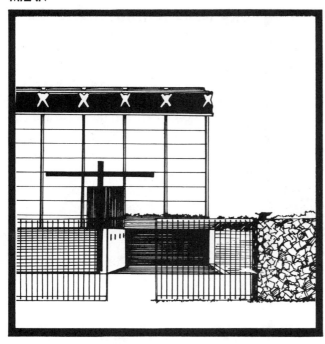

Matri Misericordiae Church (1958)

ARCHITECTS: Angelo Mangiarotti and Bruno Morasutti
LOCATION: Strada Provinciale Varesina at Via Trieste, Milan-Baranzate

Privately situated within a rubble wall in an industrial section of northwest Milan, the Matri Misericordiae Church is a remarkable structure of outstanding design. It employs only four supports of the roof, with a network of beams allowing an independent wall system. Translucent modular wall panels allow soft filtered light to flood the interior space.

MILAN

Madonna Of The Poor (1952)

ARCHITECTS: Luigi Figini and Gino Pollini
LOCATION: Via Alessio Oliveri at Via
Baggio, Milan-Baggio

This engaging church is one of the country's
first modern religious structures. Exterior and
interior brutalistic concrete is pierced with
small panes of glass, creating a striking
textural contrast. Soft indirect lighting creates
an atmosphere of quiet and meditation.

MILAN

Monument To Italian Victims Of The Nazi Concentration Camps (1948)

ARCHITECTS: BBPR Architectural Firm
LOCATION: Cimitero Monumentale, Via
Ceresio

Located in northwestern Milan, this cemetery
is one of Italy's most splendid. The open-
framed structural cube of the monument is
surrounded by highly elaborate marble tombs
that create a stunning contrast. Commemorat-
ing the numerous Italians who died in Nazi
concentration camps during World War II, a
glass case in the center of the cube has a
prisoner's bowl filled with earth from the
Mauthausan Camp in Austria. Symbolic barbed
wire and engraved quotations on black and
white marble complete the design.

MILAN

Olivetti Building (1954)

ARCHITECTS: Bernasconi, Fiocchi, and Nizzoli
LOCATION: Via Clerici

Olivetti has commissioned some of Europe's finest modern structures. This building features a series of exterior aluminum slats that are attractive as well as functional. The facade acts as a screen to protect the windows from the glare of the sun—the "brise soleil" popularized by Le Corbusier.

MILAN

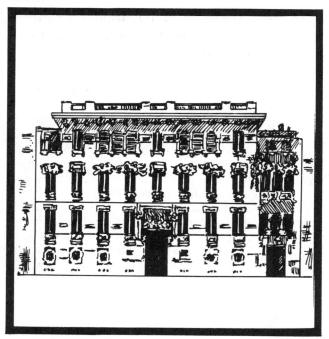

Palazzo Castiglioni (1901–03)
ARCHITECT: Guiseppe Sommaruga
LOCATION: Corso Venezia

Employing organic forms from nature, Art Nouveau was the most popular new design style throughout Europe at the turn of the century. Sommaruga was Italy's foremost exponent of the new style, and the Palazzo Castiglioni is one of the best architectural examples of Art Nouveau in the country. At first glance the Palazzo appears traditional, but on closer inspection the decorative flowers, vines, and plant forms can be seen as a break with motifs of the past.

MILAN

Pirelli Building (1957)

ARCHITECTS: Gio Ponti and others
LOCATION: Piazza Duca d'Aosta

The soaring thirty-three story Pirelli Building was one of the first major skyscrapers in Europe. The elongated hexagonal plan features two vertical spines ingeniously placed seventy-nine feet apart to support the reinforced concrete frame. Ponti's own office was in the Pirelli Building until his death in the late 70s. The elegant form of this internationally admired building contrasted significantly with its traditional surroundings when it was built and still possesses a commanding position in the city today.

MILAN

Torre Velasca (1958)

ARCHITECTS: BBPR (Belgiojoso, Peressutti, and Rogers)
LOCATION: Via Velasca at Corso di Porta Romana

Situated in an area rebuilt since World War II, this bold building caused a great deal of excitement when it was constructed. The top six of its twenty-six stories fan outward, creating a top-heavy silhouette that distinguishes the structure from surrounding traditional buildings. The oddly-shaped tower still provokes comment today.

NAPLES

Casa Del Portuale (1968–80)

ARCHITECT: Aldo Rossi
LOCATION: Calata della Marinella, by the Port

The Casa del Portuale, designed by one of Italy's foremost contemporary architects, is a supreme example of ultramodern and traditional architecture coexisting in the same neighborhood. The expressive concrete structure with clusters of slender vertical drums has been compared to "updated silos." Bold disc forms are sandwiched at various points providing a unique counterbalance to the complex.

RIOLA

Riola Parochial Church
(1966–78)

ARCHITECT: Alva Aalto
LOCATION: 35 mi. from Bologna in the Appenini Mountains

This titan of modern architecture designed a number of impressive and original buildings outside Finland. The Riola Church, situated in a lovely meadow setting by a stream was completed after his death in 1976. Strong horizontal and curved structural forms of local sandstone and concrete provide excitement. Lighting floods the nave through tiered clerestory windows topped by a sandstone roof.

British Embassy (1968)

ARCHITECT: Sir Basil Spence (England)
LOCATION: Via XX Settembre 80A

Commissioned to one of England's foremost modern architects, the British Embassy is an impressive and distinguished building in a busy downtown section of Rome. The Embassy's main structure is raised on concrete supports over a large, refreshing reflecting pond, creating a welcoming oasis in the usually hot climate. Uniformity of the exterior and interior design throughout the complex provides a sense of stability, dignity, and harmony.

Casa Baldi (1960)

ARCHITECT: Paolo Portoghese
LOCATION: Via Flaminia

Portoghese has received international acclaim for his spectacular achievements in modern residential design. The Casa Baldi sports a unique hexagonal plan. Concave walls are accentuated by expressive materials and a strong stringcourse. Deep eaves cap the structure with an Oriental feeling. Portoghese's *CASA PAPANESE* (privately owned) built in 1970 in Rome is a festive arrangement of circles and cylinders that have been compared to "organ pipes."

ROME

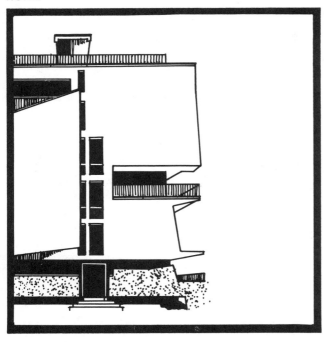

Casa Della Cooperativo (1949)

ARCHITECT: Luigi Moretti
LOCATION: 27 via Jenner

Designed by the architect of Watergate in Washington, D.C., the Casa Della Cooperativo is a good example of the clean, structural design popular after World War II. Solids and voids provide decorative interest, along with bold textural surface treatment.

ROME

Casa Roma (1970s)

ARCHITECT: Luigi Moretti
LOCATION: Viale Bruno Buozzi

Often regarded as one of Moretti's best projects, the Casa Roma features a split facade. Most of the building is arranged in a precise symmetrical treatment, but the upper roof line is designed in the individualistic and creative approach.

ROME

Fosse Ardeatatine (1951)

ARCHITECTS: April, Calcaprina, Florentino, and Perugini
LOCATION: Via Appia Antica

The Fosse Ardeatatine is a touching memorial. The structure and grounds are dedicated to 335 Italians who were brutally murdered to compensate for the loss of 32 Nazi stormtroopers killed in an accidental bombing. The architects have attempted to symbolize the horrible event by creating an immense tomb topped with a massive concrete slab roof.

ROME

Leonardo Da Vinci Airport (1960)

ARCHITECTS: Amedeo Luccichenti and Vincenzo Monaco, with others
LOCATION: Rome-Fiumicino—16 miles SW of Rome

Looking out over the ruins of ancient Ostia Antica close by, the streamlined Leonardo Da Vinci Airport provides an extreme contrast of old and new. The admirable structure of steel, glass, and concrete is planned for maximum efficiency. The design is open and inviting.

ROME

Mosque And Islamic Center (1976–84)

ARCHITECTS: Paolo Portoghese and Vittorio Gigliotti
LOCATION: Via A. Bertoloni, 22

This extraordinary religious center is a fanciful modern version of the mosque, and includes many of its familiar features. Minaret, dome, courtyard, and decorative details evoke impressions from the past. These traditional features, however, are interpreted in a structural contemporary manner. The interior is an elaborate composition of lines and forms emphasizing the ogee (reverse) curve.

ROME

Multi-Use Structure (Apartment And Offices) (1965)

ARCHITECTS: Passarelli Brothers
LOCATION: Via Campania

This fascinating structure of puzzlingly diverse design concepts functions as both an office and apartment building, with the lower level for parking. The office section is constructed of a smooth glass curtain wall that is stunningly surmounted by diagonal apartment units of raw concrete. The conglomerate of architectural approaches has been criticized as "unpure."

ROME

Offices Of The Ordine Dei Medici (1970)

ARCHITECTS: Piero Sartago with others
LOCATION: Via G.B. de Rossi

Influenced by the work of Luigi Moretti and Mario Ridolfi, this office complex is arranged in an interesting "upside down ziggurat" shape. Bold layers gradually extend outward, gradation providing a protective overhang for the lower level.

ROME

Palace Of Italian Civilisation, EUR (1942–)

ARCHITECTS: Guerrini, Lapadula, and Romano
LOCATION: On the road to Lido di Ostia and Anzio

Situated on the southern outskirts of Rome, straddling the Via Cristoforo Colombo, the EUR (site of the Espoizione Universale de Roma, an exhibition planned for 1942 and never held because of World War II) covers 1038 acres. A few of the planned buildings were constructed. Along with Nervi's Palazzetto Dello Sport built later, the stark Palace of Italian Civilization is best known. With its controlled and uniform treatment of mass and space, the structure exemplifies severe modern classicism.

ROME

Palazzetto Dello Sport (1960) and Palazzo Dello Sport (1959)

ARCHITECT: Pier Luigi Nervi
LOCATION: Via Cristoforo Colombo, E.U. 42 Grounds

These two masterpieces of prefabricated concrete architecture demonstrate Nervi's engineering expertise. The larger Palazzo, built first, seats sixteen thousand spectators and has an overwhelming exterior of reflective glass. The smaller Palazzetto is probably Nervi's finest work. This structure has a mathematically precise interior lace-like ceiling dome with bold Y-shaped supports. The structure was used for the 1960 Olympic games.

ROME

Palazzina San Maurizio (1962)

ARCHITECT: Luigi Moretti
LOCATION: 35 Via R. Roma

These apartment terraces flamboyantly express their function. Bold rounded concrete slabs wrap the structure in serpentine fashion. A solid, plain-surfaced mass provides a separated base for the tiers. The design of this housing development was innovative in the 1960s.

ROME

Railway Terminus (1948–51)

ARCHITECTS: Montuori and Calini with
Castellazzi, Vitellozzi, and Pintonello
LOCATION: Piazza dei Cinquecento

Montuori was the principal architect in charge
of remodeling the impressive Railway
Terminus, one of the finest structures of its
type in Europe. Planned around the fourth-
century ruins of the Servian wall, the
aluminum and glass structure incorporates
the existing archeological treasure into the
new design, thus preserving and enhancing
the ruins.

ROME

Rinascente Department Store (1959)

ARCHITECT: Franco Albini
LOCATION: Piazza Fiume

Known for his fabulous museum and interior
designs around the world, Albini first
exhibited in 1933 at the famous Milan
Triennale exhibition. Service ducts and an
exposed steel framework are unique features
of the Rinascente Department Store. Cornices
on each floor stabilize the design and create
unity. The structure is one of Albini's most
publicized.

TORRE DEL GRECO

Library And Cultural Center (1969)

ARCHITECTS: V. de Feo and F. Ascione
LOCATION: Town center at Torre del Greco, 7 miles SE of Naples

The Library and Cultural Center at Torre del Greco is a simple yet interesting composition of forms. The total shape of the complex resembles a farmer's shed, but design interest is achieved through the use of asymmetrical treatments, especially on the roof line. The center is typical of many public and civic buildings in Italy today in its break with traditional styling.

TURIN

Italia 61 Pavilion (1961)

ARCHITECTS: Pier Luigi Nervi and Antonio Nervi
LOCATION: Corso Polonia

Tourists flock to Turin to see the fine exhibitions held annually in the Italia 61 Pavilion and also in Pier Luigi Nervi's *PALAZZO DELLE ESPOSIZIONI* (1948) at Corso Massimo d'Azeglio—Nervi's first important building after World War II. As in many of the master architect/engineer's designs, a swirling flower-like concrete ceiling is featured. Close by, the gigantic Italia 61 Pavilion's sixteen massive columns support concrete roof slabs in an ingenious configuration.

VENICE

Teatro Del Mondo (The Floating Theater) (1980)

ARCHITECT: Aldo Rossi
LOCATION: Fusina shipyards, where it was towed after the Biennale celebration

Teatro del Mondo was built in 1980 for the Venice Biennale. In a city that is itself theatrical, Rossi has designed a marvelous small theater constructed of iron tubes welded at its base to a barge. Clad with vertical yellow pine strips, this building rises to an octagonal-pyramid roof. Rossi compared his theater design to the wonderful old lighthouses on the northern coast of America.

VIETRI-SUL-MARE

Ceramics-Factory (Early 1950s)

ARCHITECT: Paulo Soleri (USA)
LOCATION: Gulf of Salerno, 2 miles W of Salerno

Soleri, an innovative and visionary architect, migrated to America in 1947 to study with the master of organic architecture, Frank Lloyd Wright, in Taliesin, Arizona. In recent decades Soleri has been building his incredible cities in the Arizona desert north of Scottsdale, where he has become known for his extreme brutalism employing concrete in unusual forms. Soleri built this factory on a short visit to Italy.

ADDITIONAL MODERN STRUCTURES OF INTEREST

COMO

B & B Italia Offices (1971)
ARCHITECTS: Renzo Piano and Richard Rogers
LOCATION: Inquire: Information Center, Piazza Cavour

Novecomun Building (1927)
ARCHITECT: Giuseppe Terragni
LOCATION: Inquire at Information Center, Piazza Cavour

Terragni founded the avant-garde design group, Gruppo 7, in the late 1920s. The Novecomun Building, with its clean, plain white surfaces and bull-nosed corner, is one of the architect's best-known works.

FAGNANO OLONA

School At Fagnano Olona (1972)
ARCHITECT: Aldo Rossi
LOCATION: 4 miles NNE of Busto Arsizio, NE Italy

Three parallel blocks are arranged around open courtyards and accented by a rotunda that functions as a library.

FLORENCE

Stadium At Florence (1930–32)
ARCHITECT: Pier Luigi Nervi
LOCATION: Viale Manfredo Fanti, 4, Firenze

Frankly exposed structural elements are combined with a high technical level. The building brought Nervi international fame.

GENOA

Museum Of The Cathedral Treasury (1956)
ARCHITECT: Franco Albini
LOCATION: San Lorenzo Cathedral, Piazza San Lorenzo

A jewel of a modern interior setting for ancient displays, including the reputed Holy Grail. The addition is under the courtyard.

Sacra Famiglia "Parish Church" (1956–58)
ARCHITECTS: A. De Carlo, A. Mor, L. Quaroni, & A. Sibilla
LOCATION: suburb near River Bisagno, Inquire: Via Roma 11

IVREA

Olivetti Social Services And Residential Center (La Serra Residence) (1977)
ARCHITECTS: Cappai & Mainardi
LOCATION: 32 miles ESE of Aosta

A highly controversial housing plan consisting of fifty-five apartments, a cinema, a meeting hall, a restaurant, and other facilities. Also of interest in Ivrea is the *OLIVETTI FACTORY* (1952) by Luigi Figini and Gino Pollini. A clean design of unity and simplicity.

MILAN

Apartment Hotel
ARCHITECT: Luigi Moretti
LOCATION: Via F. Corridoni 22

Four handsome soaring slabs make up this apartment block designed by the architect who planned Watergate in Washington, D.C.

Biology Building (1982)
ARCHITECT: Vico Magistretti
LOCATION: Milan University campus

Repeating rectangular forms are expressively employed for the design of the impressive new Biology building designed by one of Italy's internationally known designers.

Castel Sforzesco Museum
ARCHITECTS: BBPR
LOCATION: Piazza Castello Sforzesco

A brilliantly modern treatment for displaying ancient art and artifacts.

Euro Mercato (Euromercato Brianza Paderno Dugnamo) (1970s)
ARCHITECTS: Studio Laboratories di Architettura of Milan

LOCATION: Strada Provinciale 44

A large 258,000 square foot shopping center combines elements of the past and present.

Instituto Marchiondi Spagliadi (1957)
ARCHITECT: Vittoriano Vignano
LOCATION: Spagliadi, Milan

One of the strongest examples of brutalistic architecture in Italy. Raw concrete, frankly exposed, is arranged in vigorous horizontal and vertical forms.

Newspaper Offices In Milan ("Corriere della Sera") (1964)
ARCHITECT: Alberto Roselli
LOCATION: Inquire: EPT (Information Center), Via Marconi 1

A frankly-exposed steel frame is pierced with glass to allow onlookers to see the printing machines. The function of the building is clearly related to its construction.

Office Building On The Corso Europa
ARCHITECTS: Luigi Cassia Dominioni with others
LOCATION: Corso Europa

An excellent example of commercial design on a small scale.

Residential Unit In Galloretese Quarter (The Monte Amiata) (1969–74)
ARCHITECTS: Aldo Rossi with others
LOCATION: Gallaratese Quarter of Milan

A highly praised and criticized housing complex of extreme modern design.

NAPLES

Ipogeo (1982)
ARCHITECTS: G. Borrelii Rojo, A. Beraglia, and M. Bucchignani
LOCATION: nel Campo santo

A bold underground graveyard constructed of concrete.

Stazion Della Circumvesuviana (Administration Tower And Terminal For the Railroad Station) (1970)
ARCHITECTS: Giulio De Luca and Arrigo Marsiglia

LOCATION: On Corso Garbaldi

An outstanding modern complex that contrasts significantly with its downtown setting.

The University Theology Building (Nuova Facolia Teologica) (1969)
ARCHITECT: Alberto Izzo
LOCATION: Capolimonte, Naples

A strongly expressed work with a soaring, diagonally formed chapel.

Ziggurat (1968–70)
ARCHITECT: Francesco Di Salvo
LOCATION: della 167 di Secondigliano

A striking ziggurat-shaped complex with horizontal forms extending outward in an exaggerated manner.

PESCIA

Covered Market (1951)
ARCHITECTS: Brizzi, Gori, Gori, Ricci, and Savioli
LOCATION: Piazza del Mercato

An enormous and exciting sculptural concrete shell covering a vegetable and flower market.

PIEVE EMMANUELE

Pieve Emmanuele Civic Center (1971–81)
ARCHITECT: Guido Canella
LOCATION: c. 12 km. S of Milan on Rt. No. 412

A enormous and unusual complex of brutalistic architecture.

REDIPUGLIA

Sacrarium
ARCHITECT: Giovanni Greppi
LOCATION: SW of Gorizia

A great modern memorial to Italy's dead of World War I. An effective stepped design leads up to the hillside monument.

ROME

Faculty Of Mathematics Building (1934)
ARCHITECT: Gio Ponti
LOCATION: Rome University campus

One of Ponti's first important designs employing the latest technological developments of the time.

Monte Dei Paschi Agency (1974–78)
ARCHITECT: Paolo Portoghesi
LOCATION: Inquire: EPT di Roma (Information), via Parigi 11

New Wing For The Vatican Museum (Museo Gregoriano Profano) (1970)
ARCHITECTS: Vincenzo, Fausto, and Lucio Passarelli
LOCATION: Vatican City, N of the Pinocoteca Vaticana (Picture Gallery)

A marvelous modern extension that contrasts and yet is sympathetic with the baroque architecture and gardens. Interesting forms, arches, and columns are arranged around a series of courtyards and steps.

The Vatican Audience Hall (1972)
ARCHITECT: Pier Luigi Nervi
LOCATION: The Vatican in Vatican City, Rome

This large audience space features a ceiling constructed of 41 prefabricated, V-section, concrete ribs tapering from narrow to wide shapes.

SALERNO

Sacra Famiglia Church (1969–73)
ARCHITECT: Paolo Portoghesi
LOCATION: 30 miles SE of Naples

SAN FELICE

Art Nouveau Shop At San Felice Circeo (1970s)
LOCATION: On the coast about 100 km. S of Rome in Monte-Circeo

A flamboyant and imposing structure reminiscent of the Art Nouveau style.

SAN VITO DI ALTIVOLI

The Brion-Vega Cemetery (1980s)
ARCHITECT: Carlo Scarpa
LOCATION: Near Treviso

Ironically, the first funeral held in Scarpa's modern new chapel was Scarpa's.

SESTRIERE

RESIDENTIAL HOTEL (1981)
ARCHITECTS: Roberto Gabetti and Aimaro d'Isola
LOCATION: 8 miles E. of Montgenevre Pass, about 35 miles W. of Turin

With a strong emphasis on the horizontal line, this wood, glass, and metal complex nicely conforms to the sloping site and is a good example of Postmodern architecture.

TURIN

Fiat Works (1915–21)
ARCHITECT: Matte Trucco
LOCATION: S of Turin in the suburb of Lingotto

A reinforced concrete complex, including a testing run for Fiat cars.

Museum For Modern Art (1954–59)
ARCHITECTS: Carlo Bassi and Goffredo Boschetti
LOCATION: Corso Galileo Ferraris

Based on a Z-shaped plan, modern exhibits are interestingly displayed at various angles.

URBINO

Art Institute (1972–74)
Student Apartments (1963–66)
ARCHITECT: Giancarlo de Carlo
LOCATION: University at Urbino campus, 1/2 mile from city center

One of the most progressive universities in Italy, the university at first used two abandoned palaces. Since de Carlo's modern students' apartments were erected, the campus has added a number of interesting modern buildings including the Art Institute.

VENZONE

Town Hall (1982)
ARCHITECT: Roberto Pirzio Biroli
LOCATION: N.E. Italy, 4 miles N. of Gemona
del Fruili, about 100 miles NE of Venice

The first town hall in Italy designed in the
Postmodern style.

VERONA

Banca Popolare (1974–81)
ARCHITECTS: Carlo Scarpa and Arrigo Rudi
LOCATION: On the small Piazza Nogara
close to Piazza Bra

A fascinating concrete, brass, marble, mosaic,
and steel banking facility completed after
Scarpa's death.

Norway

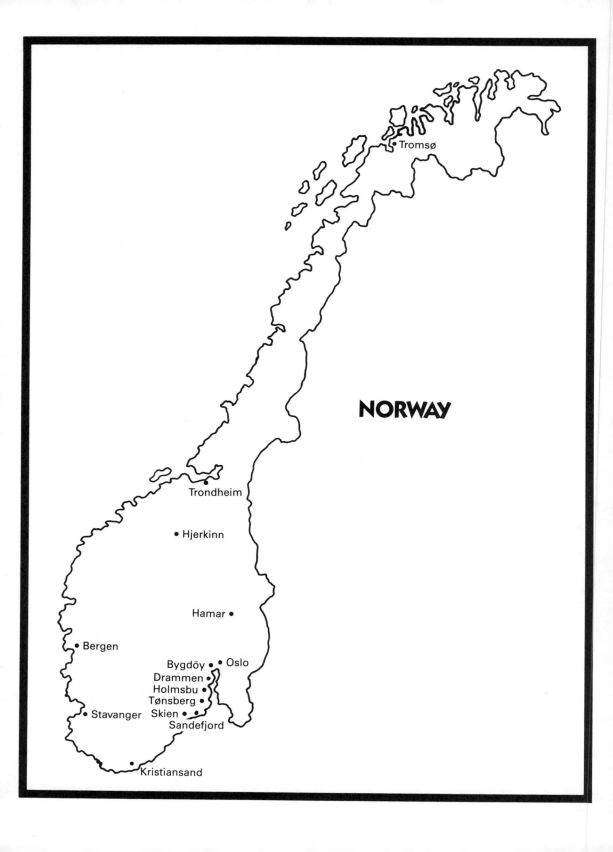

NORWAY

- Tromsø
- Trondheim
- Hjerkinn
- Hamar
- Bergen
- Bygdöy
- Oslo
- Drammen
- Holmsbu
- Tønsberg
- Stavanger
- Skien
- Sandefjord
- Kristiansand

MODERN ARCHITECTURE IN NORWAY

THE FIRST DECADES

During the first decades of the twentieth century traditional building forms dominated Norwegian architecture. As early as 1910, however, a few architects, including Bredo Greve and Olaf Nordhagen began designing in a clean structural style.

THE 1920's AND 1930's

By the 1920's and 1930's, the Bauhaus and International Style influenced many of the country's leading designers. Functionalism became an important element of architecture. The new architecture in Norway, however, was interpreted with special consideration for the country's vernacular and lifestyle.

POST WAR PERIOD

Post-War Norwegian architecture has been almost entirely modern in design. Today the architect is concerned with relating the client's functional requirements to the creation of beauty in both housing and commercial buildings. Norwegian architects know all aspects of technology and legislation in their field, but they are mostly concerned with well-being of their fellow human beings— a tradition of long standing in Scandinavia.

BYGDÖY

Norwegian Maritime Museum (Sjofartsmuseet) (1970s)

ARCHITECTS: Trond Eliassen and B. Lambertz-Nilssen with S. Nord
LOCATION: Bygdoynes, just W of Oslo

The attractive three-sided brick and glass structure is located on the waterfront, commanding a sweeping view of the ships and shoreline near Oslo. Triangular shapes are repeated everywhere, stressing the connection between the collections and the water below. From the balcony the visitor can experience the sensation of being on board a ship.

EYSTEIN

Church At Eystein (c. 1970)

LOCATION: On the E.6 Arctic Highway near Hjerkinn

With geometrically angled planes, the striking Church at Eystein makes a strong contrast to its natural setting high on a mountain plateau, a fascinating example of a new architectural approach in Norwegian ecclesiastical design. A white-rubble texture covers the concrete structure, topped with purple-gray roofing. Highlights of the building include an interesting modern rose window and wooden sculptural figure.

HAMAR

Museum In Storhamarlaven, Hamar (Hedmarksmuseet & Domkirkeodden) (Hamar Archeology Museum) (1970s)

ARCHITECTS: Sverre Fehn, Ovrum, and Schultz
LOCATION: SE Norway, 60 miles N of Oslo (W shore of Lake Mjøse) Strandveien 100

In response to the unusual challenge of preserving the existing remains of Hamar Bispegard and Storhamarlave, the museum is constructed as a "suspension museum," with ramps and catwalks through the ruins of the medieval palace. The design permits the visitor to experience history brought to life by observing the diggings firsthand. The design concept was created for both function and the visitor's enjoyment.

HOLMSBU

Holmsbu Art Gallery (Henrik Sorensen Museum) (1970s)

ARCHITECT: Bjart Mohr
LOCATION: SE Norway, 14 miles SE of Drammen

This inviting small gallery, built where Henrik Sorensen used to wander, houses some of the writer's treasures. In order to "disappear among the trees," the structure was built of timber and granite from the rock-strewn site. The gallery took many years to complete, lovingly built by Sorensen's old friends, including fishermen and farmers. The structural background, combined with natural materials, provides an effective setting for the displays.

OSLO

American Embassy (1955–59)

ARCHITECT: Eero Saarinen (USA)
LOCATION: Drammensveien 18

This internationally prominent Finnish-born American architect has built some of the world's most dynamic buildings. The bold and uniformly designed American Embassy is located on a restrictive site close to the palace. The unique facade of pulverized green-black granite produced in Norway provides an impressive surface that reflects the light. Interiors, landscaping, and details are beautifully executed throughout the complex.

OSLO

City Hall At Oslo (Radhuset) (1933–50)

ARCHITECTS: Arneberg and Poulsson
LOCATION: Pipervika Bay on Dokkveien

Situated on a prominent site by the waterfront, the majestic City Hall is Norway's first significant modern building. Constructed of dark red brick, the City Hall is an excellent example of Norwegian Nationalism popular at the time. This design approach has been combined with elements of the modern movement employed throughout the rest of Europe during the 1930s and 40s. Surrounding gardens, fountains, and plazas complement the complex in a manner that welcomes the visitor. Over two thousand yards of colorful mosaic in bold stylized designs wrap the interior walls of the main hall.

OSLO

Okern Old People's Home (1955)

ARCHITECTS: Sverre Fehn and Geir Grung
LOCATION: Okernveien and Nordalveinen

Sverre Fehn, one of Norway's most notable pioneer modern architects, gained world-wide recognition for the design of this Old People's Home. Inspired by the major modern movements in other countries of Europe, but interpreting the philosophy in his own terms, Fehn created this commendable complex reflecting his desire to create a place of warmth and welcome. The structural facility functions beautifully for its purpose.

OSLO

Ring House (Ringhuset) (Electronics Firm Gustav A. Ring A/S) (1970s)

ARCHITECTS: Torbjorn Rohdahl and others
LOCATION: Sorkedalsveien 33, Oslo 3

The dramatic horizontal forms of this five-story building for a large electrical concern are arranged in a diagonal tiered design. Slanted glass windows between rows of parapets accentuate the composition and also provide a panoramic view of the sloping wooded area and lake. The building in its country setting is compatible and engaging.

OSLO

Sandaker Center (1970s)

ARCHITECTS: John Eng's Arkitektontor A/A with Tore Drange, John Seip, and Hans Christie Bjonness
LOCATION: Vogts gate 67, Oslo 4

A functional and pleasant contemporary urban center, the Sandaker project serves over thirty thousand residents. The long, low complex is constructed of brick, glass, and steel unified by a network of interior pedestrian walkways. The new Sandaker Center's variety of facilities includes shops, restaurants, and other public services.

SANDEFJORD

Sandefjord Town Hall (1970s)

ARCHITECTS: Trond Eliassen and Birger Lambertz-Nilssen, with Finn Monies and Didrik Holm
LOCATION: 12 miles SSW of Tonsberg, SSW of Oslo

Exterior materials of brick, glass, and copper combine to create a stunning appearance. The same materials are found on the Park Hotel, a traditional landmark in Norway close to the new Town Hall—the architects wanted to link the two buildings without disturbing harmony and balance of the elements. The huge new building has a theater, concert hall, library, cafeteria, open-air theater, and office space.

SKIEN

Ibsen House At Skien (1970s)

ARCHITECTS: O. Fredrik Stoveland, H. Heyem, and I. Lykke
LOCATION: 65 miles SW of Oslo, South Norway

A lovely park-like setting provides the background for the ground-hugging Ibsen house. The building is a memorial to Norway's world famous poet and playwright whose works started a new trend in drama. (Ibsen was born in Skien.) The structural complex of wood and glass serves as a multi-activity center containing a drama theater, meeting rooms, and exhibition space arranged in a dramatic manner.

TROMSØ

Tromsdalen's Church (1965)

ARCHITECT: Jan Inge Hovig
LOCATION: 2 miles E of Tromso in Tromsdalen, Extreme N Norway, 9020 Tromsdalen

Situated in the far northern regions of Norway close to the Arctic Circle, this dramatic structure has been called "the Arctic Sea's Cathedral." Bold upward-reaching forms create a striking atmosphere. Enclosed at the peak of the soaring triangular facade of glass is a slender cross. Interior treatments and lighting complement the inspiring effect of this unique church. In 1972, Victor Sparre's brilliant stained-glass window of Christ was dedicated. The work covers an area of about 140 square meters with 86 lights set in concrete.

ADDITIONAL MODERN STRUCTURES OF INTEREST

BAERUM
Rudolf Steiner School At Baerum
ARCHITECT: Molle and Per Cappeien
LOCATION: County adjacent to Oslo
on the west

Based on the idea of an industrial hall, the
farmyard arrangement preserves the feeling of
an intimate design school.

BERGEN
City Hall At Bergen (Radhuset) (1970s)
ARCHITECTS: Herman Rolfsen and others
LOCATION: Town center, c. 300 miles
NW of Oslo

A uniform and simple complex made up of
facilities for the municipal administration of
Bergen.

BLINDERN
University Of Oslo (1930–)
ARCHITECTS: Bryn and Ellefsen
LOCATION: University of Oslo campus,
central N area of Oslo

A successful layout plan of tall and low
structures in a plain, functional manner.

DRAMMEN
**Bragernes Parish Center
At Drammen** (1970s)
ARCHITECTS: Ljoterud and Odegard
LOCATION: c. 25 miles SW of Oslo

An intriguing complex of concrete with
massive brick walls that join fifty old-people's
flats to the surroundings. A wavy, floating
shell roof dominates the design.

FANA
**Slatthaug Athletics And Swimming Hall
At Fana** (1970s)
ARCHITECTS: Olvind Maurseth

LOCATION: Suburb of Bergen, ca. 500 km.
WNW of Oslo

In an attempt to conform to the hilly site, the
architects depressed the structure into the
terrain.

HOVIK
Hovik Parish Center (1970s)
ARCHITECT: Thomas Willoch
LOCATION: Suburb of Oslo, 11 km. W of
city center

In order to incorporate the new parish
complex to the town's landmark, an ornate
neo-Gothic church, the architect designed a
simple, low structure with repeating circular
roofs.

KRISTIANSAND
**Administrative Headquarters For
A/A Avant** (1970s)
LOCATION: c. 150 miles SW of Oslo

This building is faced with Larvikit, a famous
type of blue and green stone found only on
Norway's south coast.

OSLO
Community Center West, Rea, (1970s)
ARCHITECTS: Gynt Krag and Preben Krag
LOCATION: ROA: Austiliveien 4, Oslo 7

The architect's goal was to integrate existing
buildings with this new Community Center to
form a market square.

Fellesbanken (1970s)
ARCHITECTS: Torp & Torp with others
LOCATION: Karl Johans gate 27

Situated on a busy corner site, the impressive
structure harmonizes with surrounding
buildings. A unique roof treatment.

Government Building Complex (1958)
ARCHITECT: Erling Viksjo
LOCATION: At Ibsen's Gate

An important example of early modern design in Norway after World War II.

Hotel Scandinavia (1970s)
ARCHITECT: Jan Lunding
LOCATION: Holbergs gate 30, Oslo 1

The commanding SAS Hotel contains 10,000 square meters of curtain wall built on black, anodized aluminum profiles.

Office Building—Norske Folk (1970s)
LOCATION: Platou, Oslo

A strong design emphasis on horizontal forms with depressed window bands.

Oslo Concert Hall (1972)
ARCHITECT: Gosta Abergh, MNAL (Sweden)
LOCATION: Munkedamsveien 14

A brilliant new concert hall that seats 1,600 in the large hall.

Solar Dairy (Indre Ostfold Meieri—Dairy Service) (1980s)
ARCHITECTS: Meierienes Bygnings Kontor-Dag Borgen with others
LOCATION: Mysen, near Oslo

A dazzling stainless steel and glass complex designed for a solar heating system accommodating the function of milk processing.

Sonja Henie And Niels Onstad Arts Center (1969)
ARCHITECTS: Jon Eikvar and Svein-Erik Engebretsen
LOCATION: On a hillside, a few miles S. of Oslo

An extraordinary leaf-shaped plan, this Arts Center blends nicely into its hillside setting featuring exhibit areas, an amphitheater, a restaurant, and a terrace. (Donated by the famous Norwegian ice-skater.)

Veslefrikk Cinema (1970s)
ARCHITECTS: Blakstad and Muntes-Kass
LOCATION: Roald Amundsens gate 4, Oslo 1

An unusual building project located under the Klingenberg cinema that functions as a small entertainment area.

STAVANGER

Stavanger Swimming Center (1970s)
ARCHITECT: Gert Walter Thuesen
LOCATION: c. 360 miles SW of Oslo on Western coastline

Norway boasts many fine sports centers accommodating the tremendous interest in physical fitness. This center is one of Norway's best.

TRONDHEIM

Trondheim University (1970s and 80s)
ARCHITECTS: Anne and Einar Myklebust, architects of the *LIBRARY*; Henning Larsen and others, architects
LOCATION: c. 318 mi. N of Oslo, S Shore of Trondheimsfjorden

One of the finest universities in Scandinavia, the new Trondheim campus is located in a beautiful natural setting just outside of Trondheim. A stunning series of glass covered "streets" connect many of the buildings.

Scotland

Elgin

Helensburgh

Dundee

Glenrothes

St. Andrews

Falkirk

Kilmacoln

Cumbernauld

Edinburgh

Glasgow

East
Kilbride

SCOTLAND

MODERN ARCHITECTURE IN SCOTLAND

CHARLES RENNIE MACKINTOSH

Scotland's break with traditional architecture, and in particular, the Gothic style, was ushered in by the brilliant designs of Charles Rennie Mackintosh at the turn of the century. His architecture and furniture innovations bridged the gap between the Arts and Crafts Movement, Art Nouveau, and the sophisticated International Style. Mackintosh's use of materials and geometric and structural designs influenced architects throughout Europe, becoming an important forerunner of modernism.

MODERN ARCHITECTURE IN SCOTLAND BEFORE WORLD WAR II

Beaux Arts architecture continued to dominate Scottish architecture during the 1920s and 1930s. Only a few public structures were built during this time—notably the government office in Edinburgh, St. Andrew's House by Thomas J. Tait.

MODERN ARCHITECTURE IN SCOTLAND POST WORLD WAR II

Plans for New Towns throughout Scotland became one of the principle concerns of architects in Scotland after World War II. Outstanding contributions in civic design and town planning in Scotland have been recognized internationally. Cumbernauld town is one of the best efforts and has been highly publicized. Since 1950, Scottish architects have embraced modern architecture, accepting new materials, concepts, and advanced technical possibilities. Leading architects include Sir Basil Spence and Sir Robert Matthew.

CUMBERNAULD NEW TOWN

Cumbernauld New Town (1956-)

ARCHITECTS: Hugh Wilson with others
LOCATION: 14 miles NE of Glasgow

This much-publicized new town is projected for seventy thousand inhabitants. The town center, half a mile long, includes shops, banks, restaurants, a hotel, a cinema, a swimming pool, a library, and play areas. An attempt was made to achieve the variety and life found in traditional Scottish cities, with mixed functions in the center of town. The focal point is a nine-story concrete tower that looms over the downtown section.

EAST KILBRIDE (LANARK)

St. Bride's Church And Presbytery (1960)

ARCHITECTS: Gillespie, Kidd, and Cola
LOCATION: 9 miles SE of Glasgow

Situated on a steeply falling hillside, St. Bride's Church with its soaring tower makes a dramatic silhouette on the horizon. The building, faced with rough-textured brick, is pierced with slender vertical and horizontal fenestration. The stone and brick floor's series of changing levels leads the eye toward the font. The effect is especially interesting.

EDINBURGH

Mortonhall Crematorium (1964)

ARCHITECTS: Sir Basil Spence, Glover, and Ferguson
LOCATION: Howden Hall Road

In a beautiful setting of dense woodland beside a stream, Sir Basil Spence has designed a vertical stone complex of light-colored stone that makes a dramatic contrast with the natural surroundings. The angled plan consists of a main chapel with a supporting smaller chapel and numerous other facilities for the mourner. Slender vertical slits of stained glass and lanterns on the roof wash the interior walls with light.

FIRTH OF FORTH

Bridge Over The Firth Of Forth (1881–89)

ARCHITECTS: Benjamin Baker and John Fowler
LOCATION: 9 miles W of Edinburgh

An astounding technical achievement in its time, this one-and-one-half-mile bridge has an unsupported span of 1,706 feet. The great Arts and Crafts leader, William Morris, took one look at it and said, "this is the ugliest thing I have ever seen!" The bridge was completely devoid of ornamentation, frankly revealing its construction, a design approach many despised in the late nineteenth century. Interestingly, the magnificent iron Eiffel Tower in Paris was completed the same year.

Glasgow School Of Art

(1897–1909)
ARCHITECT: Charles Rennie Mackintosh
LOCATION: 167 Renfrew Street

The brilliant design innovations of Charles Rennie Mackintosh rank as important trail blazers of modern architecture. The functional and ingeniously planned Glasgow School of Art, a masterpiece of early modern design, brought the architect international recognition. With asymmetrical detailing and composition, the structure is a good example of conservative Art Nouveau styling. Mackintosh also meticulously designed all the interior details and furnishings—mostly in a perpendicular style.

GLASGOW

Library At The University Of Glasgow (1965)

ARCHITECT: William Whitfield
LOCATION: Campus at University of Glasgow

The striking contrast of the slender modern tower complex with the traditional campus makes a dramatic impression. Charged with creating a simple "warehouse" plan with large spaces for effective library services, the architect designed large vertical clusters of cubes to house the multitude of library functions.

GLASGOW

Mains Street House

(Turn of the century)

ARCHITECTS: Charles Rennie and Margaret Mackintosh
LOCATION: Part of the University of Glasgow's Hunterian Art Gallery

The home and studio of Charles Rennie and his wife Margaret Mackintosh at 120 Mains Street was later recreated at the couple's new residence at 78 Southpark, which was in turn recreated faithfully as part of the University's Hunterian Art Gallery. The refined linear designs of Mackintosh feature leaded glass furniture, often painted white. The stark white interior was remarkable for this period.

GLASGOW

Queens Cross Church (1898)

ARCHITECT: Charles Rennie Mackintosh
LOCATION: 866 Garscube Road and Maryhill Road

This somber church by Scotland's greatest modern architect combines both Gothic and Art Nouveau forms. It is now the headquarters of the Mackintosh Society, founded in 1973 to protect and maintain the works of Mackintosh. The bold sculptural corner tower was inspired by a medieval church in Merriot in Somerset. The interior is surprisingly spacious and modern with frankly exposed steel girders and other structural supports. Furnishings and carved wooden detailing were also executed by the architect.

The Burrell Museum (1983)

ARCHITECT: Barry Gasson Architects
LOCATION: In Pollok Park

One of the most beautiful modern art museums in Europe, this structure is surrounded by a lovely wooded area. The building, constructed primarily of wood, stone, and glass, houses a collection of art owned by Sir William Burrell (1861-1958), a wealthy Glasgow shipowner. The architect, describing this museum said, "This was to be a museum in a park, not a city. This offered the opportunity of making the grass, the trees, the woodland plants, the bluebells and bracken, a context for the display of the collection." (*The Architectural Review*, Feb. 1984, page 34/2)

HELENSBURGH

Hill House (1902)

ARCHITECT: Charles Rennie Mackintosh
LOCATION: Upper Colhoqubon St.,
On A814 NW of Glasgow

Beautifully situated on a sloping landscaped hillside overlooking the Clyde estuary, Hill House is the largest and most exquisite of Mackintosh's domestic works. Constructed of local sandstone rough-cast rendered, the house has traces of the traditional Scottish baronial mansions. All the interior details were planned by Mackintosh, including furnishings and fittings. Particularly interesting is the livingroom fireplace and the white bedroom. The house, owned by the Royal Incorporation of Architects in Scotland, is open by appointment.

KILMACOLM

Windyhill (1900–01)

ARCHITECT: Charles Rennie Mackintosh
LOCATION: Rowan Treehill Road, a few
miles W of Glasgow

The work of Mackintosh was greatly admired
by America's Frank Lloyd Wright, and
Windyhill has often been compared to the
master's Oak Park homes in Chicago. Located
at the top of a steep hill, it is constructed of
strong rough-cast masonry walls and high-
pitched slate roofs. Interior details and
furnishings are ingeniously related to the
architecture.

ST. ANDREWS UNIVERSITY

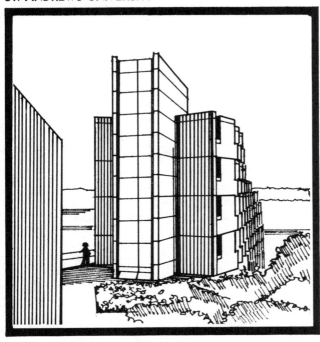

New Residence—Andrew Melville Hall (1964)

ARCHITECT: James Stirling
LOCATION: 13 miles SE of Dundee

Stirling, one of Scotland's foremost
contemporary architects, designed this
complex to include multi-faceted facades that
have provoked comparisons including "an
IBM card," "a great gray battleship," and "Op
Art sugar cubes." The architect is known for
many highly expressive projects employing
prefabricated concrete. The New Residence
has received international interest and
publicity.

ADDITIONAL MODERN STRUCTURES OF INTEREST

CAMELON

St. Mary Of The Angels (1960s)
ARCHITECTS: Gillespie, Kidd, and Cola
LOCATION: SE Stirling, W suburb of Falkirk

A unique and complex modern religious
building employing timber construction.

EDINBURGH

**Edinburgh College Of Domestic
Science** (1971)
ARCHITECTS: Renton Howard Wood
Associates
LOCATION: Edinburgh College campus

An unusual self-contained college comprised
of modern buildings.

**Arts And Social Sciences Building At
The Edinburgh Univ.**
ARCHITECTS: Sir Robert Matthew, Johnson-
Marshall, & Partners
LOCATION: Edinburgh University Campus

The dimensions of all elements and
components of this interesting building are
based on a fundamental unit of four inches.

**Chapel And Library At Edinburgh
University** (1950s)
ARCHITECT: Sir Basil Spence
LOCATION: Edinburgh University Campus

This modern complex is one of the architect's
finest works in Scotland.

St. Andrew's House (1930s)
ARCHITECT: Thomas J. Tait
LOCATION: Just below Calton Hill

One of the first modern public buildings in
Scotland. Structural design combined with
classicism.

ELGIN

New Town Hall At Elgin
LOCATION: 36 miles ENE of Inverness, c.
125 miles N of Edinburgh

A modern civic building demonstrating the
latest use of materials and technology.
Contrasts significantly with surroundings.

GLASGOW

**Nuclear Physics Building At Glasgow
University** (1950s)
ARCHITECT: Sir Basil Spence
LOCATION: Glasgow University Campus

Scotland Street School (1904–06)
ARCHITECT: Charles Rennie Mackintosh
LOCATION: Scotland Street, near Shilds
Road underground station

St. Columba's Church (1960s)
ARCHITECT: Anthony Wheeler
LOCATION: About 20 miles N of Edinburgh

An admirable example of modern religious
architecture, the parish church makes a
unique addition to the new town of
Glenrothes. Constructed of a pleasing
combination of brick, steel, and wood, the
church is in the form of a Greek cross. A
clean-structural interior provides a nice
background for mural paintings.

University Strathclyde (1960s)
ARCHITECTS: Various architects
LOCATION: George Street

An impressive new university boasting many
fine modern structures.

**Willow Tea Room (Now Part Of Daly's
Store)** (1901–04)
ARCHITECT: Charles Rennie Mackintosh
LOCATION: 199 Sauchiehall Street

Mackintosh designed a number of delightful
Tea Rooms for Miss Cranston. Simple
geometric forms and Art Nouveau designs
were employed.

Spain

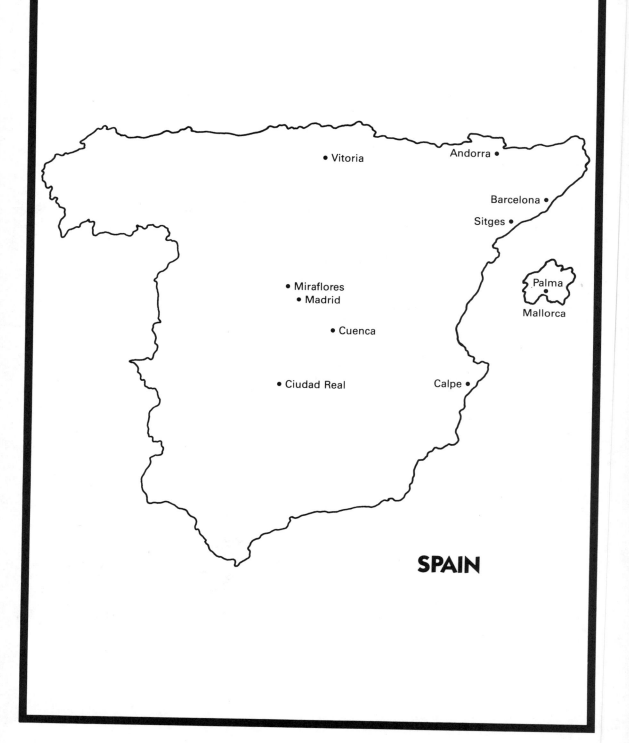

• Vitoria

Andorra •

Barcelona •

Sitges •

• Miraflores
• Madrid

Palma
•
Mallorca

• Cuenca

• Ciudad Real

Calpe •

SPAIN

MODERN ARCHITECTURE IN SPAIN

EARLY MODERN DEVELOPMENTS

As early as the 1880s Luis Domenech y Montaner began designing buildings that broke with traditional approaches. Although he incorporated historical Spanish and Moorish motifs in his work, Domenech y Montaner, along with Antoni Gaudi, was the leader of the modern movement in Spain. These two outstanding designers are national celebrities.

ANTONI GAUDI

Gaudi is one of the most imaginative if not the wildest of the designers during the Art Nouveau Period of 1890–1910. Gaudi's work incorporated a number of styles—Spanish, Moorish, Gothic—but interpreted in a modern manner. His remarkable structures have been enjoyed for many decades, especially his uncompleted Church of the Sacred Family. Gaudi was hit by a bus and killed in front of the church in 1926.

EDOUARDO TORROJA

Torroja pioneered pre-stressed concrete and gained an international reputation when he built his pavilions for the Zarzuela Race Course in 1933. He is also known in architectural circles for a number of influential books, especially *The Philosophy of Structures* (1958), and *Edouardo Torroja, an Autobiography of Engineering Accomplishment* (1958). Torroja trained the great Spanish-born Mexican architect, Felix Candela, in the use of reinforced concrete.

JOSEP LUIS SERT

Along with Torroja, Sert is considered the most important Spanish modern architect. Sert worked for a short period with Le Corbusier in Paris. Later he became Dean of the Harvard Graduate School of Design in 1953. He is known for large-scale buildings that show traces of folk architecture from his home country. He practiced architecture in the United States until his death in 1984.

CURRENT MODERN ARCHITECTURE

New, remarkably creative structures are being built in the modern style in Spain, designed by a number of well-known individualistic architects. Outstanding is the firm of Ricardo Bofill and Taller de Arquitectura.

ANDORRA

Sanctuary Of Meritxell (1979)

ARCHITECTS: Ricardo Bofill and Taller de Arquitectura
LOCATION: East Spain, 16 miles SW of Alcaniz. On a hill NE of town

The Sanctuary of Meritxell was built on the site of an earlier church destroyed by fire. The basic structure, with its flying modern Romanesque arches, is of brick block, concrete arches, and curved metal trusses covered with plywood. Polished black slate covered the interior floor spaces. The combination of copper sheathing, terrazzo, mirror, and brick creates a most unusual effect in the interior.

BARCELONA

German Pavilion At Barcelona Exhibition (1929)

ARCHITECT: Ludwig Mies van der Rohe (Germany)
LOCATION: In process of being rebuilt at Parque de Montjuich

Mies van der Rohe, Germany's foremost modern architect, was commissioned by the German Government to plan this hallmark of modern architecture. The revolutionary Pavilion featured open planning and an emphasis on structural materials and functional design. Detailing of the Pavilion, also planned by Mies, was superb. Mies designed his famous Barcelona Chair to complement the building's interior. Because of its architectural importance, the Pavilion, destroyed after the Barcelona Exhibition, is now being reconstructed.

BARCELONA

Battlo House (1904–06)

ARCHITECT: Antoni Gaudi
LOCATION: No 43, 1 Paseo de Gracia

Gaudi, Spain's visionary modern architect, designed the Battlo House for a textile manufacturer who wanted a "face-lift." Gaudi planned a facade that overwhelms visitors even today. The windows on the first floor feature deep egg-shaped stone frames. Exterior walls sparkle with a special texture created by Gaudi. The undulating balconies and supports have been compared to "bones."

BARCELONA

Casa Mila (1906–10)

ARCHITECT: Antoni Gaudi
LOCATION: Paseo de Gracia, No 92

The Casa Mila is one of Gaudi's best known works and has been photographed often for books and articles on architecture. The massive structure, occupying a unique corner site, features a serpentine facade of cut stone, inspired by ocean waves. Decorative Art Nouveau iron railings with their organic forms contrast with the structural background and provide interest. Unusual sculptured chimney pots highlight the building.

BARCELONA

Casa Vicens (1883)

ARCHITECT: Antoni Gaudi
LOCATION: Les Carolines, 24

Gaudi, with Luis Domenech y Montaner and Francesco Berenguer, worked in the English Arts and Crafts tradition, incorporating the ideals of William Morris from England. They are considered the earliest exponents of modernism in Spain. Gaudi is known as the most flamboyant and imaginative of the designers of Art Nouveau, a style he wholeheartedly embraced at the turn of the century. For the Casa Vicens, Gaudi incorporated delightful Moorish motifs.

BARCELONA

Church Of The Sacred Family (1883–1927)

ARCHITECT: Antoni Gaudi
LOCATION: East on Calle de Provenza, Calle Mallorca

Tourists flock to Barcelona to see this unfinished structure, one of the most fantastic ever designed. Construction still continues according to Gaudi's original plans. Employing past styles, particularly Gothic, Gaudi has created a modern fantasy of Art Nouveau. The church boasts four expressive mosaic towers and surfaces heavy with organic decoration of all types. Gaudi was killed by a streetcar in front of the church in 1927.

BARCELONA

Guell Palace
(Palacio Guell) (1885–90)

ARCHITECT: Antoni Gaudi
LOCATION: In Calle del Conde de Asalto, on left

Built for Gaudi's wealthy patron, the Guell Palace has a rather gloomy and austere facade. A highly decorative entry gate and sculptural chimney pots relieve large areas of plain stone construction. The simple exterior is contrasted inside by a wealth of decoration interestingly employed. Today the Palacio Guell houses a Museum of the Theater.

BARCELONA

Miro Foundation (Centro De Estudios De Arte Contemporaneo) (1974)

ARCHITECT: Josep Luis Sert (USA)
LOCATION: Avenida del Estado, Parque de Montijich

This internationally prominent architect has designed creative structures in many countries, especially in the United States, where he now practices. The striking Miro Foundation houses the works of Joan, Spain's famous modern artist. The whitewashed building interprets a Spanish flavor in an innovative contemporary approach.

BARCELONA

Parque Guell (1900–14)

ARCHITECT: Antoni Gaudi
LOCATION: North of town, Olot, s/n

Commanding a panoramic view of Barcelona, the extraordinary Parque Guell is a favorite meeting place for Gaudi admirers. Here the architect had full opportunity to freely express himself. There are whimsical structures everywhere. A meandering mosaic lizard greets the visitor on the entry steps. A playground with mosaic snake-like benches around the perimeter is supported beneath by a forest of heavy columns. Fanciful forms, buildings, grottos, and other sites are placed throughout the park. The *MUSEO GAUDI* in the park is also worth a visit.

BARCELONA

The Church At Santa Coloma (1908–14)

ARCHITECT: Antoni Gaudi
LOCATION: Santa Coloma Colonia Guell— Santa Coloma de Cervello

The lines and forms of the Church at Santa Coloma can be confusing to the visitor expecting traditional symmetry. Four central pillars of stone seem to buckle under the stress of the heavy roof. Wood benches with organic carved motifs in the Art Nouveau style were designed by the architect to further express the flowing forms of the structure.

BARCELONA

Villa 'El Capricho (1888–90)

ARCHITECT: Antoni Gaudi
LOCATION: Comillas (Santander)

One of Gaudi's most whimsical residential designs, this is one of his most photographed. Gaudi differs from other pioneer modern architects in his great creativity for each individual project. He uses decorative masonry for the Villa 'El Capricho, with colorful decorative tile and mosaics fashioned in awesome arrangements.

BARCELONA

Walden 7 (1972–76)

ARCHITECTS: Ricardo Bofill and Taller de Arquitectura
LOCATION: Sant Just, d'Esvern, Carretera Reial

Bofill is one of the most outstanding modern architects in Spain, responsible for many dramatically designed housing complexes throughout Spain and France. In the Walden 7 structure, twenty-seven stories with occasional projecting cylinders punched with holes create a unique staggered effect. The complex design has been admired around the world.

CIUDAD REAL

City Hall (1970)

ARCHITECT: Fernando Higueras
LOCATION: Town center, 100 Miles S of
Madrid

From a distance this compelling structure
suggests architecture from the past. On closer
inspection, however, modern materials such
as concrete and steel become apparent,
employed in a delightful manner. Four spear-
like towers pierce the sky and add drama to
the structure. A large pebble-concrete plaza
leads up to the new "pre-cast Gothic" City
Hall.

CUENCA

Museo De Arte Abstracto Español (1950s)

DESIGNERS: La Generacion Abstracta
LOCATION: Barrio de San Martin

Three of Cuenca's famous cliffhanging houses
have been renovated and reorganized in an
exciting contemporary manner to house a
marvelous collection of modern art by some
of Spain's most important artists. The
beautiful setting with a panoramic view below
the steep hillside is breathtaking. The
museum is an ingenious marriage of art,
architecture, and location.

MADRID

Edificio España (1949)

LOCATION: Plaza de España

Most Spanish architecture since the Civil War and World War II has been modern in expression. The stepped multi-storied buildings in the Plaza de España integrate basic structural design with decorative crowning similar to the Art Deco style of the 1920s and 1930s in America. A rooftop restaurant and swimming pool are housed within the striking structure. An early modernistic monument honoring Cervantes stands in front of the Edificio de España.

MADRID

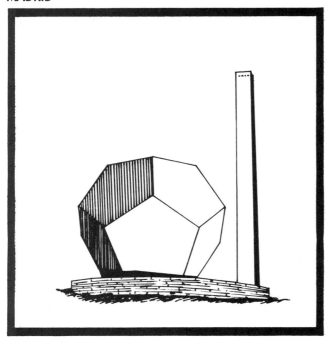

Instituto Tecnico De La Construccion Y Del Cemento

ARCHITECTS: Eduardo Torroja with Echegaray and Barbero
LOCATION: Costillares (Chamartin)

This complex of buildings engineered by Spain's famous pioneer of reinforced concrete functions as a postgraduate school and research center. A number of buildings on the campus are noteworthy, including the sculptural coal bunker. Torroja has created a striking structure out of what would be ignored by less sensitive architects.

MADRID

Pavilions Of The Zarzuela Race Course (1935)

ARCHITECT: Edouardo Torroja
LOCATION: Zarzuela, Madrid

Torroja is one of Spain's most important early modern architects, internationally known for his innovations in employing reinforced concrete. The Pavilions of the Zarzuela Race Course, Torroja's best known work, are engineering masterpieces. A series of remarkable fluted concrete cantilevers extend dramatically over the seating area. Torroja was so confident in the potential of reinforced concrete that he felt this medium would support any architectural idea.

MADRID

School Center In The University City

ARCHITECT: Miguel Fisac
LOCATION: Ciudad Universitaria de Madrid, NW Madrid

Fisac, known for his brilliant modern church at Vitoria, designed this admirable addition to the University of Madrid. With an emphasis on function, Fisac planned attractive lecture halls, laboratories, administrative space, and other facilities. The Ciudad Universitaria has become a center for advanced technology and architectural progression in Spain.

MADRID

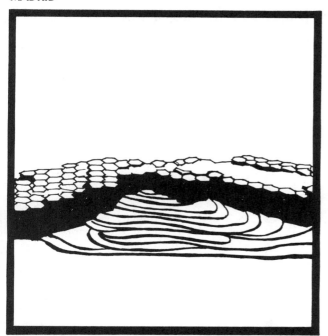

The Spanish Pavilion From The Brussels' World Fair (1958)

ARCHITECTS: Jose Antonio Corrales and
Ramon Vazquez Molezun
LOCATION: Casa de Campo,
outside of Madrid

This delightful Pavilion, erected at the
Brussels' World Fair, was dismantled and
reconstructed in Madrid after the exhibition
was over. Hexagonal shapes are arranged in a
progression of varying heights that are
effectively lit with clerestory windows. The
same spirit of graduating levels is carried out
by a tiered grand entrance. The light and airy
clusters house a number of public facilities.

MALLORCA

Studio For Joan Miro (1955)

ARCHITECT: Josep Luis Sert (USA)
LOCATION: Palma de Mallorca

Whitewashed walls of this studio for one of
Spain's most beloved modern artists dazzle in
the hot Spanish sun. High walls built of stone
masonry typical of this Mediterranean island
location are connected with flights of stone
stairs that lead up to the two levels of the
house and studio. Bold concrete in curved
and straight forms makes a striking
background for Miro's abstract art. Huge fixed
windows with colorful hinged wooden panels
are highlighted against the plain white walls.

SITGES

La Muralla Roga
(The Red Wall) (1975)

ARCHITECTS: Ricardo Bofill and Taller de Arquitectura
LOCATION: On the Mediterranean, 5 miles E of Villanueva

Painted in a range of strikingly brilliant reds, this controversial housing complex makes a commanding silhouette on the Spanish coastline. The much-photographed complex is composed of a fascinating configuration of four-unit clusters in a " + " plan. In this latest phase of La Manzanera, sometimes referred to as "The Red Wall," Bofill has sought a functional, economical, and creative solution to architectural problems.

SITGES

Los Tres Coronas
(Three Crowns) (1967)

ARCHITECTS: Ricardo Bofill and Taller de Arquitectura
LOCATION: By La Muralla Roga

Each of the square units of Los Tres Coronas is a self-contained apartment hotel. Note the three-crown motif on the top unit. The entire complex has been compared to Moshe Safdie's famous Habitat '67 built for the World's Fair at Montreal in 1967. The Three Crowns, which Bofill refers to as "Kafka's Castle," is painted a strong purple hue. Like the Muralla Roga close by, Los Tres Coronas has provoked much comment ranging from outlandish to outstanding.

VITORIA

Church Of The Coronation Of Our Lady (1960)

ARCHITECT: Miguel Fisac
LOCATION: Calle de Eulogio Serdan

The Church of the Coronation of Our Lady makes a powerfully direct statement in its use of strong materials interestingly softened by the filtered light of stained-glass windows. Walls designed in a serpentine form are balanced by a starkly straight wall. The dramatic result is emphasized by light pouring across the altar, highlighting a slender stylized crucifix designed by Pablo Serrano.

VITORIA

The Church Of Our Lady Of The Angels (1959)

ARCHITECTS: Javier Carvaljal Ferrer and Jose Garcia de Paredes
LOCATION: Calle Norte-Sur at Calle Bastiturri

A unique aspect of this extraordinary church is its continuity of triangular form—the site is a triangle, and the structure picks up this theme with dramatic effects. The garden entrance introduces soaring forms of brick, wood, and slate. Light streams between the "floating" roofs and wall. A suspended angel by J. Garcia Donaire hovers over the altar.

ADDITIONAL MODERN STRUCTURES OF INTEREST

BARCELONA

Church Of The Sagrada Corazon De Jesus (1961)
LOCATION: On a hill by the Tibidabo Station from Calle de Balmes.

Concrete Factory Converted Into Architect's Office For Ricardo Bofill and Taller De Arquitectura (1972–76)
ARCHITECTS: Ricardo Bofill and Taller de Arquitectura
LOCATION: Juan Sebastian Bach, 28

Vigorous forms of a previous concrete factory provide office space for one of Spain's most important architectural firms.

Icart Perfume Factory (Fabrica Traci) (1978)
ARCHITECTS: L. Cantallops, J. Martinez, E. Torres, M. Espar
LOCATION: Guipuzcoa, 159

A striking ten-story building emphasizing a strong vertical line, designed for a large perfume firm.

Museo De Arte Moderno
LOCATION: Parque y Jardines de la Ciudadela

A new addition to Palacio Real.

Casa Lleo Morera (Turn of the century)
ARCHITECT: Domenech y Montaner
LOCATION: Inquire at the Avenida de Jose Antonio for directions.

An interesting work by one of Spain's important early modern architects. Open to the public.

BURGOS

New Theater At Burgos (1967)
ARCHITECT: Fernando Higueras
LOCATION: N Spain, 130 miles N of Madrid

Higueras has received many honors and awards throughout Europe for his innovative work.

CALPE

Xanadu (1967)
ARCHITECTS: Ricardo Bofill and Taller de Arquitectura
LOCATION: Along the coast SW of Barcelona

Beautifully situated on a slope overlooking the sea, the structure of seventeen apartments is designed in an exciting mixture of curves, cantilevers, and paraboloids.

MIRAFLORES DE LA SIERRA

Summer Home For Children
ARCHITECTS: J. A. Corrales, R. V. Molezun, and A.d.l. Sota.
LOCATION: 45 miles North of Madrid

A commendable summer home, nestled in the hillside, for about 100 boys and girls.

MADRID

Teatro Real
LOCATION: Opposite the Palace, entrance in Plaza Isabel II

A new modern facility for the performing arts.

Sweden

SWEDEN

- Kiruna
- Luleå
- Umea
- Sundsvall
- Storsatern
- Idre
- Mora
- Gävle
- Fors
- Uppsala
- Eskilstuna
- Stockholm
- Vallingby
- Nyköping
- Oxelösund
- Göteborg
- Borås
- Varnamo
- Halmstad
- Angelholm
- Klippan
- Orrefors
- Helsingor
- Kalmar
- Hoor
- Lund
- Malmö
- Ronneby

MODERN ARCHITECTURE IN SWEDEN

THE STOCKHOLM EXHIBITION OF 1930

A number of Swedish architects made impressive contributions to the modern movement during the first decades of the twentieth century, but most art historians pinpoint the real beginning of modern Swedish design to the year 1930, the date of the great Stockholm Exhibition. Gunnar Asplund planned the Stockholm Exhibition and designed some of the buildings. The theme for the exhibition was "More beautiful things for everyday life," a philosophy still important in Scandinavian design today. This exhibition introduced to the public light and airy buildings with clean, pure design. The impact of the exhibits, structures, and projects for functional living made a tremendous contribution to the development of modern architecture and design in Scandinavia.

GUNNAR ASPLUND, PETER CELSING, SIGURD LEWERENTZ, AND SVEN MARKELIUS

These architects pioneered modern architecture in Sweden. Aware of major movements in modern architecture throughout Europe, they adopted ideas to the Scandinavian lifestyle, developing design with special considerations for their unique environment and traditions.

MODERN ARCHITECTURE IN SWEDEN TODAY

Sweden has a reputation for a high standard of living with excellent facilities for both residential and commercial buildings. Architects from Sweden consider the function of a structure without sacrificing beauty and comfort. Design solutions incorporate the latest technical advancements, materials, and space planning. Concern for man and nature is always effectively blended into many aspects of the total environment. Some of the leading modern architects are Tage Hertzell, Bengt Lindroos, Carl Nyren, Wello Uuskyla, Sten Samuelson, Ralph Erskine, and many other designers of a new generation of architects creating some of the world's finest buildings.

ANGELHOLM

Town Hall In Angelholm (1975)

ARCHITECT: Sten Samuelson
LOCATION: c. 25 miles NNE of
Helsingborg, city center

Commanding a prominent position in
downtown Angelholm, this unique Town Hall
is arranged in a "boomerang" shape to
accentuate the winding River Ronne close by.
The effect is intriguing. Repetitive arches
follow the meandering structure's ground-
hugging form. The Town Hall by Samuelson,
one of Sweden's most esteemed modern
architects, is considered one of the nation's
finest new public buildings.

FORS

Cardboard Factory (1953)

ARCHITECT: Ralph Erskine
LOCATION: North of Avesta and Krylbo,
107 miles NW of Stockholm

Erskine, the English-born Swedish architect,
has met the challenge of creating a suitable
factory for manufacturing cardboard, a
process requiring air so hot and cold it could
affect the materials used for construction. He
ingeniously employed materials, form, and
space to solve these problems with an
aesthetically pleasing design. The undulating
facade captures the spirit of the natural
surroundings.

GÄVLE

Crematory Chapels (1959)

ARCHITECTS: Engstrom, Landberg, Larsson, and Torneman
LOCATION: New City Cemetery, via Rikshuvudvag 10

Crematory chapels abound in Sweden, and this structure is one of the best. The building blends harmoniously with the pine forest. The effect of seemingly suspended planes of glass and wood is carried throughout the interior as well. The complex, composed of three chapels, is built around open courtyards that unify the structures.

GÖTEBORG

Art Museum At Göteborg (1968)

ARCHITECTS: White Arkitekter AB
LOCATION: Goteplatsen

The modern addition to Göteborg's Art Museum adds to its aesthetics as well as to its function. The gleaming small wing contrasts significantly with the huge existing traditional structure. The lower wing features a new main entrance, restaurant, additional exhibition space, and other facilities. The higher wing, facing the park, is a terraced room connected to the main art museum. The art is greatly enhanced by the clean structural background of the new addition.

HALMSTAD

Martin Luther's Church In Halmstad (1970)

ARCHITECTS: Bertil Engstrand and Hans Speek
LOCATION: 70 miles SE of Goteborg

A nationwide competition was held to select the architect for this place of worship. The winning architects integrated harmoniously modern expression. The exterior features a strong repetitive line that is capped by a softly rolling roof. The sacristy, nave, aisles, and tower are reminiscent of traditional building approaches. The principal worship room accommodates four hundred people.

HELSINGBORG

City Theater At Helsingborg (1974–75)

ARCHITECTS: Arton Consulting Architects, Ltd.
LOCATION: Kal Johans gata 1

The modern City Theater is close to the *CONCERT HOUSE* built in the 1920s by early modern architect Sven Markelius. The complex is an appealing arrangement of tiers, angles, and rounded forms providing facilities for a variety of activities associated with the performing arts. The intimate auditorium, seating up to six hundred people, is designed for varying set changes.

HELSINGBORG

Office Building— Frigoscandia (1969)

ARCHITECT: Sten Samuelson
LOCATION: Rusthallsgatan 21

Located just south of the city's center on a lovely sloping site, the fan-shaped building juts out dynamically toward the sound. Anodized aluminum and heat-reflecting glass were selected to withstand the salty winds of the locality. Housed inside are offices, conference rooms, an auditorium, a lobby, and other functional facilities for the seventy employees. The esteemed architect has designed modern commercial structures around the world.

HOOR

The Chapel At Hoor (1971)

ARCHITECT: Bernt Nyberg
LOCATION: Parish of Hoor, 20 miles NE of Lund

Two impressive free-standing roofs in square forms are constructed of concrete waffle slabs supported on steel columns, providing unique lighting treatment within. Textural play of light on natural building materials is evident throughout the chapel. Classic modern "ant" chairs by the internationally known Danish designer, Arne Jacobsen, make up the seating arrangement.

Majolkudds Church (1969)

ARCHITECT: Bertil Franklin
LOCATION: 450 miles NNE of Stockholm

The enhancing setting plays up a slender blue bell tower that functions as a focal point for the church. The entire building group is sheathed with multi-colored natural ceramic blocks that create an innovative contrast with the natural surroundings. Brilliant light reflection makes the huge multi-faceted dome look like a huge rock crystal. Harmonious interior backgrounds complement the exterior design.

LULEÅ

Shopping Center (1960)

ARCHITECT: Ralph Erskine
LOCATION: Storgatan at Kungsgatan

Erskine, born and trained in England, practices architecture in Sweden. He has received international acclaim for his innovative design solutions, and the shopping center at Lulea is one of his finest. Only seventy miles from the Arctic Circle, Lulea has a severely cold climate. Erskine planned a warm and inviting enclosed shopping complex geared for comfort and convenience without loss of aesthetic appeal. The massive enclosure also provides facilities for amusement and cultural activities.

MALMÖ

Caroli City (1970s)

ARCHITECTS: Various architects and town planners
LOCATION: Downtown Malmo, Southern Sweden

Caroli City is a unique five-block urban development consisting of over one thousand dwellings. Included in the huge project are offices, shops, a park, and hanging gardens. The area of former slum dwellings has been turned into a beautiful environment for living that has been much applauded in Sweden. In the shopping center note the dazzling floating glass sculpture "Dream of the Flying City" by Bertil Vallien. The project was designed to depict a balloon and a zeppelin.

MALMÖ

City Theater At Malmö (1943)

ARCHITECTS: Hellden, Lallerstedt, and Lewerentz
LOCATION: Fersensvagen and Ronneholsmvagen

Situated at the end of Malmö's main street, the City Theater makes a commanding impression, especially at night when lights flood the building and grounds. The theater is regarded as one of Europe's finest. The spacious interior houses well-designed promenades, staircases, a snack bar, and the theater itself. A smaller actors' theater adjoins the larger structure.

MALMÖ

Malmo Art Gallery (1975)

ARCHITECT: Klas Ansheim
LOCATION: Malmohusvagen

An inviting visual experience for the museum goer, the Malmo Art Gallery is constructed of concrete, aluminum, and glass. Untreated spruce floors run throughout the entire complex, integrating the exhibit areas. Huge skylights enhance the workshop and exhibit areas. The architect, in order to save a large tree, modified his design by bending a wall.

ORREFORS

Orrefors Exhibition Hall And Museum (1957)

ARCHITECT: Bengt Gate
LOCATION: 26 miles NW of Kalmar

Swedish glass design is known over the world for its beauty and excellence of craftsmanship. The Exhibition Hall and Museum are superbly arranged to display the exquisite glass objects. Lighting is artfully placed, and the open and closed cases further play up the glassware. The sleek museum is close to the old Orrefors factory, and the *KOSTA GLASS MUSEUM*, thirteen miles away, is also of interest.

OXELÖSUND

St. Botvid's Church (1957)

ARCHITECT: Rolf Bergh
LOCATION: Kyrkogatan, Oxelosund—SW of
Stockholm near Nykooing

St. Botvid's Church, set on a hill by a small fishing village, is remarkable. The structure's peculiar shape has been compared to a giant buoy standing protectively on shore. It functions both as a religious building and as a beacon. The raw concrete is reminiscent of the traditional wooden towers so admired by the rest of the world. The interior treatment is intricate, busy, and perhaps a little distracting.

STOCKHOLM

City Hall (1911–23)

ARCHITECT: Ragnar Ostberg
LOCATION: Waterfront at end of Norr
Malarstrand

Beautifully situated on the edge of Lake Malaren, the Stockholm City Hall is Stockholm's most popular landmark. The stately buildings are arranged around open courtyards that are neatly landscaped. The building, with simplified traditional overtones, is constructed of dark red brick. The 144-foot-long Golden Hall is covered with impressive mosaics in stunning stylized designs. The City Hall has been called "the most beautiful building of this century in Europe."

STOCKHOLM

Forest Crematorium (1941)

ARCHITECT: Gunnar Asplund
LOCATION: Sockenvagen, via Gotgatan and
Nynasvagen

Forest Crematorium, one of the pioneer
modern architect's most memorable works,
was finished shortly before his death in 1940.
The simple structures of the chapel and the
symbolic cross are set in a beautifully
landscaped setting, also created by Asplund—
the relationship between nature and
architecture is superb. An inner courtyard
was planned around a stylized sculpture by
Joel Lundqvist.

STOCKHOLM

Garnisonen—Office Building (Government Building) (1970s)

ARCHITECT: Tage Hertzell
LOCATION: Entire block, situated on
Karlavagen

The Garnisonen Office Building complex is
one of the largest office buildings in all of
Europe, providing working space for nearly
three thousand people. Emphasis was placed
on efficiency, without sacrificing comfort and
beauty. Glass, concrete, and metal combine in
an effective arrangement of form and space.

STOCKHOLM

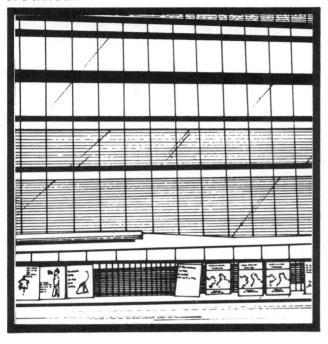

Kulturhuset— "The House Of Culture" (1968–73)

ARCHITECT: Peter Celsing
LOCATION: At Sergel's Square, Sergels Torg

The brilliant glass-walled "House of Culture" in the center of Stockholm houses exhibition space that opens onto Sergel's Square. Other facilities include a library, a theater, an auditorium, cafes, a children's section, a workshop, and Stockholm's information center. A large flat roof space functions as an outdoor exhibit area. Complementing the reflective facade of the structure is a super-elliptic fountain.

STOCKHOLM

Parliament Building (1968–71)

ARCHITECT: Peter Celsing
LOCATION: Sergelstorg

The Parliament Building is one of Sweden's finest modern structures, admired internationally. Sheathed with gleaming stainless steel, the structure makes a dazzling impression on Stockholm's skyline. The large complex boasts one of the world's most efficient and beautiful parliament rooms. The interior and furnishings throughout the complex are harmoniously planned to complement the architectural background.

Stockholm City Library

(1924–28)

ARCHITECT: Gunnar Asplund
LOCATION: Sveavagem 73

On the waterfront park, the Stockholm City Library, with its cleanly simple exterior, is a landmark of modern design in Sweden. Originally, the library was planned to feature the more traditional dome over a rotunda. Instead, the innovative "circle within a square" design was employed by the architect, a complete departure from more conventional design.

Stockholm Exhibition Buildings (1930)

ARCHITECT: Gunnar Asplund
LOCATION: Massvagen 1

Few countries can pinpoint an actual starting date for modern design, but the great Stockholm Exhibition, spearheaded by Asplund, marked a significant beginning in Sweden. The theme for the modern exhibition was "More beautiful things for everyday life." Asplund built structures that were light, airy, and functional, setting a high standard throughout Scandinavia and bringing international recognition to Asplund's work.

Stockholm's Savings Bank (1970s)

ARCHITECT: Carl Nyren
LOCATION: On corner of Hamngatan and Regeringsgatan

This streamlined building is located in a new area of Stockholm called the "Brunkeberg." A continuous multi-leveled horizontal glass treatment is accented by the sharp, gabled roof line. With its first floor raised to accommodate shops and other facilities, this is one of Nyren's most interesting accomplishments.

STOCKHOLM

The Stockholm TV Tower (Kaknas Tower) (1970s)

ARCHITECT: Bengt Lindroos
LOCATION: Morka Kroken

A familiar landmark on the Swedish horizon, the Stockholm TV Tower looms 155 meters high. It is the tallest structure in all of Scandinavia. The boldly formed tower was made of concrete employing an advanced sliding form technique. The slender tower gains interest with the sandwiched concrete slabs that angle outward.

STOCKHOLM

Storkallan's Chapel Crematory At Nacka (1968–70)

ARCHITECT: Wolfgang Huebner
LOCATION: Nacka, just E of Stockholm, SE of Alta gard along Tyresobaden

The soaring bell tower of Storkallan's Chapel can be seen for a great distance; it serves as an effective focal point for the structure. An interesting U-shaped plan accommodates two small chapels and a number of other religious facilities with a clean, simple, and direct design throughout.

STOCKHOLM

Swedish Film Institute (Filmhuset) (1971)

ARCHITECT: Peter Celsing
LOCATION: North Stockholm, university campus

Designed the same year as the House of Culture, the Swedish Film Institute is equally fascinating. The complex is constructed of raw concrete slabs covering a steel support. Housed inside this special building for the university are a theater, film studios, cinemas, and a national film library.

STOCKHOLM

Trade-Union Center
(Folkets Hus) (1960)

ARCHITECT: Sven Markelius
LOCATION: Barnhusgatan, Stockholm

The Folkets Hus, built on a limited site in an older section of Stockholm, has an impressive combination of facilities—meeting rooms accommodating from 25 to over 1,500 persons, a theater, a restaurant, a congress hall, and offices. These facilities are ingeniously arranged to take best advantage of the available space. Folkets Hus is one of the great architect's most important works.

STOCKHOLM

University Of Stockholm
Library (1983)

ARCHITECTS: Ralph Erskine, Bengt Ahlqvist, Peter-Ove Skanes, and Erich Muhlbach
LOCATION: Universitetsvagen 10, S-106, campus

The extraordinary new Library at the University of Stockholm is Erskine's latest project. Of the impressive structure *Architectural Review* wrote: "Ralph Erskine has never been reluctant to exploit technology but, in his lifelong pursuit of an architecture intended to enhance humanity, he has never worshipped the machine and its products. Instead, he has used them to give new freedoms to the people who use his buildings. Nowhere can this approach be more clearly seen than in his new library."

STORSATERN MOUNTAIN

Church In Storsatern,
Idre (1968)

ARCHITECTS: Jack Hanson and Gosta Lilliemarck
LOCATION: At Storsatern Mountain, close to the Norwegian border, NW Sweden

The Storsatern Mountain Chapel mirrors the majestic surrounding Norwegian mountain range. The stern triangular design has been compared to a "giant lapp kut" (hut). Constructed of huge laminated beams anchored into the ground, the entire structure is completely faced with tarred wood shingles that blend harmoniously with the natural terrain.

SUNDSVALL

Nacksta Church At
Sundsvall (1968–71)

ARCHITECT: Peter Celsing
LOCATION: At Sundsvall 200 miles N of Stockholm

The first impression of the Nacksta Church is a dynamic ship's form nestled in the trees. Two strong horizontal glass window bands emphasize the curving form of the structure. Two levels contain a myriad of functional facilities, including areas for photography, sewing, hobbies, and play areas, in addition to spaces for religious activities.

VALLINGBY

Satellite Town Of Vallingby
(From 1956)

ARCHITECTS: Sven Markelius and others
LOCATION: Bergslagsvagen—via
Drottningholmsvagen

Known as one of Sweden's finest "new towns," Vallingby is Markelius' greatest architectural contribution. As chief planner for the monumental project, the architect arranged marvelous living areas around parks. Motor vehicles are restricted in many sections of the town, and there are well planned facilities for shopping, cultural and sports activities, amusement, and other commercial establishments. Markelius, influenced by Le Corbusier, was one of the first architects to introduce the International Style to Scandinavia—reflected in the design approach at Vallingby.

VALLINGBY

Vasterort Church (1956)

ARCHITECT: Carl Nyren
LOCATION: Vallingbyvagen 186

Vasterort Church has a marvelous interior arrangement of materials, light, form, and space. Nyren was faced with the challenge of giving the church a separate identity from the high rise structure that had to be attached due to development restrictions. The surface treatment of raw concrete combined with acute angles provides the church with its own character.

ADDITIONAL MODERN STRUCTURES OF INTEREST

BORÅS

Grand Hotel (1970s)
ARCHITECT: Wello Uuskyla
LOCATION: 35 miles E of Goteborg

A fine example of the type of deluxe modern hotel built in Sweden since World War II to accommodate the tourist boom. The main facade is covered with fiberglass-reinforced polyester sheets combined with natural aggregate stone.

ESKILSTUNA

Froslunda Centrum (1957)
ARCHITECTS: Jan Hojer and Sture Ljungqvist
LOCATION: Skogstorpsvagen at Sturegatan, 79 miles W of Stockholm

Froslunda Centrum is a unique and inviting residential and shopping complex for a nearby industrial city.

GOTHENBURG (GÖTEBURG)

Church At Gothenburg (Härlanda Church) (1958)
ARCHITECT: Peter Celsing
LOCATION: Harlandavagen 23

Known for his striking Parliament and House of Culture designs in Stockholm, Celsing is particularly noted for his many modern churches throughout Sweden. The church at Gothenburg is one of his best.

Court House At Gothenburg (1937)
ARCHITECT: Gunnar Asplund
LOCATION: Gustaf Adolfs Torg 1-2

A simple and complementary addition to an existing traditional building by Sweden's great pioneer modern architect. The frame of the new building expresses the pilasters of the old structure.

Kviberg Crematorium (1938)
ARCHITECT: Gunnar Asplund

LOCATION: Kortedalavagen

Known for his many crematorium projects, Asplund designed the Kviberg Crematorium during the last few years of his life.

Masthugg Church (1916)
ARCHITECT: Sigried Eriksson
LOCATION: Storabackagatan

One of the very earliest departures from eclecticism in Sweden, the Masthugg Church is more structural in design with limited ornamentation.

Ostra Nordstan Commercial Centre (1959)
ARCHITECTS: White Arkitektkontor AB
LOCATION: Just north of the city, Spannmalsgatan

Originally, the design consisted of two buildings with a covered street for pedestrians—now the plan has expanded to include a hotel, offices, and more shops.

Recreation Building For SKF Kristinedal (1971–73)
ARCHITECTS: Contekton arkitektdontor
LOCATION: Byfogdegatan 2

A streamlined glass-walled structure that houses numerous facilities including a large restaurant, a swimming pool, a hall for sports, an exhibition hall, and education and employment office space.

KALMAR

St. Birgitta Church At Kalmar (1973–75)
ARCHITECTS: Ove Hidemark and Goran Mansson
LOCATION: 190 miles SSW of Stockholm

Heavy brick masonry, wood, and steel are combined with a colorful mosaic ceramic flooring for this distinctive contemporary religious building.

KIRUNA

Kiruna Town Hall (1963)
ARCHITECT: Artur von Schmalensee
LOCATION: c. 165 NW of Lulea, N Sweden

The design of this well-known modern town hall reflects the wealth and dignity of this mining town. A dramatic emphasis on the square building is a soaring cast iron clock tower.

KLIPPAN

St. Petri Church At Klippan (1966)
ARCHITECT: Sigurd Lewerentz
LOCATION: Just SE of Angelholm

Built of brick, a material much loved by Swedish architects, St. Petri Church is considered one of Sweden's classic modern designs.

LUND

Park Recreation Center (1977)
ARCHITECT: Bengt Edman
LOCATION: In the People's Amusement Park at Trollebergsvagen

A delightful complex that replaces an old dance rotunda. Built of wood, brick, and glass in a triangular form, the building functions as a dance hall, a theater, and a place for various other recreational activities.

Sparta Student Centre, Tunavagen (1971)
ARCHITECT: Bengt Edman
LOCATION: Tunavagen, Lund

This large masonry structure has a facade highlighted with changes in form and line. Facilities include an auditorium, club rooms, shops, offices, and other student services.

MALMÖ

Chapel At Malmö, South Crematorium (1944)
ARCHITECT: Bengt Nyman
LOCATION: Inquire: Tourist Information, Hamngatan 1

This simple chapel is one of many in Sweden by the great early modern architect and is considered one of his finest.

County Administration Offices At Malmö (1972–74)
ARCHITECT: Bengt Nyman
LOCATION: Inquire: Tourist Information, Hamngatan 1

A principal design concern for this well-planned office building was efficiency without sacrificing an attractive appearance. A pedestrian bridge spans the area.

Ostra Kyrkogarden Cemetery (1969)
ARCHITECT: Sigurd Lewerentz
LOCATION: Inquire: Tourist Information, Hamngatan 1

A starkly executed structure, the cemetery was one of Lewerentz's last works. It was designed for the sale of flowers on the cemetery grounds.

MORA

St. Michael's Chapel (1954)
ARCHITECT: Borje Blome
LOCATION: Cemetery at Mora, 220 Miles NW of Stockholm

An interesting feature of this modern church is a stunning mosaic cross of black, gray, and white located behind the altar.

RONNEBY

Addition To Ronneby Brunnshotell (1971)
ARCHITECT: Sten Samuelson
LOCATION: c. 235 miles SW of Stockholm, on the S Coast

The new hotel addition is interestingly terraced, with the structures integrated with the surrounding hillside.

STOCKHOLM

Farsta New Town (1960–)
ARCHITECTS: Stockholm Town Planning Office and others
LOCATION: Agestavagen (via Nynasvagen)

Located south of Stockholm, Farsta is a sister "new town" to Vallingby to the west and helps contribute to a more pleasant environment for its residents, away from city congestion.

Gallerian Pedestrian Mall (1970s)
ARCHITECTS: Malmquist & Skooghs
LOCATION: Runs the block called Storviggen from Hamngatan in the north to Jakobsgatan in the south.

A handsome indoor pedestrian shopping street that has dramatically high ceilings.

Huddinge University Hospital (1971–75)
ARCHITECTS: HLLS Arkitektkontor AB
LOCATION: SW Stockholm, Halsovagen, S-141

The largest health care complex in Sweden, boasting all the latest technical advancements and medical facilities.

Loen, Government Office Building (1970s)
ARCHITECT: Nils Tesch
LOCATION: Corner of Jakobsgatan and Karduansmakargatan

A variety of government departments are located in this structural complex. A unique treatment of arched windows was selected to enhance the design.

The National Bank Of Sweden (1975–76)
ARCHITECT: Peter Celsing
LOCATION: Brunkebergstorg 11, S-111

The dignified National Bank of Sweden is considered one of the country's most beautiful structures.

The Royal Technical Institute School Of Architecture (1970)
ARCHITECT: Gunnar Henriksson
LOCATION: By Ostermalm's street pattern

Containing lecture rooms, offices, workshops, and studios, this functional structure is part of the Technical Institute of Stockholm.

St. Marks Church (1955)
ARCHITECT: Sigurd Lewerentz
LOCATION: Skarpnack, Stockholm

Rough textured brickwork is expressively employed in this commendable church. It is considered one of Lewerentz's finest works.

Scandia Cinema Center (Now the Cinema Look) (1922–1923)
ARCHITECT: Gunnar Asplund
LOCATION: Drottninggatan 82, S-111

Asplund, one of Sweden's most important modern architects, has created a fantasy design for movie-goers with the creation of the Scandia Cinema Center.

Stockholm Building Society (1953)
ARCHITECT: Sven Markelius
LOCATION: Noorlandsgaten

One of Markelius' many well-designed structures that have received national praise.

Stockholm Underground Stations, Jarva Line, Taby Line, Botkyrka Line (1973–78)
ARCHITECTS: SL Arkitektkontor, Michael Granit, and Per Reimers
LOCATION: Network of stations under central Stockholm

A marvelous underground "modern cave" environment. The unusual modern plan is efficient and functional for the task. Many artists have contributed to the design of these underground stations in Stockholm.

Student Center And University Of Stockholm (1970s)
ARCHITECTS: Ralph Erskine and others
LOCATION: University of Stockholm campus, Universitetsvagen 10 S-106

The university campus boasts many excellent examples of modern building design including Ralph Erskine's well-planned Student Center.

Sverigehust, Sweden House (1969)
ARCHITECT: Sven Markelius
LOCATION: In Hamngatan at west corner of Kungstradgarden

The Tourist Travel Association and the Tourist

Center Information Stand are just a few of the facilities located in this well-designed structure planned by one of Sweden's most illustrious modern architects.

Varby Church (Varby Gards Church) (1975)
ARCHITECT: Harald Thafvelin AB
LOCATION: S Stockholm, Varby Alle 5, S-143

Vivid forms and colors are arranged in a delightful and functional manner for this parish and youth center.

UMEA

Alidhems Church At Umea (1973–74)
ARCHITECT: Carl Nyren
LOCATION: 320 Miles NNE of Stockholm, just NE of Umea

Nicely sited on a hill in the middle of a housing area, the church of glass, steel, and natural materials is arranged in a neat unified box plan.

UPPSALA

Student Union (1963–66)
ARCHITECT: Alvar Aalto (Finland)
LOCATION: Uppsala University campus, 40 miles NNW of Stockholm

An individualistic artistic expression by the world famous Finnish architect with a special regard for the indigenous regional characteristics of Sweden.

VALLINGBY (STOCKHOLM)

Church At Vallingby (1960)
ARCHITECT: Peter Celsing
LOCATION: Inquire: Sverigehuset, Hamngatan 27, Stockholm

Celsing is especially noted for his brilliantly designed churches throughout Sweden. A striking feature and focal point on this church is a soaring, open concrete tower enclosing twenty-two bells.

VARNAMO

Church Square And City Hall (1961–69)
ARCHITECT: Carl Nyren
LOCATION: 40 miles S of Jonkoping, South Sweden

The Town Square, as well as the surrounding buildings, were designed by Nyren, one of Sweden's best known modern architects.

Switzerland

SWITZERLAND

MODERN ARCHITECTURE IN SWITZERLAND

Modern movements in England, France,
Germany, and Austria had little influence
in Switzerland before Moser.

CARL MOSER

This important Swiss architect trained at the
Zurich Technical High School and the Ecole
des Beaux Arts in Paris. After a partnership
with Curjel in Karlsruhe, Germany, from 1888
to 1915, Moser settled in Zurich. His buildings
of simple, plain concrete were some of the
first modern structures in Switzerland. Moser
is particularly famous for his modern
churches. His most notable work is St.
Anthony's Church at Basel.

LE CORBUSIER

Charles Edouard Jeanneret, known as Le
Corbusier, was born at La Chaux-de-Fonds.
With Frank Lloyd Wright in America, Alvar
Aalto in Finland, and Ludwig Mies van der
Rohe in Germany, he is one of the four great
titans of modern architecture. Le Corbusier
rejected the traditional Beaux Arts education
and trained with Auguste Perret in Paris and
Peter Behrens in Germany. After extensive
travel he settled in Paris, where he opened
his own practice on the Rue des Sevres. He
developed modern approaches to architecture
that are still influential throughout the world.
He coined the aphorisms, "A house is a
machine for living," and "All houses should
be painted white—by law!"

CURRENT MODERN ARCHITECTURE
IN SWITZERLAND

The Swiss have built many modern hotels and
resorts to accommodate foreign visitors to
their country. Traditional Swiss Chalet style
remains dominant. But numerous modern
private and public buildings can be seen
throughout Switzerland, especially in large
city centers.

BADEN

The Home Of Sculptor Hans Trudel (Galerie Trudel-Haus) (1969–70)

ARCHITECTS: Urs Burkard, Adrian Meyer, and Max Steiger
LOCATION: In the historical part of town, 13 miles NW of Zurich

This structure of steel framework and wood floors was added to the existing house for use as gallery space with three floors of exhibition area. Concrete columns and prefabricated vaults were used to build the annex. On the lower level a portico leads to the gallery and a cafeteria. The entire complex is beautifully terraced into its town setting, complementing the traditional architecture.

BALDEGG

The Motherhood Of Sisters Of Divine Providence (1968–72)

ARCHITECTS: Marcel Breuer (USA) with others
LOCATION: SE shore of Baldeggersee

This large Swiss convent has been described as "a rectangular island floating in a sea of apple trees." The complex is constructed of precast concrete and rubble stone arranged around four courtyards. Deeply set windows placed on an angle add interest to the design. Facilities include a chapel, a dining hall, a library, classrooms, offices, and private areas for the Sisters, postulants, and novices.

BASEL

All Saints Church (1953)

ARCHITECT: Hermann Baur
LOCATION: Neubadstrasse at Laupen-Ring

Baur has designed many impressive modern structures in Switzerland including this fine example of ecclesiastical architecture. The exterior of gray brick set in a concrete frame conveys a simple and dignified appearance. The interior is harmoniously integrated on a light scale with slender concrete columns, delicate barrel-vaulting, and lacy window grills. The soft gray-and-white color scheme accents the dark granite altar.

BASEL

St. Anthony's Church (Antoniuskirche) (1926)

ARCHITECT: Professor Karl Moser
LOCATION: Kannenfeldstrasse 4056

The design of St. Anthony's Church won Moser international acclaim and is considered the early modern architect's finest work. The structure is Switzerland's first modern church and is regarded as a national treasure. Built primarily of concrete, the triple-nave basilica is softened by large stained-glass windows designed by Hans Stocker and Otto Staiger. The church is noted for its clean, simple architectural treatment.

BASEL

Stadttheater At Basel (1969–75)

ARCHITECTS: F. Floor, R. Gutmann, H. Schupbach, and F. Schwarz
LOCATION: Central Basel by the Cathedral, on Theaterstrasse 4051

The city theater commands a prominent position in the heart of Basel. The unconventional structure features a diagonally stepped area with a striking prow-shaped exterior. Close by is an old church that contrasts with the sleek modern design of the new theater. A nicely landscaped square introduces and welcomes the visitor to the facilities.

BERNE

Halen Estate, Near Berne (1959–61)

ARCHITECTS: Atelier 5 (Eritz, Gerbers, Hesterberg, Hostettler, Morgenthaler, Pini, and Thormann)
LOCATION: 4.5 kilometers N of Berne

This fascinating modern community perches high on a hilltop overlooking the river. The complex consists of seventy-four privately owned terrace houses, a swimming pool, a playground, woods, a clubroom, and other common facilities for the residents. Halen Estate served as an early prototype for the condominium plans popular in the United States today.

BETTLACH

Roman Catholic Church—St. Klemens (1965–68)

ARCHITECT: Walter M. Forderer
LOCATION: A few miles NE of Biel

Among the remarkable architectural contributions of Switzerland are the striking modern churches found throughout the mountainous countrysides. Many are constructed of raw concrete like the Church at Bettlach. The focal point of this building is a unique belfry of staggered forms and voids that culminate around a simple cross. Inside, solid dark oak furnishings bring a warmth to the building materials.

BIEL

Congress Hall With Swimming Bath (The Programme) (1961–66)

ARCHITECTS: Max Schlup with others
LOCATION: 17 miles NW of Berne

This immense modern public center consists of a large convention building, three halls, a restaurant, swimming pools, a gymnasium, a school of sciences, offices, and other public facilities. The trendsetting structure of reinforced concrete, aluminum facades, and glass windows is punctuated by dynamic forms and materials.

BRIG

Parochial Center At Brig (1968–69)

ARCHITECTS: ACAU (M. Baud-Bovy, J. and N. Iten, M. Rey, J.P. Dellenbach, and R. Gaulis)
LOCATION: 26 miles S of Interlaken

The commanding church center radiates outward from a central tower. In an attempt to integrate the modern complex with surrounding traditional Swiss architecture, the architects employed corresponding building materials of plastered brick, timber and asbestos-cement. The fan-shaped church seats 750 persons, the parish hall 400. A strong, rectangular bell tower tops the structure, creating an interesting focal point.

CHAMBÉSY

The Center Of The Orthodox Church (1976)

ARCHITECT: A Bugna
LOCATION: A few kilometers N of Geneva, on W shore of lake

Beautifully situated on a green hillside overlooking Lake Geneva, the Center of the Orthodox Church makes an impressive sight. The structure was built around the lovely old trees and integrated into the gentle slope through a stepped terrace plan and the use of rounded achitectural forms. Strong architectural forms contrast with the natural setting, bringing variety to the large complex.

CLARENS-MONTREUX

The Karma House (1904–06)

ARCHITECT: Adolf Loos (Austria)
LOCATION: East Shore of Lake Geneva, just north of Chillon

One of the first examples in Switzerland of modern residential design. Loos, the great Austrian architect, was an important pioneer for the modern movement in Europe. The rectangular Karma House, built on an old farm site, demonstrates the architect's use of simple, direct planning. Many critics of the time denounced this structure as radically austere.

DORNACH

Goetheanum Dornach So. (1925–26)

ARCHITECT: Rudolf Steiner
LOCATION: 5 miles S of Basel

This powerfully expressive structure functions as a meeting place for the Anthroposophical Society of which Steiner was a member. The Goetheanum seems to have been organically sculpted in bold deep forms—a new approach made possible at the time with reinforced concrete. The structure is one of the first and most important examples of Expressionist architecture in Switzerland, a movement popular in Germany during the 20s and 30s.

GENEVA

The International Conference Center At Geneva (1970–72)

ARCHITECTS: Francis Gaillard, Alberto Camenzind, and others
LOCATION: Rue de Voreuble, 15

This superb example of space planning provides areas for conference halls, foyers, offices, restaurants, a television studio, a post office, a communications exchange, and other facilities. A flexible diagonal arrangement allows maximum efficiency. The mammoth complex has a striking facade constructed primarily of brush-hammered reinforced concrete colored with iron oxide.

GRENCHEN

Park Theater And Hotel At Grenchen (1949–55)

ARCHITECT: Ernst Gisel
LOCATION: Bahnhofplatz, SW Switzerland, 6 miles W of Solothurn

An inviting modern tourists' accommodation and theater located close to Berne, the popular mountain retreat is located in a beautiful natural setting. Gisel is known for his innovative use of form, space, and materials. The walls of the complex are of brick and the roof is copper. A wide courtyard provides an ideal setting for a delightful abstract sculpture by Max Bill.

LA CHAUX-DE-FONDS

The International Museum Of Watches (Musee International D'Horlogerie)

(1974)

ARCHITECTS: Pierre Zoelly and Georges-Jacques Haefeli
LOCATION: 9 miles NW of Neuchatel

The architects have created a subterranean structure in a park setting instead of building a tall structure for this brilliant museum complex in Le Corbusier's hometown. With only entrance and roof visible, the structure allows constancy of air and light for the precious watch collections.

LANGENDORF

The Ecclesiastical Center (1970–71)

ARCHITECTS: M. Pauli with W. Egli and W. Ledermann
LOCATION: Adjacent to Solothurn 25 miles S of Basel

This large complex, one of the first religious centers in Switzerland and one of the most impressive, is a meeting place for both Protestant and Catholic congregations. The dual center has a common plaza channeling traffic to all functional areas. The boldly formed buildings were constructed of prefabricated concrete elements clad with marble and white cement. The complex makes a striking contrast to the natural surroundings.

LICHTENSTEIG

Church Of Saint Anthony (1968–70)

ARCHITECT: Walter Förderer
LOCATION: c. 20 miles SW of St. Gallen, just N of Wattwil

This intriguing religious building radiates outward in stepped blocks of concrete. The asymmetrical massing of forms is repeated in the landscaping and retaining wall. The hillside setting complements the staggered forms that culminate in a clock tower. Straight lines and angled forms enhance a simple cross placed to the side of the walkway. The original and imaginative structure is one of Forderer's best-known works.

LUCERNE

Art Gallery And Congress Hall (Kunstmuseum) (1930–33)

ARCHITECT: Armin Meili
LOCATION: Robert-Zund Strasse 1, near the Bundes-platz

The Art Gallery and Congress Hall complex is one of the first buildings of modern structural design in Lucerne. The simple, uniform design functions admirably for its purpose. The flexible plan allows the art gallery space to be transformed easily into a functional congress hall with fifteen conference rooms.

LUCERNE

High-Rise Block
(Wohnhochhaus) (1965–68)

ARCHITECT: Alvar Aalto (Finland)
LOCATION: Wohnhochhaus Schonbuhl

A titan of modern architecture, this Finnish
designer and architect was awarded
numerous commissions outside his home
country. Aalto planned this fourteen-story
apartment block to connect with a shopping
center. An arrangement of staggered angles
contains 83 flats interestingly positioned
relative to the sun. The plan is typical of
Aalto's concern for creating pleasing human
environments. Aalto was known as "the
humanist architect."

LUCERNE

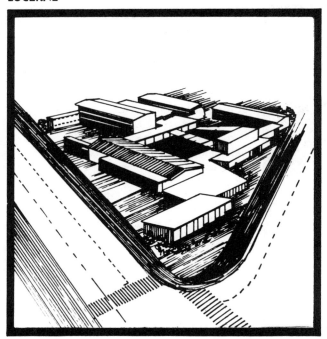

Museum Of Transport And
Communications (1959)

ARCHITECTS: Otto Dreyer with Jean Huber
LOCATION: Lidostrasse at Seeburgstrasse

Adults as well as children are intrigued by the
exhibits of all types of water, land, and air
transport at this large modern museum
complex. The architects had the challenge of
housing such exhibits as locomotives and
streetcars in a setting that would enhance the
visitor's experience. The natural and artificial
lighting of the interior is superb. An old Swiss
steamboat, the oldest in the country, functions
as a restaurant and snack bar in the
courtyard.

LUGANO

Chiesa Di Cristo Risorto (1975)

ARCHITECT: Rino Tami
LOCATION: By the Lugano Cemetery

This severe but fascinating Roman Catholic Church and Funeral Chapel is set close to the cemetery. The plan is based on strong diagonal forms and lines accentuated by raw concrete inside and outside. Natural lighting washes the altar wall, playing up an interesting abstract wall design that functions as a focal point in the chapel.

MOSCIA, TESSIN (PORTO RONCO)

The Koerfer House (1964–67)

ARCHITECTS: Marcel Breuer (USA) with R. Meyer
LOCATION: Hills above Porto Ronco, overlooking Lake Maggiore (privately owned)

This terraced house cascades down a rugged hillside overlooking Lake Maggiore. The design combines elements of the International Style, that Breuer, the famed German-American architect, helped to develop, with new architectural techniques. Rubble walls contrast with large panels of glass and exposed concrete that complement the natural surrounding environment.

PASSUGG

Evangelist Church
At Passugg GR (1971–72)

ARCHITECTS: Andres Liesch, with R. Vogel
and A.P. Muller
LOCATION: A few kilometers SE of Chur

Perched dramatically just above the road from
Chur to Tschiertschen, this small but
delightful church introduces the small village
of Passugg. Exposed concrete, employed for
both the interior and exterior, makes a
significant impression against the sloping
green mountain setting. A copper and wood
roof effectively contrasts, with the raw
concrete, adding interest to the structure. The
sharp angles of the church echo the feeling of
the surrounding mountain terrain.

RIGI KALTBAD

The Protestant Church
(Evangelisch-Reformierte)
(1962–63)

ARCHITECTS: E. Gisel with others
LOCATION: North Central Switzerland
between Lake Lucerne and Zug

Designed mainly for tourists, this church is
situated on a steep mountainside surrounded
by tall trees. The building faces away from
the panoramic view, distinguishing it as a
place of worship and meditation. The
unimposing church is built below the
entrance level in an interesting composition
of right angles and straight lines.

SAINT GALLEN

Municipal Theater (Stadttheatre) (1964–68)

ARCHITECTS: C. Paillard with H. Gugler
LOCATION: NE Switzerland by Lake Constance

This boldly expressive hexagonal building is situated in a lovely public park. The primary construction material for both interior and exterior is raw concrete. That textural effect combined with dynamic forms creates a stimulating environment for the performing arts. The strong design of the complex makes a vivid impression in its setting.

SAINT GALLEN-WINKELN

Bruder-Klaus-Kirche At St. Gallen-Winkeln (1959)

ARCHITECT: El Brantschen
LOCATION: Hauptstrasse

A commendable Catholic Church located in an industrial area just west of the city. A sweeping concave roof suspended over a square plan provides a dynamic feeling. The extraordinary interior space is emphasized by the bold waving form of the ceiling and soft shafts of light that flood the simple altar wall.

SCHWARZENBURG

The Schwandbach-Bridge (1933)

ARCHITECT/ENGINEER: Robert Maillart
LOCATION: 9 miles SW of Bern

This world famous designer began building extraordinary concrete bridges as early as 1901. He created over forty revolutionary bridges in his lifetime. The imposing Schwandbach-Bridge, spanning a deep ravine, is one of his most photographed projects. The graceful bridge is constructed on an elliptical groundplan that allows easy continuity of the roadway.

VADUZ

The Center For Art (1975)

ARCHITECT: Riccardo Porro
LOCATION: NE Switzerland, S of Lake Constance by Buchs

The art center, tucked away from the main stream of tourist traffic, provides a festive atmosphere for the exhibits of paintings, books, and sculpture. Areas for displaying art are combined with spaces for concerts, readings, and lectures. Fascinating swirls of lines and forms are created in steel and concrete. Vertical aluminum sections anodized in black and gold are integrated with gilt panels and white walls.

VEVEY

"En Bergère," International Headquarters Of Nestlé (1956–64)

ARCHITECT: Jean Tschumi
LOCATION: In a park on the shore of Lake Geneva, W of Vevey

Attractively located in a well-landscaped park, the Headquarters for Nestle's chocolate manufacture makes an impressive sight. A huge concrete slab supports the steel frame that is raised above ground level by a series of flayed columns. The enormous Y-shaped complex was awarded the Reynolds prize for the use of aluminum in architecture in 1960.

WALCHWIL

The Small Protestant Church (1963–64)

ARCHITECT: Hans-Peter Ammann
LOCATION: South of Zurich on the Zugersee

This small but dynamic church of exposed concrete perches high on a projecting hillside. Visible from the Gotthard Road, the church clearly contrasts with its beautiful natural setting. The strong diagonal shape of the structure is further emphasized by its diagonal placement on the terrain. An interior spiral staircase leads up to the nave, where 120 seats are placed diagonally on the square floorplan.

ZUG

Terrace Apartments (Terrassenhauser At Zug) (1958–61)

ARCHITECTS: Fritz Stucky and Rudolf Meuli
LOCATION: 18 miles South of Zurich

A creative development of 25 blocks, the extraordinary complex is supported on stepped concrete walls that conform to the steep slope of the mountainside. The apartments vary in size, with a spacious terrace provided for all units—a remarkably attractive architectural solution for a difficult site. The terraces command a breathtaking view of the Zugersee.

ZÜRICH

Annex To The Art Museum (1973–75)

ARCHITECTS: Erwin Muller and others
LOCATION: Inquire: Zurich Information Ctr., Railroad Station (Bahnhofstrasse)

The architects have created a daylight museum through the use of prismic skylights supported in a free-span steel roof truss. The ground floor descends three levels to an outside entry area crowded with old trees. An unusual exhibition area fills four levels free of solid partitions. The delightful arrangement is as engaging as it is effective for its function.

ZÜRICH

Centre Le Corbusier (1966–67)

ARCHITECT: Le Corbusier
LOCATION: Hoschgasse, in the Zurichhorn Park

Le Corbusier, one of the world's most important pioneers of modern architecture, was born in Switzerland. Located in the Zurichhorn Park by the Lake of Zurich, this Pavilion is based on modular dimensions. It was commissioned by Heidli Weber as an exhibition space for Le Corbusier's work. Paintings, sculpture, and graphic art are wonderfully arranged in the uniform and simple structure. A good example of the International Style that Le Corbusier promoted.

ZÜRICH

Church Center (1975)

ARCHITECT: Walter Moser
LOCATION: Leimbach, Pfarrzentrum

Tightly situated on a steep hillside close to the station, the Church Center features the nave at its highest level. An open courtyard directs foot traffic to various facilities, including community and club rooms. A unique combination of dark-blue glazed tile on the church and belfry gives the center individuality. Walter Moser is one of Switzerland's most prominent modern architects and has designed many outstanding structures.

ZÜRICH

Doldertal Apartments (1935)

ARCHITECT: Marcel Breuer
LOCATION: Inquire: Zurich Information Ctr.,
Railroad Station (Bahnhofstrasse)

Breuer, the famous Bauhaus member who
fled Nazi Germany before World War II,
received a number of important commissions
abroad after setting up practice in New York
City. Employing design theories from the
International Style, the Doldertal Apartments
are situated at an angle to the street to take
full advantage of the southern exposure for
the terraces. The steel, brick, and asbestos
cement structure features a garden space
between its two blocks.

ZÜRICH-ALTSTETTEN

Reformed Church (1941)

ARCHITECT: Werner Moser
LOCATION: Badener Strasse at
Pfarrhausstrasse

Moser sympathetically planned this new
Reformed Church to complement an old
church nearby. Natural light streaming
through vertical and horizontal window strips
is soft and subtle, emphasizing an interesting
wall screen behind the altar. Unexpected
angles lend additional interest to the church.

ADDITIONAL MODERN STRUCTURES OF INTEREST

BALERNA

Craft Center (1977–79)
ARCHITECT: Mario Botta
LOCATION: Far S. Switzerland, 4 miles NW of Como, Italy

This Craft Center was designed by one of Switzerland's most innovative architects.

BASEL

Bis (Bank For International Settlements)
ARCHITECTS: Burckhardt & Partner
LOCATION: Centralbahnplatz 2, near Central Station

One of the most interesting modern banking towers in Switzerland.

Bruder Klaus Church At Birsfelden, Basel (1958)
ARCHITECT: Hermann Bauer
LOCATION: Hardstrasse at Im Lerchengarten

The Cantine And Administrative Building (Geigy Ltd) (1966)
ARCHITECT: Martin Burckhardt
LOCATION: Ciba-Geigy, Schoren

European World Trade And Convention Center (1984)
ARCHITECTS: Architect's collaborative, Suter & Suter in charge
LOCATION: Riehenring 45

This impressive new center is one of Europe's finest.

Johanneskirche (Church) (1936)
ARCHITECTS: K. Egender and E.F. Burckhardt
LOCATION: Metzerstrasse and Mulhauerstrasse

Museum Of Contemporary Arts (1980)
ARCHITECTS: Wilfried & Katharina Steib, Architekten BSA/SIA
LOCATION: St. Alban-Tal 2

This fascinating and structural building is an extension of an ancient factory, providing an excellent background for art exhibits.

Reformierte Tituskirche (The Church Center) (1964)
ARCHITECT: Benedikt Huber
LOCATION: im Tiefen Boden 75

University Library (1964–68)
ARCHITECT: Otto
LOCATION: Near Petersplatz at the University of Basel

BELLINZONA

Museo Civico Nei Castello De Montebello (The Storza Castello) (1974)
ARCHITECTS: Mario Camp, Franco Pessina, Niki Pizzoli
LOCATION: 92 miles SE of Berne, a few miles E of Locarno

A modern museum nestled by an old 13th–14th century castle.

BUCHS

Katholische Church Herz Jesu (1963–65)
ARCHITECT: J. Dahinden
LOCATION: c. 20 miles SE of St. Gallen

A square church plan placed on the diagonal and constructed of concrete, timber, and copper.

LA CHAUX-DE-FONDS

Villa Schwob (1916)
ARCHITECT: Le Corbusier
LOCATION: 9 miles NW of Neuchatel, NW Switzerland

A fascinating early work of the world-renowned early modern architect. The design, in many respects, is an outgrowth of the Secession in Vienna.

DAVOS

The Cultural And Sports Center At Davos (1963–65)
ARCHITECT: E. Gisel
LOCATION: c. 20 miles SE of Chur

EFFRETIKON

The Reformed Church (1959–61)
ARCHITECTS: E. Gisel and others
LOCATION:

An interesting church on a hill overlooking the village.

ENNETBADEN

St. Michael's Church (1961–65)
ARCHITECT: Hermann Baur
LOCATION: c. 12 miles NW of Zurich, just NE of Baden

FRIBOURG

Fribourg State Bank (1982)
ARCHITECT: Mario Botta
LOCATION: Adjacent to the railroad station

Modern building material's combine with traditional materials in an exciting manner. Besides the bank, the facility contains a disco and restaurant.

GENEVA

Eglise Neo Apostolique (1950)
ARCHITECT: Werner M. Moser
LOCATION: Rue Liotard, 14

Maison Clarté (1930)
ARCHITECT: Le Corbusier
LOCATION: Rue Saint-Laurent, 2

An apartment complex of 45 flats by the master architect.

GLARUS

Art Gallery (Kunsthaus) (1951)
ARCHITECT: H. Leuzinger
LOCATION: 25 miles SW of St. Gallen, E Central Switzerland

An interesting modern gallery in a park near the station.

HÉRÉMENCE

Centre Paroissial Church (1971–72)
ARCHITECTS: Walter M. Förderer and others
LOCATION: c. 60 miles S of Berne, a few miles SE of Sion

HERREN-SCHWANDEN

Terraced Housing—Siedlung Thalmatt (1974)
ARCHITECTS: Atelier 5
LOCATION: 300 meters to the east of the famous Halen Estate (Near Berne)

LAUSANNE

Ecole Des Beaux-Arts (1961–63)
ARCHITECT: F. Brugger
LOCATION: Inquire: 60 Ave. d'Ouchy, Tourist Office

Kodak Administration Building (1961–63)
ARCHITECT: F. Brugger
LOCATION: Inquire: 60 Ave. d'Ouchy, Tourist Office

Mortuary (Centre Funeraire De Montoie) (1972)
ARCHITECT: Frederic Brugger
LOCATION: Inquire: 60 Ave. d'Ouchy, Tourist Office

LENGNAU

Romisch-Katholisches Pfarrzentrum (Church Hall) (1975)
ARCHITECT: Franz Fueg
LOCATION: c. 17 miles NW of Berne, just SW of Grenchen

LENK IM SIMMENTAL

The Vacation Center—Ferienzentrum Der Schwizer Reisekasse (1975)
ARCHITECT: Hans Hostettler
LOCATION: A few miles E of Gstaad in W Central Switzerland

MEGGEN

Catholic Church At Meggen (1964–66)
ARCHITECT: Franz Fueg
LOCATION: A few miles ENE of Lucerne, on the shoreline

MÉZIÈRES

Theatre Du Jorat (1907–08)
ARCHITECTS: Maillard and Chal
LOCATION: 20 kilometers from Lausanne

A remarkable early structure design constructed entirely of wood.

MUTTENZ

The Municipal Center (1958)
ARCHITECT: Hermann Baur
LOCATION: Suburb of Basle, Hardstrasse at Im Lerchengarten

RAPPERSWIL

Kinderzoo (Children's Zoo Of Knie's Circus) (1961–62)
ARCHITECT: Wolfgang Behles
LOCATION: S of the station on Upper Zurich Lake

REINACH

Evangelist Reformation Church (1961–63)
ARCHITECTS: Ernst Gisel and others
LOCATION: c. 5 miles S of Basel

RIEHEN

Kornfeldchurch (Small Parish Center) (1964)
ARCHITECT: Werner Moser
LOCATION: c. 5 miles NE of Basel city center

RIGI KALTBAD

Hostellerie Du Rigi (Mountain Resort) (1965)
ARCHITECT: Justus Dahinden
LOCATION: S side of Rigi

ST. GALLEN

Faculty Of Economics And Social Sciences (1957–63)
ARCHITECTS: Forderer, Otto, and Swimmpfer
LOCATION: On the Rosenberg overlooking St. Gallen

SARNEN

Church At Sarnen College (1964–66)
ARCHITECTS: J. Naef, E. Studer, and G. Studer
LOCATION: On the Brunigpass road at Sarnen College

SONCEBOZ

Community Center (Batiment Communal) (1964–65)
ARCHITECTS: Baumann and Tschumi
LOCATION: On street connecting Sonceboz railway station with road to St. Imier

TROGEN

Kultraum Pestalozzidorf (Church) (1967–68)
ARCHITECT: Ernst Gisel
LOCATION: 4 miles ESE of St. Gallen, NE Switzerland

UDORF

The Church And Church Hall (1970–71)
ARCHITECTS: Floor, Gutmann, Schupbach, and Schwarz
LOCATION: A few miles W of Zurich

VEVEY

Une Petite Maison (1923)
ARCHITECT: Le Corbusier
LOCATION: By Lake Geneva

One of the few structures in Switzerland by the great modern architect.

ZÜRICH

Ape House At The Zurich Zoo (1956–57)
ARCHITECTS: M.E. Haefeli and A.M. Studer
LOCATION: Inquire: Information Ctr., Railroad Station (Bahnhofstrasse)

Feliz Und-Regula-Church (1948–49)
ARCHITECT: Fritz Metzger
LOCATION: Inquire: Information Ctr., Railroad Station (Bahnhofstrasse)

Ferrolegeringar AG (Administrative Building) (1967–70)
ARCHITECT: Justus Dahinden
LOCATION: On Seefeldquai, in park alongside the lake

Freizeitzentrum Heuried (Recreation Center) (1963–65)
ARCHITECTS: H. Kitz and F. Schwarz
LOCATION: Inquire: Information Ctr., Railroad Station (Bahnhofstrasse)

Geschaftshaus Und Kino Zett-Haus (The Zett House) (1930)
ARCHITECTS: R. Steiger and C. Hubacher
LOCATION: Inquire: Information Ctr., Railroad Station (Bahnhofstrasse)

One of the first modern office buildings in Zurich.

The Mensa At The University Of Zürich (Student Center) (1969)
ARCHITECT: Werner Frey
LOCATION: University of Zurich campus

Trade School And Museum Of Arts And Crafts (1931)
ARCHITECTS: Steger and Egender
LOCATION: Inquire: Information Ctr., Railway Station (Bahnhofstrasse)

The Trades School Hardau (1964)
ARCHITECTS: Otto Glaus and R. Lienhard
LOCATION: N of Bullingerstrasse between Herdernstrasse and Hardstrasse

ZÜRICH-SCHWAMENDINGEN

Church Complex (Kirche Saatien) (1961–64)
ARCHITECT: Claude Paillard
LOCATION: Near the trunk road to Winterthur

theNetherlands

THE NETHERLANDS

Zwolle

Haarlem

Aerdenhout

Amsterdam
Amstelveen

Hilversum

Apeldoorn

Amersfoort

The Hague

Leiden

Utrecht

Otterlo

Hook of Holland

Arnhem

Rotterdam

Helmond

Eindhoven

Geleen

MODERN ARCHITECTURE IN THE NETHERLANDS

EARLY CONTRIBUTIONS

Modern architecture in Holland can be traced from the beginning of the twentieth century with the advanced ideas of a number of pioneer architects. Leader of the early modern movement in Holland was Petrus Berlage, who had tremendous impact on architects throughout Europe.

THE DE STIJL GROUP

The most important contribution from Holland to the modern design movement was made by the De Stijl Group formed in Leiden in 1917 by Theo van Doesburg. This group of twelve designers, including Piet Mondrian, J.J.P. Oud, and Gerrit Rietveld, developed a theory called "neo-placticism." They vowed to:

Use only right angles, employ only abstract design, use only primary and non-primary colors, and use smooth, shiny textures.

These ideas had a profound influence on architects and designers throughout the world, including the famous Bauhaus school of design in Germany. The artistic credo of this group can be seen today in all branches of the arts.

ARCHITECTURE AFTER WORLD WAR II

The De Stijl Group disbanded around 1932, bringing modern developments to a standstill until after the war. The destruction of the war provided need to rebuild many areas of Holland, especially in and around Rotterdam. Modern developments evolved around building more economical, simple, and functional buildings. Architects like Piet Blom, Aldo van Eyck, Herman Hertzberger, and Frank van Klingeren exhibit dynamic innovation in their contemporary architecture.

AERDENHOUT

Reformed Church (1958)

ARCHITECT: Karel L. Sijmons
LOCATION: Leeuweriken Laan, SW of
Haarlem

A boldly designed Dutch Reformed Church, this structure captures the spirit of its members and doctrine. An interesting wall with a series of deeply set windows, some colored, floods the nave with light. The undulating ceiling gives additional drama to the space. A small cross to the left of the altar is set against a plain white horizontal slab, creating an effective focal point.

AMERSFOORT

Zonnefhof Exhibition Hall And Museum (1959)

ARCHITECT: Gerrit T. Rietveld
LOCATION: Arnhemseweg, Amersfoort, 30 miles SE of Amersterdam

Rietveld aimed at bringing rhythm into space through the lines and colors employed in this complex, reflecting the architectural approach of the De Stijl philosophy. The simple box-shaped Zonnefhof Museum is relieved by an interesting asymmetrical window treatment. Brick, steel, and glass employed throughout the interior become an effective background for modern displays.

AMSTELVEEN

Van Leer Building (1957–58)

ARCHITECT: Marcel Breuer (USA)
LOCATION: Amsterdamseweg 206, 5 miles
SW of Amsterdam

After leaving Nazi Germany and settling in the United States in the late 1930s, Breuer received commissions in many European countries. The uniform and stately Van Leer Building is pleasantly located by lakes and canals. The long exterior walls are of glass, with the end partitions of Roman travertine. The windows are protected by solar glass sunshades. A folded concrete roof is supported by tapered triangular columns, a design feature often employed by Breuer.

AMSTERDAM

Bickerseiland Housing
(1972–76)

ARCHITECTS: Van den Bout and De Ley
LOCATION: Bickersgracht 230-240, 244-254;
Grote Bickersstraat 305-319

Many contemporary architects in Europe have attempted to maintain the basic feeling of traditional native building styles in modern structures. The Bickerseiland Housing project accomplishes this goal. The attractive design conveys a suggestion of the old Dutch house interpreted with a refreshingly modern outlook.

AMSTERDAM

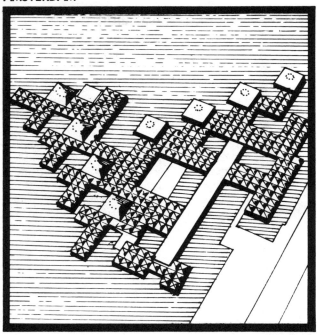

Children's Home (1955–60)

ARCHITECT: Aldo van Eyck
LOCATION: In Ysbaarnpad, Amsterdam

Van Eyck is one of Holland's new generation of modern architects internationally recognized for innovative design. Functional space planning, the challenge in the design of the Children's Home, was met by efficient clusters centered around open courtyards. The textural effect of the roof creates an aerial view of the complex that has been compared to a giant set of Lego building pieces. Interestingly, Legos are very popular with children in Holland.

AMSTERDAM

De Dageraard Housing Estate (1918–23)

ARCHITECT: Piet Kramer and Michael de Klerk
LOCATION: Th. Schwartzeplein 15-33 and 1-13, H. Ronnerstraat 233

The stunning exterior resembles many structures throughout Europe and America in the Art Deco style. Expressive modern brickwork and simple decorative detailing add interest to the housing complex. A fascinating feature of the building is the unusual corner site. The architects capitalized on this characteristic by creating a corner entry emphasized by tiered forms that extend the full height of the facade— "rhythm by gradation" often employed by Art Deco architects during the 1920s.

AMSTERDAM

Hotel Okura (1968–71)

ARCHITECTS: Yoshiro Taniguchi, Yozo
Shibata (Japan), Bernard Bijvoet, and
G.H.M. Holt
LOCATION: 46 Joseph Israel Street

Admirable collaborative effort by Japanese
and Dutch architects has created a truly
international hotel. Located along a quiet
canal, the 23-story reinforced-concrete and
steel structure makes a striking contrast on
the skyline. Careful urban planning initiated
the construction, with future developments to
incorporate the new civic opera house. The
interior of the hotel is a fascinating blend of
Dutch and Japanese themes. Many of the
rooms are totally planned in the Oriental
style.

AMSTERDAM

Housing For Single Parent Families (Mothershouse) (1976–80)

ARCHITECT: Aldo van Eyck
LOCATION: Plantage Middenlaan 33

A colorful and whimsical composition, this
complex features mirror strips on columns
and brightly painted steel panels. The lightly-
scaled concrete structure with its eye-catching
treatment of red, yellow, and blue components
fits nicely into the surroundings even though,
with its industrial materials, it is a thorough
departure from its traditional neighbors.

AMSTERDAM

Open Air School (1930–32)

ARCHITECT: Johannes Duiker
LOCATION: Cliostraat 36 - 40

The concept of the Open Air School, completely innovative for the time, stimulated architects to rethink educational building designs. The school is Duiker's most admired structure. Expansive glass walls with terraces on each of its five stories are interestingly placed on the diagonal. Natural lighting floods the spacious classrooms to enhance the open feeling.

AMSTERDAM

Opstanding Church (1956)

ARCHITECT: M.F. Duintjer
LOCATION: Bos en Lommer Plein at van Artvelde Straat

The exuberantly designed tower of the unusual Opstanding Church is striking. A U-shaped interior is composed of a string of "sliced" wall partitions topped with wooden ceiling beams, a unique arrangement that allows slivers of indirect natural lighting to penetrate the room. A tall, slender cross provides an effective backdrop for the simple altar.

AMSTERDAM

Scheepvaarthuis (1911–16)

ARCHITECT: Johan Melchior van der Meij
LOCATION: Far NW end of Prins Hendrick Kade

Scheepvaarthuis, built for a shipping company, is one of Holland's first examples of the Expressionist Style popular in Germany. A structural grid expressed on the brick, terracotta, and concrete facade gives a decorative interest to the structure. Exterior design motifs are carried into the interior spaces, providing a unified theme. The remarkable shape of the complex creates a commanding impression on the waterfront.

AMSTERDAM

Stock Exchange Building (1898–1903)

ARCHITECT: Petrus Berlage
LOCATION: Beursplein 1-3

Berlage, one of Holland's first pioneer modern architects, is thought of as "the father of modern Dutch architecture." The Stock Exchange Building is internationally recognized as an early modern landmark. Its emphasis on structure instead of decorative detail was unique at the turn of the century. The traditional red brick, popular throughout Holland, combines interestingly with the advanced construction of the iron-and-glass roof.

AMSTERDAM

Vincent Van Gogh Museum (1974)

ARCHITECTS: Gerrit Rietveld, J. van Killen, & J. van Tricht
LOCATION: Between Museum Straat and Paulus Potter Straat, Museumplein

Originally designed by the Great De Stijl master, Gerrit Rietveld, the Vincent Van Gogh Museum was completed by his partner ten years after his death. The remarkable structure has been called a "giant chunky cubic mass spinning off lesser bodies." The interior lighting and clean white backgrounds for the treasure, consisting of over two hundred works by the famous neo-impressionist painter, is superb. The *STEDELIJK MUSEUM* across the street houses Holland's largest modern art collection.

APELDOORN

Central Beheer Office (1968–74)

ARCHITECT: Herman Hertzberger
LOCATION: Prins Willem Alexanderlaan 651

Hertzberger is one of the country's most important modern architects. After designing his highly successful Factory Extension clip-on system in Amsterdam, he planned this efficient complex. The office, planned for 1,000 workers, consists of 56 cubes or "work islands" organized in a grid of interior "streets"—an ingenious solution for working spaces.

ARNHEM

Arnhem Pavilion (1966)

ARCHITECT: Aldo van Eyck
LOCATION: Sonsbeekpaviljoen,
Zijpendaalseweg 30

An aerial view of the stunning Arnhem
Pavilion reveals a fascinating parallel design
in the Dutch De Stijl manner of the 1920s.
The heavy masonry walls are arranged in a
linear series of flat and curved planes almost
like a labyrinth. The huge glass ceiling adds
to the unfolding sensation of viewing the
exhibits in the gallery of this remarkable art
museum.

EINDHOVEN (LELYSTAD)

Agora (1968–73)

ARCHITECT: Frank van Klingeren
LOCATION: Agorahof 2, Lelystad,
Eindhoven

The unique tent-like forms of this Structuralist
complex house two schools, a library, a
restaurant, a supermarket, and other
community facilities in open yet well-defined
spacial unity. Agora has been called "a major
triumph of Dutch Structuralist architecture."
The design has also been described as "a
cluster of modern-day sheds." Van Klingeren's
't KARREGAT," built 1972–73, is located at the
corner of Broekakkerseweg/Urkhovenseweg in
Eindhoven, and is another unique
arrangement of shops, a school, a medical
center, and other cooperative activities.

EINDHOVEN

Evolution Museum (Evoluon)
DESIGNER: James Gardner (England)
LOCATION: NW edge of town at junction of ring road, the road to Tilburg and Noord Brabantlaan

One of the most fantastic museums in Europe, the Evolution Museum is a popular tourist attraction. This structure, the shape of a flying saucer on stilts, was designed to commemorate the founding of the firm of Philips. The striking displays, with explanations, include communications, pollution, food production, population explosion, industry, and other facets of evolution artfully presented to the visitor. The architectural background is symbolically expressive of man's imagination and skill through the ages.

GELEEN

Reformed Church (1956)
ARCHITECT: Bart van Kasteel
LOCATION: Parklaan at Op de Vey, 12 miles N of Maastrict

A sweeping ramp, symbolic of elevation to a higher spiritual plane, leads up to the entry of this innovative Dutch Reformed Church. The interior and exterior are simply designed, relying on form, texture, and color for interest. A colorful stained-glass window, designed by Karel Appek, one of Holland's best-known modern artists, augments light from roof windows.

HELMOND

Speelhuis Art And Leisure Center ("The Playhouse") (1975–78)

ARCHITECT: Piet Blom
LOCATION: Markt 99

Representing the individualistic approach to architecture typical after World War II, Blom is one of Holland's most creative contemporary designers. The unique design of the Speelhuis Arts Center, with its brightly painted units, features a cube set on its point, producing an abstract "cubic windmill." The Helmond Leisure housing complex, consisting of 188 units, is a good example of Post-Modern architecture. Tourists flock to see this unusual Center that has become an architectural curiosity.

HILVERSUM

Hilversum Town Hall (Raadhuis) (1928–31)

ARCHITECT: Marinus Dudok
LOCATION: Town center, 800 meters W of the station

Dudok's individualistic and rational architectural approach won him acclaim throughout Europe. He preferred traditional Dutch brick for use in his modern work. The Hilversum Town Hall, arranged in a series of asymmetrically arranged blocks, is his best-known building. Most of Dudok's work is located in Hilversum. The V.V.V. offers a city guide of Dudok's projects in Hilversum.

HILVERSUM

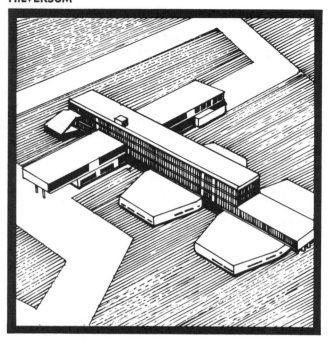

World Broadcasting Center (1961)

ARCHITECTS: Van den Broek and Bakema
LOCATION: Lage Naarderweg, hoek Nieuwe Crailooseweg

This fascinating complex combines simply designed units with more diverse sections to achieve both unity and variety. With irregular shapes and predictable forms the whole complex is connected by means of functional and attractive intersections. The architectural team of van den Broek and Bakema, among Holland's most respected designers, influenced building throughout Europe. The World Broadcasting Center is one of their finest efforts.

HOOK OF HOLLAND

Housing Estate (1926–27)

ARCHITECT: J.J.P. Oud
LOCATION: SW of Rotterdam, Inquire at V.V.V. 130 B Rietdijkstraat

Undoubtedly Oud's most famous work, the Housing Estate on the Hoek van Holland was an innovative and influential multi-dwelling complex for the period, incorporating many imaginative ideas for clustered living and anticipating modern condominiums. Featuring many aspects of De Stijl philosophy, the design is devoid of ornamentation and color. Horizontal lines, flat roofs, and bold curves characterize the complex.

HOGE VELUWE NATIONAL PARK (OTTERLO)

Soonsbeek Sculpture Pavilion And Rijksmuseum Kröller-Müller

ARCHITECTS: Gerrit Rietveld (Soonsbeek Pavilion, 1954), Henri van de Velde (Kroller-Muller, 1938)
LOCATION: 6 kilometers N of Arnhem by Otterlo

In a beautiful park setting, formerly the private estate of the Kröller family, is situated one of the most exciting modern museums in Europe. The T-shaped museum by van de Velde houses a famous collection of Van Gogh and other artists presented to the state by the Kröllers. The creative Sculpture Pavilion by Rietveld, the famous De Stijl member, was designed as an effective background for modern art. *THE NEW WING* by W. G. Quist is also notable.

ROTTERDAM

De Bijenkorf Department Store (1953–57)

ARCHITECT: Marcel Breuer (USA) with Elizas and Schwartzman
LOCATION: Coolsingel 105

This impressive modern structure occupies a prominent position in the reconstructed downtown central area of Rotterdam. The striking exterior of the building is sheathed with Roman travertine pierced with window slits. Bold lettering is backed by fluorescent lights that give emphasis to the facade. Widely spaced concrete columns, a teakwood ceiling, and suspended lighting animate the interior spaces.

ROTTERDAM

Lijnbaan Shopping Center (1953)

ARCHITECTS: J.B. Bakema and H. van den Broek
LOCATION: Lijnbaan

This famous architectural team was responsible for rebuilding Rotterdam after it had been leveled by bombs in World War II. Conveniently located in the downtown area, the Lijnbaan Shopping Center is a favorite meetingplace for townspeople and tourists. The attractive modern facility is surrounded by well-planned structures also designed by Bakema and van den Broek.

THE HAGUE

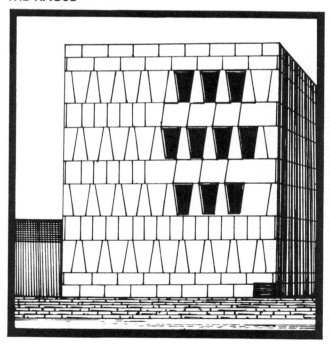

United States Embassy (1954–58)

ARCHITECT: Marcel Breuer (USA)
LOCATION: Corner of Korte Voorhout and Vois in Tuin

A stunning facade of trapezoidal and rectangular panels of rough limestone and smooth granite is asymmetrically placed and highlights the boxy exterior. The L-shaped structure commands a busy corner site with its unusual design treatment. Ten windows arranged in three rows picks up the design theme creating a fascinating focal point.

UTRECHT

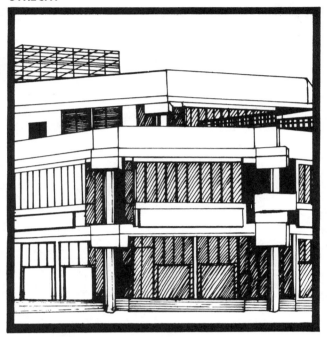

Music Center (Muziek Centrum) (1980)

ARCHITECT: Herman Hertzberger
LOCATION: Corner of Vredenburg and Vrendenburg Lange

The unpretentious contemporary structure is situated on a busy corner of the huge Catharijne development. A repeating vertical pattern of narrow sash-stepped wall sections helps relate the new building to the city's traditional architecture at the same time it maintains its own identity.

UTRECHT

Schröder House (1924)

ARCHITECT: Gerrit Rietveld
LOCATION: Prins Hendriklaan 50

Designed for Rietveld's patron, Mrs. Schröder, this house is the most important architectural contribution by the famed De Stijl member, incorporating all aspects of the artistic group's philosophies. The structure's clean white flat sections project beyond each other and are accented by primary colors of red, yellow, and blue. Large panes of glass and the absence of decoration were a complete departure from traditional architecture at the time. The house, recently restored and functioning as an apartment complex, is a fascinating example of the International Style developed in the 1920s.

ADDITIONAL MODERN STRUCTURES OF INTEREST

AMSTERDAM

Dutch Diamond Workers Society (1898)
ARCHITECT: Petrus Berlage
LOCATION: Inquire: V.V.V., 5 Rokin,
just S of Dam

An interesting early example of modern architecture in Holland.

New Town Hall (1967)
ARCHITECT: Fernando Higueras (Spain)
LOCATION: Inquire: V.V.V., 5 Rokin
(just S of Dam)

A modern structure by one of Spain's most important contemporary architects.

Old Age Home (1975)
ARCHITECT: Herman Hertzberger
LOCATION: Inquire: V.V.V., 5 Rokin,
just S of Dam

A much publicized structure of repetitive spaces that has been compared to "white crosses containing black coffins."

Olivetti Building (1970)
ARCHITECT: Hans Hollein (Austria)
LOCATION: Inquire: V.V.V., 5 Rokin
(just S of Dam)

The Olivetti Building was designed by one of Austria's most innovative architects.

Nederlandsche Handel-Mallscappij (Algemene Bank Netherlands) (1919–1926)
ARCHITECT: Karel P.C. De Bazel
LOCATION: Inquire: V.V.V., 5 Rokin,
just S of Dam

An abstractly designed building with polychrome masonry. De Bazel's most important work.

ARNHEM

Bio Health Resort (Bio-Revalidatiecentrum) (1952–60)
ARCHITECT: J.J.P. Oud
LOCATION: Wekeromseweg 6

A starkly designed structure and one of the famous De Stijl member's last important works.

HILVERSUM

Public Baths (1930s)
ARCHITECT: Marinus Dudok
LOCATION: Tours: Inquire: V.V.V., Stationsplein, E of inner town

A structural design of brick featuring strong horizontal planes and a contrasting soaring tower.

ROTTERDAM

Bergpolder Flats (1934)
ARCHITECTS: J.A. Brinckmann and L.C. van der Vluckt
LOCATION: Abraham Kuyperlaan/Borgesiusstraat

An early modern steel-framed apartment building employing galvanized sheet steel sheathing. A prototype widely copied throughout Europe.

Kiefhoek Housing Development (1928)
ARCHITECT: J.J.P. Oud
LOCATION: Kiefhoekstraat/Heer Arnoldstraat/Lindtstraat

The design philosophy of the De Stijl group is evident throughout this important housing development.

New Wing Of The Boymans-Van Beuningen Museum (1972)
ARCHITECT: A. Boden
LOCATION: Back of the museum's park on Westzee Dijk

An effective new wing providing an interesting contrast between the old and new.

Van Nelle Chocolate And Tobacco Factory (1928)
ARCHITECTS: J.C. van der Vluckt and J.A. Brinckmann
LOCATION: van Nelleweg 1

A striking feature of this much photographed work is the use of an expansive glass curtain wall.

THE HAGUE

Congresgebouw (1969)
ARCHITECT: J.J.P. Oud
LOCATION: Just off Stadhouderslaan close to Gemeente Museum

A clean modern design and one of the last important works of the famous De Stijl member.

Gemeente Museum (Haags Gemeentemuseum) (1927–35)
ARCHITECT: Petrus Berlage
LOCATION: Just N of Stadhouderslaan

An early modern building of warm Dutch brick employed in a simple structural treatment.

Villa Henny (1898)
ARCHITECT: Petrus Berlage
LOCATION: Oude Scheveningse Weg 42

An important work by "the father of modern architecture in Holland" and one of the first examples of early modern residential design in the country.

UTRECHT

Julianahal (Jaarbeurs) (1956)
ARCHITECT: Gerrit Rietveld
LOCATION: Just W of the station

A large public center designed a few decades after the De Stijl design group disbanded. Used for exhibition fairs.

Hoog Catharijne (1973–77)
LOCATION: A large covered shopping center complex just west of the old city center.

ZWOLLE

Zwolle Housing (1975–77)
ARCHITECTS: Aldo van Eyck and Theo Bosch
LOCATION: c. 75 miles NE of Amsterdam

Zwolle housing design features a new planning concept with sixteen different residential types maintaining the feeling of the traditional Dutch facade.

Bibliography

Adler, Florian, ed. *Architectural Guide—Switzerland*. Zurich: Architectural Publishers, 1969.

Ball, Victoria Kloss. *Architectural and Interior Design*. New York: John Wiley and Sons, Inc., 1980.

Baedeker's Austria. Englewood Cliffs, New Jersey: Prentice-Hall, Inc.

Baedeker's Italy. Englewood Cliffs, New Jersey: Prentice-Hall, Inc.

Baedeker's Spain. Englewood Cliffs, New Jersey: Prentice-Hall, Inc.

Baedeker's Germany. Englewood Cliffs, New Jersey: Prentice-Hall, Inc.

Bastland, Knud. *Jose Luis Sert*. New York: Frederick Praeger, Publications, 1980.

Beer, Eileene Harrison. *Scandinavian Design: Objects of a Life Style*. New York: Farrar, Straus and Giroux and The American-Scandinavian Society, 1975.

Besset, Maurice. *New French Architecture*. New York: Frederick A. Praeger, Publishers, 1967.

Bill, Max. *Le Corbusier, Vol. 3, 1934-1938*. New York: Praeger Publishers Inc.,

Bjerregaard, Kirsten, ed. *Architecture from Scandinavia*. Copenhagen: World Pictures AS., 1970s.

Bode, Peter M. & Gustav Peichl. *Architektur aus Osterreich seit 1960*. Salzburg und Wien: Residenz Verlag. 1980.

Boesiger, Willy. *Le Corbusier, Vol. 1, 1910-1929*. New York: Praeger Publishers Inc., 1966.

Boesiger, Willy. *Le Corbusier, Vol. 2, 1929-1934.* New York: Praeger Publishers Inc., 1966.

Boesiger, Willy. *Le Corbusier, Vol. 4, 1938-1946.* New York: Praeger Publishers Inc., 1966.

Boesiger, Willy. *Le Corbusier, Vol. 5, 1946-1952.* New York: Praeger Publishers Inc., 1966.

Boesiger, Willy. *Le Corbusier, Vol. 6, 1952-1957.* New York: Praeger Publishers Inc., 1966.

Boesiger, Willy. *Le Corbusier, Vol. 7, 1957-1965.* New York: Praeger Publishers Inc., 1966.

Boesiger, Willy. *Le Corbusier, Vol. 8, Last Works.* New York: Praeger Publishers Inc., 1970.

Borsi, Franco, and Ezio Godoli. *Paris 1900.* New York: Rizzoli International Publications, Inc., 1978.

Bussmann, Klaus. *Dumont Guide-Paris and The Ile De France.* New York: Stewart, Tabori, and Chang Publications, 1984.

Conti, Flavio. *The Grand Tour—Individual Creations.* Boston: HBJ Press, 1978.

Conti, Flavio. *The Grand Tour—New Techniques.* Boston: HBJ Press, 1978.

Cooper, Jackie, Ed. *Mackintosh Architecture.* New York: St. Martin's Press, 1978.

Craig, Maurice. *Architecture in Ireland.* Dublin: Department of Foreign Affairs, 1978.

Delevoy, Robert L., Wieser, Giovanni, and Maurice Culot. *Brussels 1900 Capital of the Art Nouveau.* Bruxelles: Ecole Nationale Superieure d'Architecture et des Arts Visuels, 1972.

Design From Denmark. World Pictures AS. Copenhagen. 1970s.

Dezzi Bardeschi, Marco, ed. *Italian Architecture 1965-1970.* Rome: IsMEO, Istituto Italiano per il Medio ed Estremo Oriente, 1973.

Faber, Tobias. *New Danish Architecture.* New York: Frederick A. Praeger, Publisher, 1968.

Fleming, John and Hugh Honour. *Dictionary of the Decorative Arts.* New York: Harper & Row, 1977.

Fodor's Scandinavia. New York: Fodor's Travel Guides, 1983.

Frampton, Kenneth. *Modern Architecture: A Critical History.* New York: Oxford University Press, 1980.

Frampton, Kenneth, and Futagawa, Yukio. *Modern Architecture 1851-1945.* New York: Rizzoli, 1983.

Galardi, Alberto. *New Italian Architecture.* New York: Frederick A. Praeger, Publishers, 1967.

Geretsegger, Heinz and Peintner, Max. *Otto Wagner 1841–1918.* Residenz Verlag Salzburg. Salzburg, Austria. 1964.

Harling, Robert, Ed. *Dictionary of Design and Decoration.* New York: Viking Press, 1973.

Heineman, Hans-Erland, Ed. *New Towns and Old—Housing and Services in Sweden.* Stockholm: The Swedish Institute, 1975.

Herbert, Gropius, Walter and Ise Gropius, eds. *Bauhaus.* New York: The Museum of Modern Art, 1975.

Heyer, Paul. *Architects on Architecture.* New York: Walker and Company, 1978.

Hitchcock, Henry Russell. *Philip Johnson Architecture: 1949–1965.* New York: Holt, Rinehart & Winston, 1966.

Hofmann, Werner and Udo Kultermann. *Modern Architecture in Color.* New York: Viking Press, 1970.

Huches, Robert. *The Shock of the New.* New York: Alfred A. Knopf, 1980.

Jacobus, John, Ed. *James Stirling: Buildings and Projects.* London: Thames and Hudson, 1975.

Janson, H.W. *History of Art*. New York: Prentice-Hall, Inc. and Harry Abrams, Inc., 1969.

Jencks, Charles. *Late Modern Architecture*. New York: Rizzoli International Publications Inc., 1980.

Jencks, Charles. *The Language of Post-Modern Architecture*. New York: Rizzoli International Publications, Inc., 1981.

Jencks, Charles and William Chaitkin. *Architecture Today*. New York: Harry N. Abrams, Inc., Publishers, 1982.

Jones, Edward and Christopher Woodward. *A Guide to the Architecture of London*. New York: Van Nostrand Reinhold Company, 1982.

Kane, Robert S. *London A to Z*. Garden City, New York: Doubleday, 1974.

Kane, Robert S. *Spain*. New York: Rand McNally, 1980.

Klein, Dan. *Art Deco*. New York: Crown Publishers, 1974.

Landau, Royston. *New Directions in British Architecture*. New York: George Braziller, 1968.

Mang, Karl. *History of Modern Furniture*. New York: Harry N. Abrams, Inc., Publishers, 1979.

Marrey, Bernard. *Rhone-Alpes. Les Guides du XX siecle*. Edition L'Equerre. 1982.

Maxwell, Robert. *New British Architecture*. New York: Praeger Publishers, 1973.

Michelin Paris. London: Michelin Tyre Co. Ltd., 1976.

Mower, David. *Gaudi*. New York: The Two Continents Publishing Groups, 1974.

Myklebust, Einar. *10 Years Norwegian Architecture*. Oslo: Norsk Arkitekturmuseum, 1978.

New York, The Museum of Modern Art. *Aalto: Architecture and Furniture*. 1938.

Nicholson, Robert. *Nicholson's Complete London Guide*. London: Robert Nicholson Publications, 1980.

Papachristou, Tician. *Marcel Breuer New Buildings and Projects*. New York: Praeger Publishers, 1970.

Pehnt, Wolfgang. *Expressionist Architecture*. Thames and Hudson. 1973.

Peter, John. *Masters of Modern Architecture*. New York: Bonanza Books, 1958.

Pevsner, Nikolaus, Fleming, John, Honour, Hugh. *A Dictionary of Architecture*. Woodstock, New York: The Overlook Press, 1976.

Pevsner, Nickolaus. *Pioneers of Modern Design: From William Morris to Walter Gropius*. Rev. and partly rewritten. New York and Harmondsworth, England: Penguin Books, 1975.

Portoghesi, Paolo. *Postmodern*. Rizzoli International Publications, Inc., 1983.

Reid, Richard. *The Book of Buildings*. Chicago: Rand McNally, 1980.

Richards, J. M., Editor. *Who's Who in Architecture from 1400 to the Present*. New York: Holt, Rinehart and Winston, 1977.

Romer, Karl, ed. *Facts about Germany*. Lexikon-Institut Bertelsmann, Edition for the Press and Information Office of the Government of the Federal Republic of Germany. 1979.

Roos, Frank J. Jr. *An Illustrated Handbook of Art History*. New York: The Macmillan Company, 1954.

Schnell, Hugo. *Der Kirchenbau Des 20. Jahrhunderts in Deutschland*. Munchen: Verlag Schnell & Steiner, 1973.

Scully, Vincent Jr. *Modern Architecture: The Architecture of Democracy*. New York: George Braziller, 1974.

Smith, G. E. Kidder. *The New Architecture of Europe*. Cleveland and New York: The World Publishing Company, 1967.

Smithson, Alison and Peter Smithson. *The Heroic Period of Modern Architecture.* New York: Rizzoli International Publications, Inc., 1974.

Steinegger, Huber and Jean-Claude, ed. *Jean Prouve.* New York: Praeger Publishers, 1971.

Suomi Rakentaa Finland Bygger. Suomen Rakennustaiteen Museo Finlands Arkektumuseum. 1982.

Suomi Rakentaa Finland Bygger. Suomen Rakennustaiteen Museo Finlands Arktektumuseum. 1976.

Tempel, Egon. *New Finnish Architecture.* New York: Frederick A. Praeger, Publishers, 1968.

Tomes, John. *Blue Guide to Holland.* New York: W. W. Norton & Co., Inc., 1982.

The SAR Guide to Contemporary Swedish Architecture 1968–78. Stockholm: The National Association of Swedish Architects, 1978.

Waddell, Roberta. *The Art Nouveau Style.* New York: Dover Publications, Inc., 1977.

Warren, Geoffrey. *Art Nouveau Style.* London: Octopus, 1972.

Weihsmann, Helmut. *Art Nouveau in Vienna.* Ars Nova Media. 1983.

West, T. W. *A History of Architecture in Scotland.* University of London Press Ltd., 1967.

Windsor, Alan. *Peter Behrens: Architect and Designer 1968–1940.* New York: Whitney Library of Design, 1981.

Whiton, Sherrill. *Elements of Interior Design.* New York: J. B. Lippincott Company, 1974.

Yarwood, Doreen. *The Architecture of Europe.* London: Chancellor Press, 1974.

PERIODICALS CONSULTED

Progressive Architecture

Architectural Record

A.I.A. Journal

Architectural Forum

RIBA Journal — 25 Years of British Architecture, 1952-1977

CASA VOGUE

Domus

L'Architecture D'Aujourd'Hui

Living Architecture Scandinavian Design

Design from Scandinavia

Architecture from Scandinavia

Index